D0805494

Seashore Chronicles

Seashore

Three Centuries o

Edited b

Chronicles

the Virginia Barrier *Islands*

Brooks Miles Barnes *and* Barry R. Truitt

University Press of Virginia — *Charlottesville and London*

The University Press of Virginia
© 1997 by the Rector and Visitors of the University of Virginia
All rights reserved
Printed in the United States of America

First published 1997

♾ The paper used in this publication meets the minimum requirements of the American National Standard for Information Sciences—Permanence of Paper for Printed Library Materials, ANSI Z39.48–1984.

Library of Congress Cataloging-in-Publication Data

Seashore chronicles : three centuries of the Virginia Barrier Islands / edited by Brooks Miles Barnes and Barry R. Truitt.

p. cm.

Includes index.

ISBN 0-8139-1748-4 (cloth : alk. paper)

1. Barrier islands—Virginia—History—Sources. 2. Virgina—History—Sources. 3. Natural history—Virginia. I. Barnes, Brooks Miles. II. Truitt, Barry R.

F232.A19S43 1997
975.5′1—dc21

97-2489
CIP

FOR

Thelma M. Barnes

Anne E. Barnes

Maude L. Truitt

Anne P. Truitt

and

In memory of

Roland Van Zandt

Contents

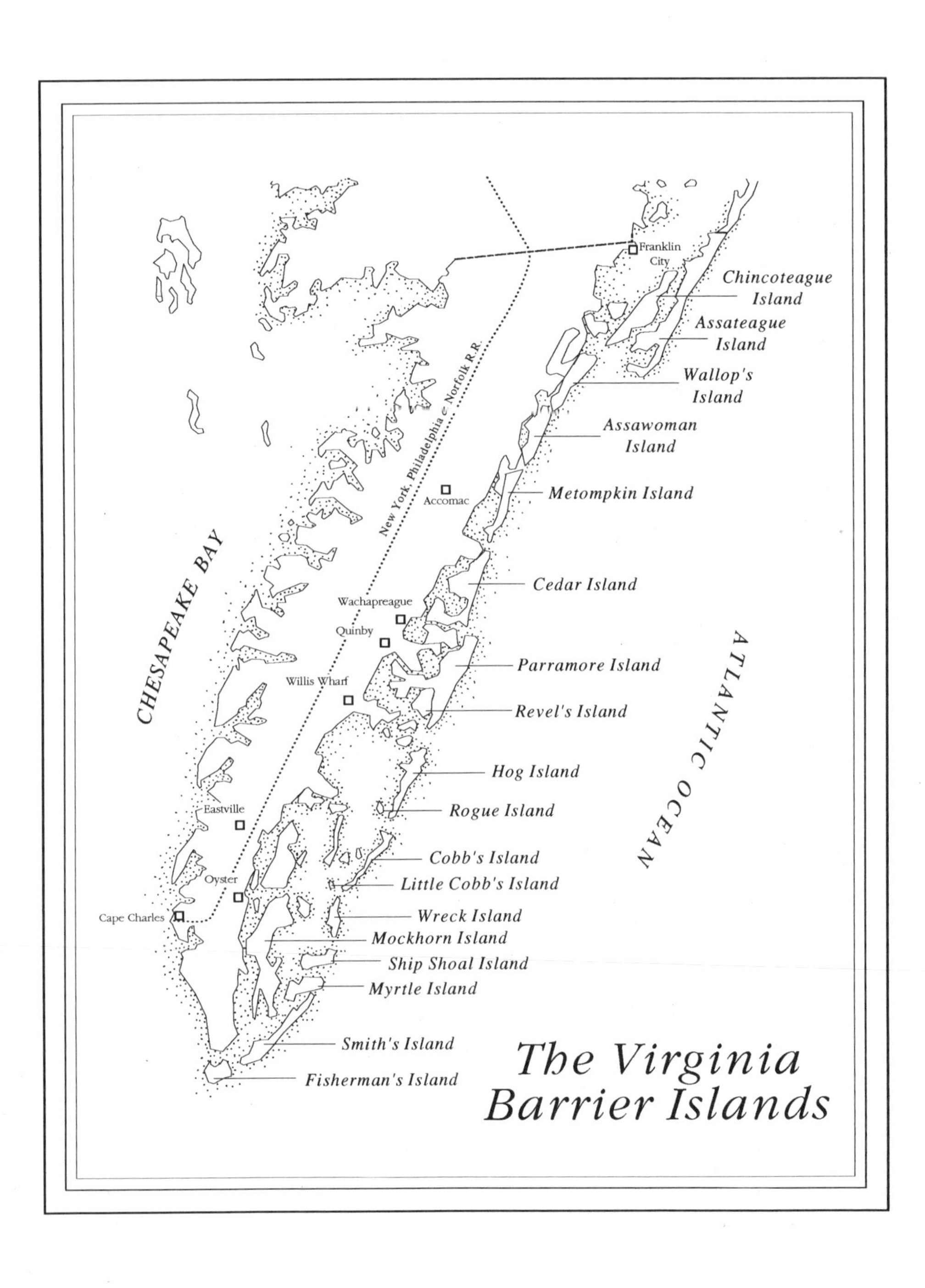

Franklin City
Chincoteague Island
Assateague Island
Wallop's Island
Assawoman Island
Metompkin Island
Accomac
New York, Philadelphia & Norfolk R.R.
CHESAPEAKE BAY
Cedar Island
Wachapreague
Quinby
Parramore Island
Willis Wharf
Revel's Island
ATLANTIC OCEAN
Hog Island
Eastville
Rogue Island
Cobb's Island
Oyster
Little Cobb's Island
Cape Charles
Wreck Island
Mockhorn Island
Ship Shoal Island
Myrtle Island
Smith's Island
Fisherman's Island
The Virginia Barrier Islands

Foreword

Driving south on U.S. 13 below Pocomoke City, Maryland, the roadside landscape seems gradually to become older and quieter, as though time had slowed or passed it by. There are few great manors, as in other parts of Maryland's Eastern Shore. Instead there are mainly small farms with checkerboard fields of potatoes or soybeans bordered by stands of oak and loblolly pine. The highway itself changes. It no longer resembles an interstate with broad medians, but more a county highway that passes through (not around) small towns with names like Oak Hall, Temperanceville, and Nassawadox. An occasional grain elevator borders the highway, as do abandoned farmhouses with hogged roofs and silver-grey shingles.

By these signs you will know that you have crossed the line, the line long disputed three centuries ago by the Lords Baltimore and the London Company. You have entered the State of Virginia. The Eastern Shore of Virginia, that is, so physically separate and so different from all that is the rest of the Old Dominion.

Even as these words are written, however, the signs are fast changing. A throughway, complete with wide medians and urban bypasses, is now being planned to replace the old highway. It will connect with the extra lanes that are now being added to the eighteen-mile Chesapeake Bay Bridge-Tunnel that joins the Virginia peninsula with the Norfolk–Portsmouth–Virginia Beach megaplex. Thus the once-quiet U.S. 13 will presently give way to a major north-south artery, a coastal alternative to the heavily traveled Interstate 95.

Happily, though, you may still find peace and quiet in the area's back roads. More than that, you will be doubly rewarded if you head east or west following small signs to such villages as Willis Wharf, Oyster, or Cherrystone, which suggest something other than the area's agrarian character. Drive west five or ten miles and you will find the waters of the Chesapeake Bay at its broadest. Better, drive east a short distance and you will soon come to a wide expanse of shallow bays, marsh, serpentine creeks, tidal flats, and small hammocks of firm land dotted with stunted oak and cedar. The refreshing tonic of sea air is already with you and you sense that something bigger is near at hand. Raise your binoculars and you may find it. Depending on your location you may catch a glimpse of distant sand dunes and perhaps even a stray plume of storm-tossed spray.

There on the far horizon lie Virginia's barrier islands, the thin first line of defense against the ever-restless Atlantic Ocean. Follow these islands down from Chincoteague some eighty miles south to Cape Charles at the entrance to the Chesapeake Bay. Metompkin, Cedar, Parramore, Hog, Cobb's, Wreck, Ship Shoal, Myrtle, and Smith's—the very names entice. Together they constitute what one author of this volume has called the Atlantic's crown jewel of "vintage wild seacoast." The islands also have the distinction of being what some call the earth's least stable landform. Others, especially scientists, prefer to regard the islands as dynamic, since what the sea takes from one will often accrue to another. I like to think of them as restless, as restless as the sea that shapes them, sometimes overruns them, divides them, and ultimately moves them inexorably toward the mainland.

It may thus come as a surprise for all those who know the islands in their present wild state to learn that they have long been the scene of settlement. The islands, in short, have a history of human habitation. Fortunately, this is what Brooks Barnes and Barry Truitt, the author-editors of this fine collection of *Seashore Chronicles,* as they call them, wish to bring foremost to our attention. Efforts at human habitation, we might better say, few of which have been successful for very long. Some were purposeful. Others were chance encounters, where men found themselves on the barriers' shifting sands through circumstances not of their choosing.

The list is long. In 1650 the heartless captain of the *Virginia Merchant* left fourteen starving passengers stranded on one of the outer islands after a frightful transatlantic winter passage of three months. Nine survived, eventually to be rescued by friendly and extremely generous Indians. Two hundred years later George W. Bonsall found himself sailing with Company D of the Ohio Volunteer Infantry to Hog Island, there to guard against the Confederates who a year before had raided Smith's Island and smashed the Cape Charles lighthouse. Bonsall found the island's ten families to be good and loyal Unionists, but there was another enemy in the form of "gallinippers," or "sketters," of incredible size and ferocity that attacked the troops night and day until some of the men were "disfigured with red, black and blue marks, swollen eyes, and other marks of the of the terrible charge." "We all supposed Hog Island was . . . a little paradise," Bonsall sardonically noted.

Barnes and Truitt have also wisely included the writings of many who journeyed to the islands for pleasure or imagined profit. In 1808 we find George Washington Parke Custis, Martha Washington's grandson whom the President adopted as his son, inspecting the sheep that shared Smith's Island's "succulent herbage" with wild cattle and a few pigs. In the florid rhetoric for which he was well known, Custis praised the sheep and their wool as fine as any in the world and described himself as "lost in astonishment at this wonderful interposition of Providence in our behalf." But twenty-four years later Custis's son-in-law Robert E. Lee visited Smith's and found the island gale-wracked and "in many places levelled [so that] the water at common high tide finds its way into them & renders the Pasturage not so good." The wool of the surviving sheep looked "very *ragged*" and by Lee's estimate not worth a quarter of the prevailing market value.

Other efforts, particularly those designed to attract visitors, had greater success. Foremost among these were the various hotels and private hunting and fishing lodges that sprang up on nearly all the islands in the course of the nineteenth century. One of the first of these, Cobb's Island, was purchased and settled by one Nathan Cobb and family from Cape Cod in Massachusetts during the 1830s. Initially the islands provided the Cobbs with a lucrative salvage business rescuing the schooners and other coasting vessels that ran afoul of the offshore breakers and racing tides that are characteristic of the inlets between all of the islands. But by the second half of the century the Cobbs had devoted the greater part of their efforts and the island's "dry" or "high-tide" acreage to tourism. Joseph Morgan's delightful account of his 1877 "Trip to Cobb's Island" describes the family's hotel and outbuildings capable of accommodating over one hundred guests, as well as privately owned clubs such as the Baltimore Cottage and the Virginia House, where well-stocked bars provided island proprietaries for a long day of hunting or fishing.

But by 1896 a reporter from the *Baltimore Sun* found the Cobb's Island Hotel a complete wreck, the victim of a storm that washed over the island. There were "about three feet of sand . . . in the dancing pavilion" and the barroom, the billiard room, the bowling alley and a number of outbuildings were described as "tumbled down in one heap and broken up so they were of no use whatever." Fortunately no lives were lost, thanks to the heroic work of the keeper and surfmen of the United States Life-Saving Service who launched their surf boat at the height of the storm to rescue islanders from the roofs and second stories of their homes. Elsewhere in the *Chronicles* Barnes and Truitt include a fitting tribute to the service, predecessor to today's Coast Guard, which established lifesaving stations on all the Atlantic coast's major barrier islands, each manned by a keeper and crew of six or eight surfmen whose duty it was, as tradition has it, "never to refuse the sea." Little wonder, then, that in forty years the Virginia barrier island stations alone went to the aid of 383 vessels, 174 of which were total losses.

With the advent of fast rail service, the latter part of the nineteenth century saw boom markets develop for the plentiful oysters, clams, crabs and fish of the "broadwater" bays and marsh creeks in the lee of the islands. Chincoteague, a center for much of this activity, not to mention its rough-and-tumble annual wild pony penning, is described in the rollicking and not always flattering prose of a youthful Howard Pyle in one of his first literary efforts. In a different vein is Thomas Dixon's "Along Shining Shores." Dixon, an avid hunter, delights in recounting his success in outwitting the wily "jack curlews," or today's whimbrels, and occasionally letting fly his scatter shot at huge flocks of "robin snipe," now known as red knots.

Those who now enjoy the magnificent procession of shorebirds journeying north along the barriers every spring owe a special thanks to the scientists and naturalists, both trained and empirical, who began visiting the islands at the beginning of this century. Among them George Shiras III, Olin Sewall Pettingill Jr., and Tom Horton deserve special mention. Shiras, a responsible hunter, wildlife photographer, and member of Congress from Allegheny, Pennsylvania, grew alarmed at the hunters who fired round after round at the thousands of "handsome robin snipe" that came to the islands each spring, took easy aim at the larger curlews, and brought down as many as a dozen ruddy turnstones and small plovers in a single shot. This, Shiras noted, was to say nothing of all "the eggers . . . a large proportion of the natives of the Eastern Shore," who delighted in collecting and consuming the eggs of virtually every species of gull, shorebird, and waterfowl. Thus prompted to action, Shiras introduced the first Federal Migratory Bird Bill in 1904, which in its final form banned all spring shooting, prohibited market hunting, and set bag limits for geese and ducks.

In June of 1933 the noted ornithologist Olin Sewall Pettingill Jr. and his bride had the unique experience of honeymooning on Cobb's Island and surviving a fierce northeaster that brought the storm tides up through the floorboards of the cottage of George Cobb, grandson of Nathan, with whom they took refuge. But worse was yet to come for Cobb, who lived a solitary life on the island protecting its bird life. Later that same summer what islanders always remember as the great August hurricane took Cobb's life. It also prompted a general exodus from all the islands. Hog Island, which once boasted a school, a church, and a population of 150 was the last to go. By 1941, in fact, the last family to live on the barriers had left the island.

Then there is Tom Horton's "Ultimate Edge," a thoughtful essay inspired by a visit to Parramore Island. It is required reading for all who would learn more of how and why the islands change—*migrate* is now the preferred term—as they do. Why, for example, standing on the beach at Smith's Island you may see a stump of stone out beyond the surf at low tide. It is all that remains of the old Cape Charles Lighthouse, once situated on the island's highest ridge. Horton also tells of the long, difficult, and ultimately successful effort by the Nature Conservancy to acquire fourteen islands that stretch for fifty-five miles at the heart of the barrier system, along with considerable acreage of marsh and broadwater behind them. These islands—Smith's, Myrtle, Mink, Godwin, Ship Shoal, Cobb's, Little Cobb's, Hog, Rogue, Revel's, Sandy, Parramore, Cedar, and Metompkin—now constitute the Conservancy's Virginia Coast Reserve. It has been granted world-class status as a United Nations Biosphere Reserve because of the islands' rich diversity of species, the result of being a meeting ground of both northern and southern plant and animal life. Thanks to the Conservancy, therefore, dark clouds of waterfowl may still be seen in autumn skies and so, too, shorebirds in spring, still by the thousands, in fact.

The reserve has not been entirely popular with all local residents, who once dreamed of a chain of seashore resorts and second-home developments. It is for this reason, I suspect, that Barnes and Truitt have added a coda to their collection, a closing tone poem of appreciation to the newly wild islands by a native Eastern Shoreman. He is Curtis J. Badger and he tells of the pleasures of beachcombing with his ten-year-old son, of the "thunderous noise of breaking surf; the cries of terns and skimmers; the discovery of jingle shells; . . . the immensity of ocean, sky, and beach; the thrill of being part of something wild and undefinable."

In time we will all come to similar appreciation, I am sure, local residents included. The Virginia Coast Reserve is part of what is already the longest continuous stretch of undisturbed beachfront along an Atlantic coast that is fast becoming a continuous chain of vacation homes, hotels, boardwalks, amusement parks, sun-tanned lifeguards, and parking lots.

For myself it is ample reward to stand atop an island dune and watch long rows of wind-plumed breakers rolling in from the Atlantic. Sometimes I walk the beach, fishing rod in hand, on the lookout for schools of marauding bluefish just beyond the surf, marked by sprays of small fish breaking the surface and the screams of gulls and terns. At other times, especially in autumn, it is enough to stretch out on the sand and watch long wavy lines of scoters winging their way south. Or train my binoculars in either direction, as far as vision will carry, until the seemingly endless beach becomes a mirage where sand, sea, and sky come together in a common haze.

We must therefore thank the Nature Conservancy for such experiences, for letting the islands come full circle back to the way they were for the castaways of the *Virginia Merchant* in 1650. Equal thanks must also go to Brooks Barnes and Barry Truitt for the deeper appreciation that comes with knowledge of the islands' history. They have told it well in their informative short history, their notes, and their splendid collection of *Seashore Chronicles.*

William W. Warner

Acknowledgments

The following individuals and institutions helped us obtain manuscripts, essays, and photographs: Curtis J. Badger; Richard Chenery III; Duke University, Special Collections Library; Eastern Shore of Virginia Historical Society, especially Director John Verrill; Eastern Shore Public Library, especially Director W. Robert Keeney, Sandra G. Scoville, and Wyllie B. Thornton; Virginia Cardwell Eldredge; R. Michael Erwin of the Patuxent Wildlife Research Center, National Biological Service; Tom Horton; Johns Hopkins University Press; Charles E. Kincaid; Kirk C. Mariner; Mariners' Museum; National Geographic Society; Nature Conservancy, Virginia Coast Reserve, especially Director John Hall; Peabody Essex Museum; Olin Sewall Pettingill Jr.; Claude Rogers; Saint Mary's County Historical Society; Smithsonian Institution, National Museum of American Art, Photographic History Collection; Melvin M. Spence; Stackpole Books; Jean Steffens; Jerry Via of the Virginia Polytechnic and State University; and Robert Wilson.

Tommy and Cheryl O'Connor generously made available their extensive collection of barrier island photographs.

The following individuals shared their expert knowledge: Kellee L. Blake, Assistant Director, National Archives, Philadelphia; Mitchell A. Byrd, Director Emeritus, Center for Conservation Biology, College of William and Mary; Mary Linda Elliott, Deputy Clerk, Northampton County Circuit Court; Gary Guyette of Guyette & Schmidt, Inc.; Harry Holcomb; and Thelma Peterson of the Eastern Shore of Virginia Barrier Island Center.

Vladimir Gavrilovic of Paradigm Design created the map.

Edward L. Ayers of the University of Virginia, Jack Temple Kirby of Miami University, and James Tice Moore of Virginia Commonwealth University read and commented on portions of the manuscript. Ed Ayers also kindly put us in contact with the University Press of Virginia.

William W. Warner graciously consented to write the foreword.

Our wives, Anne Barnes and Anne Truitt, and our children, Morgan Truitt and Edward and Elizabeth Barnes, endured, encouraged, and sustained this project.

The Accomack Clubhouse, located off Wachapreague, ca. 1890

Oyster-shucking house, Wachapreague, ca. 1910

Sunbathing on the beach, Wallop's Island, ca. 1900

A fine catch of fish, Wallop's Island, ca. 1900

The Wallop's Island Clubhouse, ca. 1905

Model sailboat race, Wallop's Island, ca. 1900

The cottage of George Shiras III on Revel's Island, ca. 1900; photo by George Shiras III, *Hunting Wild Life with Camera and Flashlight*

Little Jerry the ox on Revel's Island, ca. 1900; photo by George Shiras III, *Hunting Wild Life with Camera and Flashlight*

View of Broadwater and Hog Island, ca. 1900; photo by Rudolph Eckemeyer

Tombstone of Maggie A. Simpson uncovered on the beach of Hog Island, ca. 1960; photo by Claude Rogers

The second Cape Charles Lighthouse (1864–1927) on Smith's Island, ca. 1890

George David Hitchens (*center*) and the crew of the U.S. Life-Saving Service, Smith's Island, ca. 1914

The harbor at Hog Island, ca. 1900; photo by Rudolph Eckemeyer

Assateague Lighthouse (1860–), ca. 1905

The Atlantic Hotel, Chincoteague, ca. 1905

Steamboat *Manzanita* at the Atlantic Hotel dock, Chincoteague, ca. 1915; "Chincoteague Memories" ms. by Victoria Pruitt

A sinkbox used for duck hunting, Chincoteague, ca. 1915

Unloading the fish boats, Chincoteague, ca. 1910

Result of one day's sport at Chincoteague, ca. 1910

En route to Chincoteague, ca. 1900, *Harper's Monthly Magazine*, October 1913

Seashore Chronicles

W. L. Sheppard

Introduction

The Virginia Barrier Islands extend from north to south along the seacoast of the Eastern Shore from the Maryland line to the mouth of Chesapeake Bay. Out of the east rolls the sleepless Atlantic. To the west across marsh and shallows lie the peninsular counties of Accomack and Northampton. The occasional island is large enough to sustain stands of cedar, pine, and myrtle but most are mere strips of beach and dune. All are under the relentless pressure of wind, surf, and tide.

Human presence on the islands is limited, for the most part, to the northernmost islands—to the National Seashore Park on Assateague, to the tourist haven of Chincoteague, and to Wallops, the site of a National Aeronautics and Space Administration facility. The rest are in the hands of the state and federal governments or of the Nature Conservancy, a national conservation organization, and are reserved as sanctuaries for a myriad of animal and plant life and as living laboratories for ecosystem research.

Today, the only regular visitors to most of the barriers are conservationists and scientists. This was not always the case. Until well into this century, men and women used the islands for fishing and shellfishing, hunting, egging, farming, and livestock raising. They plundered wrecks, founded villages, and established sporting clubs and resort hotels. The islands and their inhabitants also attracted the attention of travelers and tourists whose accounts of their journeys are herein collected. The visitors included speculators, excursionists, rusticators, sportsmen, ornithologists, and those enamored of the isolated and picturesque. Among them were George Washington Parke Custis, Robert E. Lee, illustrator Howard Pyle, sportswriter Alexander Hunter, novelist Thomas Dixon, and naturalists George Shiras, Olin Pettingill, and Tom Horton. Less famous visitors included farmers and clergymen from the Eastern Shore mainland, a Union soldier assigned to picket duty on Hog Island, and a newspaper correspondent reporting on the great storm of 1896.

Taken together, the travelers' accounts tell a curiously circular story of change over time—change not only on the ever-shifting barriers themselves but also in man's relation to the islands. Through the Civil War the barrier islands were extremely isolated, sparsely populated, and virtually undeveloped. Early travelers' accounts, relating dreams of livestock propagation and resort construction, speculate on how the barriers might be used for human benefit. After the war improved communications opened the islands to tourism and investment. Travelers' narratives from 1865 through the hurricane years at the end of the century are stories of the good life, of hunting, fishing, and recreation, of comfort, plenty, and pleasure for sportsmen and watermen alike. They depict the islands as paradise and playground.

Storms, shoreline migration, and the overharvesting of nature's bounty wrecked the resorts and depopulated the islands. Modern accounts emphasize the ancient rhythms of nature—the habits of birds, the pull of tides, the irresistible power of the surf. They conclude that man, so destructive, and, ironically, helpless, has no permanent place on the barriers. Indeed, in the twentieth-century accounts man is no longer central to the narrative. The islands have come full circle.

The travelers' accounts collected in *Seashore Chronicles* are only a small proportion of those available. In making and arranging our selections we sought chronological and geographical balance, variety of experience and viewpoint, narrative coherence, and readability. We have kept editorial intrusion at a minimum. In the interest of clarity and concision we have added the occasional word (indicated by brackets) and silently pruned superfluous text. We have also supplied endnotes that establish chronology, clarify the ambiguous, correct mistakes, identify persons and places, and indicate pertinent scholarship. When local and official spellings of place-names differ, we have used the vernacular.

Brooks Miles Barnes
Barry R. Truitt

A Short History of the Virginia Barrier Islands

BROOKS MILES BARNES
& BARRY R. TRUITT

The Virginia Barrier Islands are some of the most dynamic landforms on earth. The sea is their master, and it is restless and resistless. Its gradual rise since the end of the last ice age has driven the islands slowly westward. Its shifting currents daily build each of the barriers up on one end and tear it down on the other. Its fierce storms wash away dunes, fill marshes, and cut new inlets. Under the suzerainty of the sea, individual islands flourish, whither, and flourish again. The experience of Cobb's Island in the late nineteenth century is typical. In a span of less than forty years storms divided and reunited the island while currents dramatically reshaped its shoreline.

Cobb's, Parramore, Assateague, and the other islands that front the Atlantic vary in length from several hundred yards to a few miles, but all share a similar morphology. Behind the beach rise dunes or sandy ridges and beyond them begins a vast marsh interlaced with bays, guts, and channels. Atop the dunes pines and cedars often take root, and on the larger islands meadows and glades extend from the ridges to the marsh. Between the outer barriers and the Eastern Shore mainland, islands such as Mockhorn, Revel's, and Chincoteague rise from the tall marsh grass. They too are characterized by ridges and glades, but their beaches are abbreviated affairs caressed not by breakers but by the more placid waters of the coastal bays.

The barrier island complex is nursery and way station for a myriad of animal life. Thousands upon thousands of birds and waterfowl rest on or near the islands during their annual migrations. The marshes are spawning ground for a multitude of marine organisms, and the islands themselves are rookeries for numerous species of shore and sea birds. Mammals are not as richly represented—only deer, foxes, raccoons, muskrats, and rice rats are distributed throughout the islands—but insects abound, most obviously mosquitoes, ticks, chiggers, and horseflies.

The Eastern Shore Indians, the Accomacs and Occohannocks, visited and occasionally inhabited the barriers where they hunted, fished, and gathered shellfish, birds' eggs, and seashells. English settlement began on the Eastern Shore mainland in what is now lower Northampton County in the second decade of the seventeenth century and within fifty years had extended northward along the bayside creeks into mid-Accomack County. Other than an ill-fated saltmaking venture on Smith's Island, the early colonists were too busy growing tobacco for the lucrative London market to consider much the economic potential of the barrier islands. At mid-century, however, tumbling tobacco prices forced Eastern Shore planters to diversify into grains and the production of beef and hides. From the first days of settlement Eastern Shoremen had let their cattle run free or had fenced them into necks of land. Now, as the herds grew larger, the planters came to see that the islands were, in the words of a Northampton man, "sufficiently fenced by the Ocean and rivers" and provided abundant grazing and, usually, ample water for the subsistence of cattle and other livestock. Between 1671 and 1705, the heyday of the local cattle industry, Eastern Shoremen applied to the colonial government for land patents for almost all of the barrier islands.

In the first quarter of the eighteenth century, cattle and tobacco declined in importance on the Eastern Shore as grains achieved a primacy that continued until after the Civil War. And yet on the barriers cattle and other livestock—horses, sheep, and swine—endured well into the present century. On Smith's Island, George Washington Parke Custis in the early 1800s bred sheep that he compared favorably with the Merino. On Chincoteague, Assateague, and other islands, the patentees pastured horses. Stunted by exposure, interbreeding, and a Spartan diet of marsh grass, these developed over the generations into the distinctive island pony. Renowned for its strength, endurance, and docility, the pony was much desired for the saddle and for light cart and carriage work. The pony herds generally were owned by syndicates of peninsula planters who each summer "penned" the stock for branding, gelding, and sale. By the early 1800s, the pony penning on Chincoteague was an institution that attracted large crowds from the adjacent islands and from the Virginia and Maryland mainland. On penning day, excursionists and islanders traded horses, gossiped, danced, courted, and consumed prodigious quantities of food and liquor.

The first of the islands settled permanently by the colonists was Chincoteague, around 1690. By the time of the Revolution, settlers had crossed from the mainland to Assateague, Wallop's, Hog, and Smith's and by the Civil War to Cobb's and Prout's. The island communities generally began small—three or four families—and grew slowly, if at all. As late as 1860 only eight people resided on Smith's Island, thirty on Cobb's, eleven on Prout's, fifty-seven on Hog, and similar numbers on Wallop's and Assateague. Chincoteague, with a population of more than five hundred, was the exception. The islanders lived in one- or two-room, story-and-a-half houses, often built of red cedar and set on cedar blocks. A more prosperous household might enjoy a brick chimney, but most made do with lime and lath. Within, the sparsely furnished cabins were decorated with posters, cheap prints, and bottles stuffed with red flannel.

The barrier islanders made an easy living by hunting, egging, fishing, gathering shellfish, herding livestock, and tending garden plots. To visitors attuned to the rhythms and responsibilities of commerce and industry, the islanders seemed the epitome of ignorance and indolence, somnolent souls whose ambition had been leached out by the natural fecundity of marsh and bay. Certainly many an islander could be made deeply content with cedar shakes over his head, oysters in his cookpot, and tobacco and whiskey at his hand, but these abundant luxuries did not eliminate his interest in material gain.

Beached whales and wrecked ships delighted the islanders. These misfortunes meant lucrative salvage opportunities or, at the least, lumber and booty for island homes or for resale on the mainland. There is no evidence that the islanders deliberately lured vessels to their doom, but wrecking occasionally revealed an unsavory facet of the islander personality. In 1787 the survivors of a Maryland packet that broke up off Smith's Island were robbed by islanders of the few valuables they had saved from the wreck. "The boors of Cornwall," an Annapolis editor exclaimed, "would have blushed of such behavior." More than a hundred years later the Chincoteague skipper of a seagoing tug brought his vessel out in a storm to the shoal where the United States naval steamer *Despatch* had run aground, not to rescue the endangered sailors but to attempt to buy the ship for salvage.

Until well into the nineteenth century, the barrier islands contributed next to nothing to the swelling stream of American immigration, commerce, and industry. They did occasionally provide the setting for a minor scene in the national drama. In the seventeenth and eighteenth centuries pirates, including the infamous Blackbeard, made landfall on the more remote of the islands (one buccaneer even claimed to have buried a treasure on the mainland above Chincoteague), and smugglers stole into the inlets with cargoes of slaves and other contraband. During the American

Revolution and the Civil War, rebels circumvented the respective British and Union blockades of the Virginia capes by moving supplies through the seaside inlets, over the Eastern Shore main, and by night across Chesapeake Bay. In both wars the islands witnessed violent encounters. During the Revolution a British privateer reduced a patriot fort on Wallop's Island, and during the Civil War, Confederate raiders smashed the machinery in the Smith's Island lighthouse.

Economic change was in the seaside air during the two decades preceding the Civil War, and by the end of the conflict a boom was at hand for the barrier islands. The change was initiated and sustained by accelerating urban growth and technological innovation and by an infusion of northern capital, ingenuity, and ambition. The growing population and affluence of the northern cities created a demand for barrier island seafood and game, while the development of steam canning and refrigeration combined with the expansion of national steamboat and railroad networks to enable the efficient satisfaction of that demand.

The economic quickening came first to the northernmost islands. In 1850 a traveler observed that the men of Chincoteague annually gathered "an immense quantity of oysters and clams, which they sell to . . . Philadelphia and New York." The trade in Chincoteague Bay seafood continued brisk through the 1860s, but its true heyday began with the coming of the railroad to the western shore of the bay in 1876. Overnight, the town of Franklin City appeared on the marsh, and from its long wharf railroad cars carried northward as many as 50,000 bushels of oysters annually. Across the narrow bay on Chincoteague Island, wharves and oyster-shucking houses proliferated, and in the 1880s the island's schooner fleet grew from three to twenty-five as the seaborne trade kept pace with that of the railroad. "Our oysters," an islander boasted in 1897, "are the best in the Northern market and in the lead in prices."

Meanwhile, in 1884 the New York, Philadelphia, and Norfolk Railroad laid track from Pocomoke, Maryland, south to Cape Charles City. Although the line touched the water only at Cape Charles, its numerous depots stood within easy haul of the seaside wharves. Shucking houses soon went up in the waterfront towns of Wachapreague and Willis Wharf, a Long Island man opened an oyster cannery near Capeville, and some Philadelphia capitalists formed an oyster export company in Cape Charles City. By the turn of the century, express trains daily carried seaside oysters to Chicago, Kansas City, Minneapolis, Omaha, and other western markets.

The boom was not limited to oystering. Commercial crabbing on the seaside began with the coming of the railroad, clamming grew from a sideline into a lucrative industry, and factories for the conversion of fish into oil and fertilizer were established on Chincoteague and Cedar islands. An Eastern Shore politician told a crony that the Cedar Island factories gave work to more than seventy-five men and "are owned and managed by *Republicans* from the north." Fishermen employed by the factories netted not only the inedible menhaden but also drum, trout, and other table fare, which they shipped by rail to urban restaurants and fish markets.

The trains that carried northward oysters, clams, and fish returned with tourists—rusticators and invalids for the seashore, gunners and anglers for the bays and marshes. The vacationers came as individuals, as families, and as parties. They included the humble and the illustrious—a honeymooning couple from Staunton, the Presbyterian Fishing Club of Philadelphia, the industrialist Hamilton Disston in his steam yacht *Manatee,* former Confederate president Jefferson Davis, and President of the United States Grover Cleveland. Bathers frolicked on beaches firm enough to drive a carriage on, while hunters worked a marvelous slaughter among great flights of waterfowl and shorebirds and anglers passed happy hours in successful pursuit of anything from flounder to shark.

To entertain the tourists, hotels and boardinghouses opened between 1876 and 1905 on the islands of Assateague, Chincoteague, Metompkin, Cedar, Hog, and Mockhorn and on the mainland at Red Hills, Wachapreague, and Oyster. The buildings ranged in size from tiny cottages to the fifty-two-room Atlantic Hotel on Chincoteague. The oldest and most famous of the resorts was the Cobb's Island Hotel. The Cobb family had moved from Cape Cod to the Eastern Shore in 1833. At the end of the decade they purchased Cobb's Island, began a lucrative wrecking business (ultimately salvaging thirty-seven stranded vessels at fees ranging from 35 to 60 percent), and commenced hunting waterfowl and shorebirds for the New York restaurant and millinery markets. They also began boarding a few sportsmen in their island home, a business that rapidly expanded into a hotel and cottages accommodating more than one hundred guests. By the

1870s the Cobbs' initial investment in the island of $150 had appreciated to an estimated $100,000.

Private clubs and cottages also sprang up on seaside marsh and strand. The larger resorts included the Revel's Island Club founded by Washingtonians in 1884, clubs on Wallop's and Hog islands established by Philadelphians in 1886 and 1889, and the Accomac Club founded near Parramore Island by New Yorkers around 1890. The clubs were the retreats of people accustomed to comfort and convenience. The Wallop's Island establishment embraced a commodious two-story clubhouse with veranda, guest cottages, a cookhouse, an icehouse, numerous outbuildings, and a steam launch for use as a pleasure craft. Clubmen came to the island to escape the pressures of business and business decorum, and their spirits often were as high as their pockets were deep. In 1894 a Wachapreague newspaper correspondent observed "about a dozen very select members of the Select Council of Philadelphia, with their servants," who had come to view Cedar Island as a possible resort. The Philadelphians, the Wachapreague man reported, "employed sixteen livery horses to convey the party, their liquid refreshments and other impediments from the station to the [Wachapreague] wharf and two of the largest sloops the town afforded to carry them to the Island. . . . As men of financial as well as official weight, they advertised their liberality by spending an hour of enforced delay in throwing money at a crowd of negroes and small boys in the street. [Three days later] they returned [from the island] rather bedraggled, headachy and woe begone."

The boom in tourism and the fisheries brought prosperity to the barrier islands. Watermen's wages compared favorably to those earned on the mainland. In the 1880s an oysterman expected to make $200 for a seven-month season, more than twice as much as the average farm laborer earned in a year. Islanders catering to tourists and sportsmen also did well. A bird hunter complained in 1876 that the Cobb's Island Hotel charged stiff rates and that its guides practiced a "mild extortion." The federal government also contributed to the islands' economy through wages paid to the keepers of the customshouse on Chincoteague, to the keepers of the lighthouses on Assateague, Hog, and Smith's islands, to the keepers and surfmen of the nine Life-Saving Service stations established on the islands in the 1870s and 1880s, and to the postmasters of offices opened on Chincoteague in 1867, Cobb's in 1873, and Hog in 1889. In the late 1880s a Chincoteague man estimated that revenue from oystering and federal wages and pensions—not to mention clamming, the fisheries, and tourism—provided an income of $108 per annum for every man, woman, and child on the island.

This influx of money fueled the construction of residences, churches, schools, hotels, wharves, shucking houses, fish factories, storehouses, and sawmills. A common complaint from Chincoteague in the 1880s and 1890s was the shortage of carpenters and brickmasons. Population grew as the good times kept islanders at home and attracted immigrants from the Eastern Shore mainland and from the North. The growth was most dramatic on Chincoteague, where the population soared from 500 in 1860 to 1,600 in 1880 and 2,700 in 1900. Many of the newcomers came from Maryland, Delaware, and New Jersey. In 1880, only 70 percent of the people living on Chincoteague and Assateague had been born in Virginia compared to more than 90 percent on the Eastern Shore as a whole.

Unfortunately, amidst growth and prosperity, disquieting trends emerged. By the late 1890s the increased number and activity of watermen had placed an insuperable burden on the seaside oyster supply. The Virginia government sought a remedy in leasing sections of barren public grounds to private citizens willing to plant seed oysters. The leaseholders, often wealthy and well-connected mainlanders, succeeded in increasing oyster production only to attract poachers who regarded the bounty of the sea as irrevocably in the public domain. The leaseholders discouraged depredations by erecting over their grounds watchhouses manned by shotgun-toting guards.

Meanwhile, the flights of shorebirds and waterfowl had been devastated. Vacationing sportsmen played their part, but locals wrought the greater destruction as they met the demands of northern restaurants and millineries. The birds stood not a chance. The market hunters used traps and nets, blinds and sinkboxes, breech-loading shotguns, battery guns, and mammoth puntguns. They spread bait and shot birds on the water and by torchlight. The slaughter was immense. An ornithologist learned of fourteen hundred least terns killed on Cobb's Island in a single day for New York milliners. Short-term gain obliterated long-term profit as many sportsmen, finding scarcity where once they had found abundance, quit the islands in disgust.

And yet the ravages of man paled in comparison with those of nature. Hurricanes and northeasters, always an unpleasant fact of barrier island life, entered an especially vicious cycle in the later years of the nineteenth century. Severe storms raked the coast in 1888 (twice), 1889 (twice), 1893, 1895, 1896, 1897 (twice), 1899, 1903, and 1905. The hurricane of October 1897 was perhaps the worst. Wind and high water inundated the business district on Chincoteague, wrecked the hotel on Metompkin beach, and, in the words of a local newspaperman, "levelled [Cedar Island] to a mere flat breath of sand."

Less dramatic but equally pernicious was shoreline migration. Throughout the late nineteenth century, shifting sand and encroaching surf necessitated the relocation of lighthouses, lifesaving stations, and other buildings. The ocean's most noteworthy victim was the Cobb's Island Hotel. Once five hundred yards from the surf, the hotel by the mid-1890s stood within fifty feet of the onrushing waves. In 1895 a powerful northeaster swept away some guest cottages, and the next year a hurricane submerged the island and demolished the hotel, remaining cottages, and private dwellings. By the fall of 1897, Cobb's Island had been abandoned and the hotel furniture sold. An era of barrier island history had come to a close.

During the twentieth century, the free-for-all that had characterized the island economy gradually gave way to commercial activity encouraged, regulated, and restricted by government agencies and private conservation organizations. Market hunting declined early in the century because of greatly diminished stocks of game but also as a result of pressure applied to the state and federal governments by outraged sportsmen and bird lovers. The federal Migratory Bird Act of 1913 established seasons and bag limits while the Eastern Shore Game Protective Association, the American Ornithologists' Union, and the National Aubudon Society employed wardens to prevent breaches of state and federal law. Within a decade, ornithologists noticed dramatically increased numbers of hitherto depleted species.

Shrinking shellfish harvests also prompted government intervention. Over the course of the century, the commonwealth regulated harvest locations, seasons, methods, and equipment. It also introduced a marine police force and established at Wachapreague a research facility of the Virginia Institute of Marine Science. The state failed, however, to arrest the decline of the shellfish industry as the wiles of scofflaw watermen and the political clout of seafood dealers constrained the efforts of the scientific bureaucracy.

On Chincoteague, government combined with business to stimulate the island's economy. In response to the growing popularity of automobile travel, in 1922 the Chincoteague Toll Road and Bridge Company opened a causeway joining the island to the Eastern Shore mainland. Eight years later the commonwealth assumed operation of the causeway and dropped the toll. In 1962 another Chincoteague company built a bridge to Assateague Island. Soon thereafter the federal government turned the lower end of Assateague into a national seashore park. While the causeway maintained Chincoteague's tourist trade, the bridge expanded the trade exponentially. By the mid-1990s, crowds of around forty thousand attended the annual pony penning (now a fund-raiser for the island's volunteer fire department) while more than two million persons a year visited the wildlife refuge and beach on Assateague. Motels, restaurants, and gift shops replaced wharves and shucking houses on the Chincoteague waterfront, and the island's realtors enjoyed a brisk traffic in vacation and retirement properties.

After World War II, diminishing natural resources, disappearing wilderness areas, and advancing scientific knowledge heightened awareness of the ecological importance of the barrier island complex. The state and federal governments responded by expanding and protecting the public domain. The United States government created wildlife refuges on its recently acquired portion of Assateague Island (1942) and on its old holding of Fisherman's Island (1970), while the commonwealth of Virginia purchased Mockhorn (1959), Bone (1960), and Wreck (1961) islands for refuges. Wallop's Island experienced a different fate. Obtained by the federal government from the Wallop's Island Club soon after the war, Wallop's developed as a flight center of the National Aeronautics and Space Administration.

Much more deeply involved in barrier island conservation than government was the Nature Conservancy, a well-funded private organization based in Arlington, Virginia. In 1969, after federal wetlands regulations and a national recession combined to thwart a plan to develop Smith's, Myrtle, and Ship Shoal islands, the conservancy bought out the developers and began to purchase other island property. Within six years it controlled almost the entire coast from Smith's northward to Metompkin. The Nature Conservancy welcomed scientists engaged in ecosystem research but otherwise tightly restricted human activity on its island reserve. At first the conservancy's acquisition and management of its string of islands excited controversy. Eastern Shore businessmen and politicians complained that the conservancy had robbed the peninsula of an opportunity for much-needed economic growth while locals accustomed to thinking of the barriers as a common resented the organization for its emphatic assertion of real property rights. Antagonism lessened, however, as time passed and as the conservancy articulated its vision of the barrier islands as a model of ecosystem conservation and sustainable development.

Meanwhile, the sea continued to demand its forfeit. The fierce storm cycle at the turn of the century abated, but still hurricanes and northeasters periodically pounded the coast. The hurricane of 1933 became the benchmark against which all Eastern Shore storms were measured. On the barriers below Chincoteague the storm surge swept away most of what was left of the tourist industry. It destroyed the hotel on Cedar Island and badly damaged the clubhouses on Wallop's, Parramore, Revel's, Hog, Cobb's, Mockhorn, Skidmore, and Smith's islands. Already reeling from the Great Depression, the clubs never recovered from the hurricane of 1933 and a subsequent storm of 1936.

Shoreline migration also sustained its insidious assault. With the demise of the Cobb's Island resort, Broadwater, a village of 160 souls on the lower end of Hog Island, became the last community on the barriers south of Chincoteague. Around 1930 the sea began to wear at the buffer of dune and woods protecting Broadwater. The hurricanes of the 1930s hastened encroachment, and soon abnormally high tides inundated the ground floors of island homes. In 1941 the last of the Hog Islanders abandoned the two-centuries-old settlement. A cycle had been completed.

The sea was no respecter of persons living or dead. By the early 1950s the Hog Island cemetery, once more than a mile from the beach, was awash in the surf. A headstone, toppled, wet with spray, and nearly covered by sand, attracted the attention of a visitor. He recorded its inscription:

Maggie A. Simpson
Oct. 29, 1844
Dec. 5, 1914
How many hopes lie buried here.

1650

A Voyage to Virginia

HENRY NORWOOD

In early January 1650 the English sailing ship the Virginia Merchant *made landfall somewhere north of the line of white settlement on the Eastern Shore of Virginia. More than three months at sea, the* Virginia Merchant *had been battered by storms and driven by contrary winds. The ship's stores of food and water were depleted and its surviving passengers and crew exhausted. To the weary travelers, the barrier island now before them and the wilderness beyond were objects of both hope and fear.*

The younger son of a Somerset barrister, Henry Norwood (1615–1689) took the side of Charles I in the English civil wars. After a brief exile in Virginia in the early 1650s, Norwood returned to England where he soon was imprisoned in the Tower for plotting against the Commonwealth. Following the restoration of the monarchy in 1660, Charles II gave Norwood the treasurership of Virginia (which he held in absentia from 1661 to 1673) and several other civil and military posts in North America, North Africa, and France. In 1669 Norwood retired to his family's ancestral seat in Gloucestershire.

We approach'd the shore the night of *January* 3d. with little sail; and, as the morning of the fourth day gave us light, we saw the land; but in what latitude we could not tell, for that the officers, whose duty it was to keep the reckoning of the ship, had for many days past totally omitted that part; nor had we seen the sun a great while, to take observations, which (tho' a lame excuse) was all they had to say for that omission. But in truth it was evident, that the desperate estate of the ship, and hourly jeopardy of life did make them careless of keeping either log or journal; the thoughts of another account they feared to be at hand, did make them neglect that of the ship as inconsiderable.

About the hours of three or four in the afternoon of the twelfth eve, we were shot in fair to the shore. The evening was clear and calm, the water smooth; the land we saw nearest was some six or seven *English* miles distant from us, our soundings twenty-five fathoms in good ground for anchor-hold.

And when the anchor was let loose, mate *Putts* was ordered to make the first discovery of what we might expect from the nearest land. He took with him twelve sickly passengers, who fancied the shore would cure them; and he carry'd major *Morrison* on shore with him in pursuit of such adventures as are next in course to be related; for according to the intelligence that could be got from land, we were to take our measures at sea, either to proceed on in our voyage in that sad condition that has been in some proportion set forth, or to land our selves, and unload the ship, and try our fortunes amongst the *Indians*.

In four or five hours time we could discover the boat returning with mate *Putts* alone for a setter, which we look'd upon as a signal of happy success. When he came on board his mouth was full of good tidings, as namely, That he discovered a creek that would harbour our ship, and that there was a depth of water on the bar, sufficient for her draught when she was light. That there was excellent fresh water, (a taste whereof major *Morrison* had sent me in a bottle.) That the shore swarm'd with fowl, and that major *Morrison* stayed behind in expectation of the whole ship's company to follow.

I opened mine ears wide to the motion, and promoted the design of our landing there with all the rhetorick and interest I had. The captain was no less forward for it, hoping thereby to save the lives of the passengers that remained: and that he might not wholly rely on mate *Putts's* judgment in a matter wherein he was most concern'd, he embark'd with me in the wherry, with a kinsman of his, and some others.

In our passage to the shore, the darkness of the evening made us glad to see the fires of our friends at land, which were not only our beacons to direct us to their company, but were also a comfortable relief to our chill bodies when we came near them, the weather being very cold (as it ever is) the wind northwest on that coast.

As soon as I had set my foot on land, and had rendered thanks to almighty God for opening this door of deliverance to us, after so many rescues even from the jaws of death at sea, major *Morrison* was pleased to oblige me beyond all requital, in conducting me to the running stream of water, where, without any limitation of short allowance, I might drink my fill. I was glad of so great liberty, and made use of it accordingly, by prostrating myself on my belly, and setting my mouth against the stream, that it might run into my thirsty stomach without stop. The rest of the company were at liberty to use their own methods to quench their thirst; but this I thought the greatest pleasure I ever enjoyed on earth.

After this sweet refreshment, the captain, myself, and his kinsman crossed the creek in our wherry, invited thither by the cackling of wild-fowl. The captain had a gun charged, and the moon shining bright in his favour, he killed one duck of the flock that flew over us, which was roasted on a stick out of hand by the seamen, whilst we walk'd on the shore of the creek for further discovery.

In passing a small gullet we trod on an oyster bank that did happily furnish us with a good addition to our duck. When the cooks had done their parts, we were not long about ours, but fell on without using the ceremony of calling the rest of the company, which would have been no entertainment to so many, the proverb telling us, *The fewer the better chear.* The bones, head, legs, and inwards were agreed to be the cook's fees; so we gave God thanks, and return'd to our friends, without making boast of our good fortunes.

Fortify'd with this repast, we inform'd our selves of the depth of water at the bar of the creek, in which the captain seem'd satisfy'd, and made shews in all his deportment, of his resolution to discharge the ship there in order to our safety. Towards break of day he ask'd me in my ear, If I would go back with him on board the ship? I told him, No, because it would be labour lost, in case he would persist in his resolution to do what he pretended, which he ratify'd again by protestations, and so went off with his kinsman, who had a large coarse cloth gown I borrow'd of him to shelter me from the sharpest cold I ever felt.

No sooner had the captain cleared himself of the shore but the day-break made me see my error in not closing with his motion in my ear. The first object we saw at sea was the ship under sail, standing for the capes with what canvass could be made to serve the turn. It was a very heavy prospect to us who remained (we knew not where) on shore, to see our selves thus abandon'd by the ship, and more, to be forsaken by the boat, so contrary to our mutual agreement.

In this amazement and confusion of mind that no words can express, did our miserable distress'd party condole with each other our being so cruelly abandon'd and left to the last despairs of human help, or indeed of ever seeing more the face of man. We entred into a sad consultation what course to take; and having, in the first place, by united prayers, implored the protection of Almighty God, and recommended our miserable estate to the same providence which, in so many instances of mercy, had been propitious to us at sea; the whole party desired me to be as it were the father of this distressed family, to advise and conduct them in all things I thought might most tend to our preservation. This way of government we agreed must necessarily reside in one, to avoid disputes, and variety of contradictory humours, which would render our deliverance the more impracticable; and it was thought most reasonable to be placed in me, for the health and strength it had pleased God to preserve unto me above my fellows, more than for any other qualification.

It was, to the best of my remembrance, upon the fifth day of *January* that we entred into this method of life, or rather into an orderly way unto our graves, since nothing but the image of death was represented to us: but that we might use our outmost endeavours to extract all the good we could out of those evil symptoms that did every way seem to confound us, I made a muster of the most able bodies for arms and labour; and, in the first place, I put a fowling-piece into every man's hand that could tell how to use it. Amongst the rest, a young gentleman, Mr. *Francis Cary* by name, was very helpful to me in the fatigue and active part of this undertaking. He was strong and healthy, and was very ready for any employment I could put upon him.

All our woodmen and fowlers had powder and shot given them, and some geese were killed for supper. Evening came on apace, and our resolution being taken to stay one night more in these quarters, I sent my cousin *Cary* to head the creek, and make what discovery he could as he passed along the shore, whether of *Indians* or any other living creatures that were likely to relieve our wants, or end our days. To prepare like men for the latter, we resolved to die fighting, if that should be the case; or if, on the contrary, the *Indians* should accost us in a mein of amity, then to meet them will all imaginable courtesy, and please them with such trivial presents as they love to deal in, and so engage them into a friendship with us.

My cousin *Cary* was not absent much above an hour, when we saw him return in a contrary point to that he sallied out upon. His face was clouded with ill news he had to tell us, namely, that we were now residing on an island without any inhabitant, and that he had seen its whole extent, surrounded (as he believed) with water deeper than his head; that he had not seen any native, or any thing in human shape, in all his round, nor any other creature besides the fowls of the air, which he would, but could not, bring unto us.

This dismal success of so unexpected a nature, did startle us more than any single misfortune that had befallen us, and was like to plunge us into utter despair. We beheld each other as miserable wretches sentenc'd to a lingering death, no man knowing what to propose for prolonging life any longer than he was able to fast. My cousin *Cary* was gone from us without notice, and we had reason (for what followed) to believe he was under the conduct of an angel; for we soon saw him return with a chearful look, his hands carrying something we could not distinguish by any name at a distance; but by nearer approach we were able to descry they were a parcel of oysters, which, in crossing the island, as he stept over a small current of water, he trode upon to his hurt; but laying hands on what he felt with his feet, and pulling it with all his force, he found himself possessed of this booty of oysters, which grew in clusters, and were contiguous to a large bank of the same species, that was our staple subsistance whilst we remained there.

While this cold season continued, great flights of fowl frequented the island, geese, ducks, curlieus, and some of every sort we killed and roasted on sticks, eating all but the feathers. It was the only perquisite belonging to my place of preference to the rest, that the right of carving was annexed to it, wherein, if I was partial to my own interest, it was in cutting the wing as large and full of meat as possible; whereas the rest was measured out as it were with scale and compass.

But as the wind veered to the southward, we had greater warmth and fewer fowl, for they would then be gone to colder climates. In their absence we were confined to the oyster bank, and a sort of weed some four inches long, as thick as houseleek, and the only green (except pines) that the island afforded. It was very insipid on the palate; but being boiled with a little pepper (of which one had brought a pound on shore) and helped with five or six oysters, it became a regale for every one in turn.

In quartering our family we did observe the decency of distinguishing sexes: we made a small hut for the poor weak women to be by themselves; our cabbin for men was of the same fashion, but much more spacious, as our numbers were. One morning, in walking on the shore by the sea side, with a long gun my hand loaden with small shot, I fired at a great flight of small birds called *Oxeyes,* and made great slaughter among them, which gave refreshment to all our company.

But this harvest had a short end; and as the weather by its warmth, chased the fowl to the north, our hunger grew sharper upon us. And in fine, all the strength that remained unto us was employed in a heartless struggling to spin out life a little longer; for we still deemed our selves doom'd to die by famine, from whose sharpest and most immediate darts tho' we seemed to be rescued for a small time, by meeting these contingent helps on shore, yet still we apprehended (and that on too great probability) they only served to reprieve us for a little longer day of execution, with all the dreadful circumstances of a lingering death.

For the south-west winds that had carry'd away the fowl, brought store of rain; which meeting with a spring-tide, our chief magazine, the oyster bank, was overflown; and as they became more accessible, our bodies also decayed so sensibly, that we could hardly pull them out of their muddy beds they grew on. And from this time forward we rarely saw the fowl; they now grew shy and kept aloof when they saw us contriving against their lives.

Add to this, our guns most of them unfix'd and out of order, and our powder much decayed, insomuch that nothing did now remain to prolong life, but what is counted sauce to whet, than substance to satisfy the appetite; I mean the oysters, which were not easily gotten by our crazy bodies after the quantity was spent that lay most commodious to be reach'd, and which had fed us for the first six days we had been on the island. And thus we wish'd every day to be the last of our lives (if God had so pleased) so hopeless and desperate was our condition, all expectation of human succour being vanished and gone.

[A woman] had the envied happiness to die about this time; and it was my advice to the [female] survivors, who were following her apace, to endeavour their own preservation by converting her dead carcase into food, as they did to good effect. The same counsel was embrac'd by those of our sex: the living fed upon the dead; four of our company having the happiness to end their miserable lives on *Sunday* night the——day of *January*. Their chief distemper, 'tis true, was hunger; but it pleased God to hasten their *exit* by an immoderate access to cold, caused by a most terrible storm of hail and snow at north-west, on the *Sunday* aforesaid, which did not only dispatch those four to their long homes, but did sorely threaten all that remained alive, to perish by the same fate.

Great was the toil that lay on my hands (as the strongest to labour) to get fuel together sufficient for our preservation. In the first place I divested myself of my great gown, which I spread at large, and extended against the wind in nature of a screen, having first shifted our quarters to the most calm commodious place that could be found to keep us, as much as possible, from the inclemency of that prodigious storm.

Under the shelter of this traverse I took as many of my comrades as could be comprehended in so small a space; whereas those who could not partake of that accommodation, and were enabled to make provision for themselves, were forced to suffer for it. And it was remarkable, that nothwithstanding all the provision that could possibly be made against the sharpness of this cold, either by a well-burning fire consisting of two or three loads of wood, or shelter of this great gown to the windward, we could not be warm. That side of our wearing cloaths was singed and burnt which lay towards the flames, whilst the other side that was from the fire, became frozen and congeal'd. Those who lay to the leeward of the flame, could not stay long to enjoy the warmth so necessary to life, but were forced to quit and be gone to avoid suffocation by the smoke and flame.

When the day appeared, and the sun got up to dissipate the clouds, with downcast looks and dejected, the survivors of us entred into a final deliberation of what remained to be done on our parts (besides our prayers to Almighty God) to spin out a little longer time of life, and wait a further providence from heaven for our better relief. There were still some hands that retained vigour, tho' not in proportion to those difficulties we were to encounter, which humanly did seem insuperable. The unhappy circumstance of our being coop'd up in an island, was that which took from us all probable hopes of escaping this terrible death that did threaten us every hour. Major *Morrison,* on whose counsel I had reason to rely most, was extremely decayed in his strength, his legs not being able to support him. It was a wonderful mercy that mine remained in competent strength, for our common good, which I resolved, by God's help, to employ for that end to the last gasp.

In this last resolution we had to make, I could not think of any thing worthy my proposal, but by an attempt to cross the creek, and swim to the main (which was not above an hundred yards over) and being there to coast along the woods to the south-west (which was the bearing of *Virginia*) until I should meet *Indians,* who would either relieve or destroy us. I fancied the former would be our lot when they should see our conditions, and that no hurt was intended to them; or if they should prove inhuman, and of a bloody nature, and would not give us quarter, why even in that case it would be worth this labour of mine to procure a sudden period to all our miseries.

I open'd my thoughts to this purpose to the company, who were sadly surprized at the motion; but being fully convinc'd in their judgment, that this was the only course that could be depended on (humanly speaking) for our relief, they all agreed it must be done.

To fortify me for this expedition, it was necessary that some provision should be made for a daily support to me in this my peregrination. Our choice was small; our only friend the oyster bank was all we had to rely on; which being well stew'd in their own liquor, and put up into bottles, I made no doubt, by God's blessing, but that two of them well filled, would suffice to prolong my life in moderate strength, until I had obtain'd my end. To accomplish this design, my cousin *Cary* laboured hard for oysters, hoping to make one in the adventure.

About the ninth day of our being in the island, I fell to my oyster-cookery, and made a good progress that very day; when in the heat of my labour my cousin *Cary* brought me word, That he had just in that instant seen *Indians* walking on the main. I suspended my cookery out of hand, and hastened with all possible speed to be an eye-witness of that happy intelligence; but with all the haste I could make I could see no such thing, but judg'd it a chimera that proceeded from some operation in my cousin's fancy, who was more than ordinary of a sanguine nature, which made him see (as it were by inchantment) things that were not, having many times been deluded (as I judg'd) by the same deception.

Defeated in this manner of my hopes to see *Indians* without the pains of seeking them, I returned to my work, and continued at it till one bottle was full, and myself tired: wherefore, that I might be a little recreated, I took a gun in my hand; and hearing the noise of geese on our shore, I approach'd them privately, and had the good hap to be the death of one. This goose, now in my possession without witnesses, I resolved to eat alone (deducting the head, bones, gut, *&c.* which were the cook's fees) hoping thereby to be much the better enabled to swim the creek, and perform the work I had upon my hand. I hung my goose upon the twist of a tree in a shrubby part of the wood, whilst I went to call aside our cook with his broach, and a coal of fire to begin the roast. But when we came to the place of execution, my goose was gone all but the head, the body stolen by wolves, which the *Indians* told us after, do abound greatly in that island.

Being thus over-reach'd by the wolf, it was time to return to my cookery, in order to my sally out of the island; for I had little confidence in the notice frequently brought me of more and more *Indians* seen on the other side, since my own eyes could never bear witness of their being there.

The next morning, being the ninth or tenth of our being there, I fell to work afresh, hoping to be ready to begin my journey that day; and being very busy, intelligence was brought, that a canoe was seen to lie on the broken ground to the south of the island, which was not discovered till now, since our being there: but this I thought might be a mistake cast in the same mould of many others that had deceived those discoverers, who fancy'd all things real according to their own wishes. But when it was told me, That *Indians* had been at the poor women's cabbin in the night, and had given them shell-fish to eat, that was demonstration of reality beyond all suspicion. I went immediately to be inform'd from themselves, and they both avowed it for truth, shewing the shells (the like whereof I ne'er had seen) and this I took for proof of what they said.

The further account these women gave of the *Indians*, was, that they pointed to the south-east with their hands, which they knew not how to interpret, but did imagine by their several gestures, they would be with them again to morrow. Their pointing to the south-east was like to be the time they would come, meaning nine o'clock to be their hour, where the sun will be at that time.

This news gave us all new life, almost working miracles amongst us, by making those who desponded, and totally yielded themselves up to the weight of despair, and lay down with an intent never more to rise again, to take up their beds and walk. This friendly charitable visit of the *Indians* did also put a stop to my preparations to seek them, who had so humanely prevented me, by their seeking ways to preserve and save our lives.

Instead of those preparations for my march which had cost me so much pains, I passed my time now in contriving the fittest posture our present condition would allow us to put on when these angels of light should appear again with the glad tidings of our relief; and the result was, that every able man should have his gun lying by his side, laden with shot, and as fit for use as possible, but not to be handled unless the *Indians* came to us like enemies (which was very unlikely, the premises considered) and then to sell our lives at as dear a rate as we could; but if they came in an amicable posture, then would we meet them unarm'd, chearfully, which the *Indians* like, and hate to see a melancholy face.

In these joyful hopes of unexpected deliverance by these *Indians,* did we pass the interval of their absence. Every eye look'd sharply out when the sun was at south-east, to peep thro' the avenues of the wood to discover the approaches of our new friends. When the sun came to the south we thought our selves forgotten by them, and began to doubt the worst.

About the hours of two or three o'clock it pleased God to change the face of our condition for the best; for whilst I was busy at the fire in preparations to wait on them, the *Indians,* who had placed themselves behind a very great tree, discovered their faces with most chearful smiles, without any kind of arms, or appearance of evil design; the whole number of them (perhaps twenty or thirty in all) consisting of men, women and children; all that could speak accosting us with joyful countenances, shaking hands with every one they met. The words *Ny Top,* often repeated by them, made us believe they bore a friendly signification, as they were soon interpreted to signify my friend.

After many salutations and *Ny Tops* interchang'd, the night approaching, we fell to parley with each other; but perform'd it in signs more confounded and unintelligible than any other conversation I ever met withal.

They did me the honour to make all applications to me, as being of largest dimensions, and equip'd in a camlet coat glittering with galoon lace of gold and silver, it being generally true, that where knowledge informs not, the habit qualifies.

The ears of *Indian* corn they gave us for present sustenance, needed no other interpreter to let them know how much more acceptable it was to us than the sight of dead and living corpses, which raised great compassion in them, especially in the women, who are observed to be of a soft tender nature.

One of them made me a present of the leg of a swan, which I eat as privately as it was given me, and thought it so much the more excellent, by how much it was larger than the greatest limb of any fowl I ever saw.

The *Indians* stayed with us about two hours, and parted not without a new appointment to see us again the next day: and the hour we were to expect them by their pointing to the sun, was to be at two o'clock in the afternoon. I made the chief of them presents of ribbon and other slight trade, which they lov'd, designing, by mutual endearment, to let them see, it would gratify their interest as well as their charity, to treat us well. *Ha-na Haw* was their parting word, which is farewel, pointing again at the place where the sun would be at our next meeting. We took leave in their own words *Ha-na Haw.*

The going away of the *Indians,* and leaving us behind was a separation hard to be born by our hungry company, who nevertheless had received a competent quantity of corn and bread to keep us till they returned to do better things for our relief; we did not fail to give glory to God for our approaching deliverance, and the joy we conceiv'd in our minds in the sense of so great a mercy, kept us awake all the night, and was a cordial to the sick and weak to recover their health and strength.

The delay of the *Indians* coming next day, beyond their set time, we thought an age of tedious years: At two o'clock we had no news of them, but by attending their own time with a little patience, we might see a considerable number of them, men, women, and children, all about our huts, with recruits of bread and corn to stop every mouth. Many of them desir'd beads and little truck they use to deal in, as exchange for what they gave us; and we as freely gave them what we had brought on shore; but to such of us gave them nothing, the *Indians* failed not however to give them bread for nothing.

One old man of their company, who seem'd by the preference they gave him, to be the most considerable of the party, apply'd himself to me by gestures and signs, to learn something (if possible) of our country, and occasion of the sad posture he saw us in, to the end that he might inform his master, the king of *Kickotank,* (on whose territories we stood) and dispose him to succour us, as we had need.

I made return to him in many vain words, and in as many insignificant signs as himself had made to me, and neither of us one jot the wiser. The several nonplus's we both were at in striving to be better understood, afforded so little of edification to either party, that our time was almost spent in vain. It came at last into my head, that I had long since read Mr. [John] *Smith's* travels thro' those parts of *America,* and that the word *Werowance* (a word frequently pronounced by the old man) was in *English* the king. That word, spoken by me, with strong emphasis, together with the motions of my body, speaking my desire of going with him, was very pleasing to the old man, who thereupon embrac'd me with more than common kindness, and by all demonstrations of satisfaction, did shew that he understood my meaning. This one word was all the *Indian* I could speak, which (like a little armour well plac'd) contributed to the saving of our lives.

The canoes being fitted to take us in and waft us to the main, I made a fair muster of the remnant we had to carry off, and found we wanted six of the number we brought on shore (*viz.*) four men and two women: five of those six we knew were dead, but missing one of our living women, we made the *Indians* understand the same, who as readily made us know that she was in their thoughts, and should be cared for as soon as we were settled in our quarters.

In passing the creek that was to lead us to an honest fisherman's house, we entred a branch of it to the southward, that was the road-way to it. The tide was going out, and the water very shoal, which gave occasion to any one that had a knife, to treat himself with oysters all the way. At the head of that branch we were able in a short time to discover that heaven of happiness where our most courteous host did, with a chearful countenance, receive and entertain us. Several fires were kindled out of hand, our arms and powder were laid up in safety, and divers earthen pipkins were put to boil with such varieties as the season would afford. Every body had something or other to defend and save them from the cold; and my obligation to him, by a peculiar care that he had of me, exceeded all the rest. I had one intire side of the fire, with a large platform to repose on, to myself; furrs and deer skins to cover my body, and support my head, with a priority of respect and friendly usage, which, to my great trouble, I was not able to deserve at his hands, by any requital then in my power to return.

Our bodies thus refresh'd with meat and sleep, comforted with fires, and secured from all the changes and inclemencies of that sharp piercing cold season, we thought the morning (tho' clad in sunshine) did come too fast upon us. Breakfast was liberally provided and set before us, our arms faithfully delivered up to my order for carriage; and thus in readiness to set forward, we put our selves in a posture to proceed to the place where the king resided. The woman left behind at the island, had been well look'd to, and was now brought off to the care of her comrade that came with us; neither of them in a condition to take a journey, but they were carefully attended and nourished in this poor man's house, till such time as boats came to fetch them to *Virginia,* where they did soon arrive in perfect health, and lived (one or both of them) to be well married, and to bear children, and to subsist in as plentiful a condition as they could wish.

From Peter Force, ed., *Tracts and Other Papers Relating Principally to the Origin, Settlement, and Progress of the Colonies of North America, From the Discovery of the Country to the Year 1776* (Washington, D.C., 1844), 3, no. 10

1808

The Native Sheep of Smith's Island

GEORGE WASHINGTON PARKE CUSTIS

Through the first two centuries of European settlement, Eastern Shoremen considered the barrier islands valuable primarily as pasture for livestock. George Washington Parke Custis (1781–1857) is best remembered as the step-grandson of George Washington, as a playwright, and as the squire of Arlington on the Potomac, but he also was a leading agricultural reformer. Custis intended for his experiment in sheep raising on the old family preserve of Smith's Island to serve as a model for enlightened agriculturists all along the southern coast.

I come next to speak of the Smith's Island wool, a discovery which will accrue in the happiest effects to my country, and yield the most grateful sensations to myself. This island lies in the Atlantic ocean, immediately off the eastern cape of Virginia, and contains between three and four thousand acres. Its name is derived from [Captain John] Smith, the permanent settler and improver of the colony of Virginia; the soil, though sandy, is in many parts extremely rich and productive of a succulent herbage, which supports the stock at all seasons. About one half of the island is in wood, which is pierced with glades, running parallel with the sea, and of several miles in extent. These glades are generally wet, and being completely sheltered by the wood on either side, preserve their vegetation in great measure throughout the winter, and thereby yield a support to the stock. Along the sea coast are also abundant scopes of pasturage, producing a short grass in summer, which is peculiarly grateful to the palate of most animals, and particularly sheep. The island is very long, being estimated at fourteen miles, which gives the variety and change of pasture, so necessary to the system of sheep farming. Within it, are various shrubs and plants, which the animals appear to browse on with great relish, particularly the myrtle bushes, with which the island abounds. The access to salt also forms a material feature in the many attributes which Smith's Island possesses. The stock are wild cattle, and sheep principally; hogs have been prohibited from their destroying the lambs; and some horses put on to breed many years since, but two or three remain.

The origin of the Smith's island sheep cannot be precisely ascertained, but are supposed to be the indigenal race of the country, put thereon about twenty years since, and improved by the hand of Nature. When we come to compare the Smith's Island wool, with the native wool of the country at large, we are lost in astonishment at this wonderful interposition of Providence in our behalf, which serves to shew what a benefit we enjoy, and how little we have estimated the gift.

The Smith's Island wool is, without question, one of the finest in the world, and has excited the praise and astonishment of all who have seen it. To recapitulate the various opinions given of its merits is unnecessary. It only remains to be judged in Europe, whither a specimen has been sent, to determine its value, when compared with the famous Merino, hitherto the unrivalled material in the woollen manufacture. The Smith's Island is a great deal longer than the Spanish, being, in full growth, from five to nine inches in length, and in some instances much more. In quantity it is also vastly superior, as the sheep yield at least twice as much, and in some instances still more. And, lastly, the size and figure of the animal admits of no comparison, being entirely in the favor of the Smith's Island.

The only question remaining is the texture. If the Merino is fine in grain—the Smith's Island is so fine as to answer every purpose to which the other can be appropriated, and so much larger in quantity as to yield a better profit to the breeder. No cloth which the Merino manufactures, will be disgraced by the introduction of the Smith's Island: and many fabrics manufactured by the one, at a great price, can be formed by the other, at a much less. The Smith's Island is as white as snow, and perfectly silky and soft to the touch, and of delicate grain.

It is to be remembered that the specimens which have been shewn to the world were sheared from an ewe promiscuously seized on the island, and sent to Arlington. If such be the product of an indiscriminate choice, may we not expect a much superior sample, selected by the eye of judgment and experience.

The sheep on Smith's Island are perfectly wild, and so unconscious of the care of man as to fly his approach. They are taken twice a year, in spring and fall by certain stratagems, and sheared at each time, after which they are again given to liberty and uncontroul. The growth of wool must certainly be very rapid, since the period of a few months produces a second harvest for the shears.

The number of sheep formerly on Smith's island amounted to between five and six hundred, but depredations and other casualties, have very much reduced this quantity. The number which the island would carry, when fully stocked, may be computed from the stocking of similar pasturage in other countries. From two visits made in 1800 and 1804, I supposed the prime pasturage consisted of twelve or fourteen hundred acres, this, the glades in the interior, and the flat ground on the west end; but added to this is a vast range extending from the termination of the wood, on the east, to the Ship Shoal, or eastern extremity. The sea shore, in many places, also, produces a short and pleasant herbage, much coveted by stock.

It would not be too great an average to allow four sheep to the acre, but for the sake of certainty in the calculation, four thousand sheep might fairly be allowed to the whole.

The wild cattle are so very shy as to be approached with great difficulty, and are exceedingly fierce when wounded. Their size is not large, but the flesh well tasted, and sometimes very fat. The sheep are by no means so wild, being more timorous from nature, but cannot be approached without much circumspection, and when wounded or taken, shew every symptom of fear, at beholding the great destroyer, man.

It may be rather adviseable to retain the stock of Smith's island in this primitive state of nature, since it affords a partial security from depredation, and no doubt contributes to their health, and the superior quality of their fleece.

Sheep are particularly delicate in some respects, and are very liable to be injured by an unwholesome atmosphere. We know that those which frequent the mountainous parts of most countries are a very hardy vigorous race; those again which resort to the salt marshes are unconscious of diseases common in other parts of the country. As a proof of the salubrity of our sea islands, in this respect, I remember shooting a ram on Smith's island so very old as to have worn his teeth entirely away, and his eyes were almost obscured from age. Perhaps he had numbered fifteen or twenty years, and from his size had, no doubt, been once master of the flock.

The rot, a disease fatal to sheep in all countries, is unknown upon Smith's island, and is not incident to any salt pasturage. The island, being of sandy soil, affords dry places on which they can repose; and from its insular situation, is not capable of receiving contagion from abroad.

The sheep of Smith's island will answer, I believe, in all parts of our country, particularly in the southern latitudes of Virginia, the states of Tennessee and Kentucky, the Mississippi and all southward thereof. Upon the Sea islands of the Carolinas and Georgia they might be pastured to great advantage, and very many situations now lying idle and unprofitable, might be turned to use by the introduction of this valuable race of animals. They are so very active in pursuit of their food, as to cover a great space of ground in a very short time, and will brouse upon many plants which are at present converted to no use whatever. In situations similar to their native island they will be supported without any expence; and where the climate is colder, and the pasturage less abundant, they will be found to subsist at least as well as any other species.

During my visit in 1804, I had great opportunity of judging of the mutton, and can affirm, that it was truly epicurean, and very high flavored;

whether this would continue if the animals were domesticated, I much doubt, since the flavor is as much derived from the habits as the food of the animal. The bone is remarkably small, which will cause them to weigh well, and to fatten sooner, than those of a different description.

The difficulty of obtaining fresh water upon the Sea islands is not so great as may be imagined, for in digging four or five feet in the sand it rises in abundance, and perfectly fit for use. The persons who live upon the island form ponds of this description for the use of the stock.

From *An Address to the People of the United States, on the Importance of Encouraging Agriculture and Domestic Manufactures; . . . Together with an Account of the Improvements in Sheep at Arlington, the Native Sheep of Smith's Island, and the Plan Proposed of Extending this Valuable Race of Animals, for the Benefit of the Country at Large* (Alexandria, Va., 1808), pp. 15–19

1832

Something Relative to Smith's Island

ROBERT E. LEE

In 1832 Robert E. Lee (1807–1870) was many years from entering the Confederate Valhalla. A second lieutenant of engineers stationed at Fort Monroe, Lee had come to Smith's Island to view the property for its owner and his father-in-law, George Washington Parke Custis. Lee's letter to Custis is a concise yet vivid soldier's report of the island's terrain, inhabitants, livestock, and natural bounty.

Old Point May 22nd 1832

My dear Father

Supposing you may feel an interest in hearing something relative to Smith's Island, I take advantage of the first leisure day since my return, to give you an account of my visit there. And also to submit to your better judgement my views of the manner of turning it to profit. The whole Island is nearer the level of the sea than I expected to find it; & the Tenants told me that the Gale of 27th April 1831 nearly covered it with water. In fact only some of the *highest* ridges escaped upon which the cattle & sheep took refuge. Their little patches of corn around their houses were destroyed & the salt not having yet left the ground, deprived them of a crop for this year. You may recollect that the surface of the Island is composed of alternate Ridges & Glades, running as near as I could judge from North, to South, & from one extremity to the other. The soil of the glades is as rich as possible & covered with fine grass, that of the ridges contains a great deal of sand & is covered with Pine. But as the part of the Island exposed to the ocean is wearing away, & the Beach which used to protect the glades, has been in many places levelled the water at common high tide finds its way into them & renders the Pasturage not so good. There are four families residing there, Thomas Roberts, Hamilton, Hamby & Hitchings. The first has an uncommonly good character with every one I met with both on the Island & Main. He has built himself a very comfortable house & Dr. Simkins considering him entirely honest & trustworthy, has given him immediate charge of all the Property. Hamilton & Hamby are both respectable men, but Hitchings by the united testimony of all is drunken & dishonest & he has received orders to leave the Island. Each of these families have from 30 to 40 head of cattle, which they milk, take care of &c and as they rapidly increase will be at last valuable. There are besides 150 *wild* cattle, as near as can be estimated, which perhaps increase as fast as the Tame. The females are of course valuable for their increase. But the males only for their *hides.* I therefore think the best plan would be to shoot *all* the *old Bulls* in the Fall, & to catch the calves in the Spring (if possible) & alter the males. They would then make steers, or beef in the Fall. I saw a drove of about 60 of these fellows early one morning on the Beach where they had taken refuge the night previous to get rid of the moschettoes (which are *always very thick*). But they would not let me get nearer than about 300 yds. of them. They were all small & had not recovered from the hard winter. There were a great many calves & yearlings among them. I suppose the breed must have very much degenerated. The tame cattle were somewhat larger & in better order. The number of sheep is not accurately known, but is supposed to be over 100. They are nearly as wild as the cattle, & looked very *ragged.* The shearing had not commenced, and I directed that they should then be counted & marked. I could learn of no one who wished to purchase, nor do I believe there is any one who would give for it ¼ of its value. I think it would improve the Island, to sell some of the timber & wood off of it, as it would render the interior dryer, diminish the quantity of *ticks* (of which I got full) & moschettoes which must harass the cattle very much & might tend to *civilize* the stock. Timber is much wanted on the Main for Ship & House building & I might make some arrangement with those, who supply Norfolk with pine wood to cut it of[f] the land. It is even carried to N. York from Carolina, for the Steam Boats. The Keeper of the light house & tenants were very kind & attentive to me, gave me plenty of milk [&] butter & eggs & fish. They had plenty of sea birds eggs. Those of the willet & sedge hen were the best. Fish is so common there that they cooked a large dish of the *Roes* for me. The season for Rock & the *streaked* Bass was just commencing, & in a few days that of the Drum would begin. As I had to see Dr. Simkins, I went first to the E. S. He was very polite & is a gentlemanly & sensible young man. He was prevented from going to Smith's Id. with me by business. As I knew you objected to *long* letters, I have tried to make this as short as possible, but wishing to be minute it has been spun out to this great length. I will now stop & wishing you all kinds of happiness, will hope that you believe me your truly & sincerely

R. E. Lee

From Robert Edward Lee Papers, Duke University, Durham, North Carolina

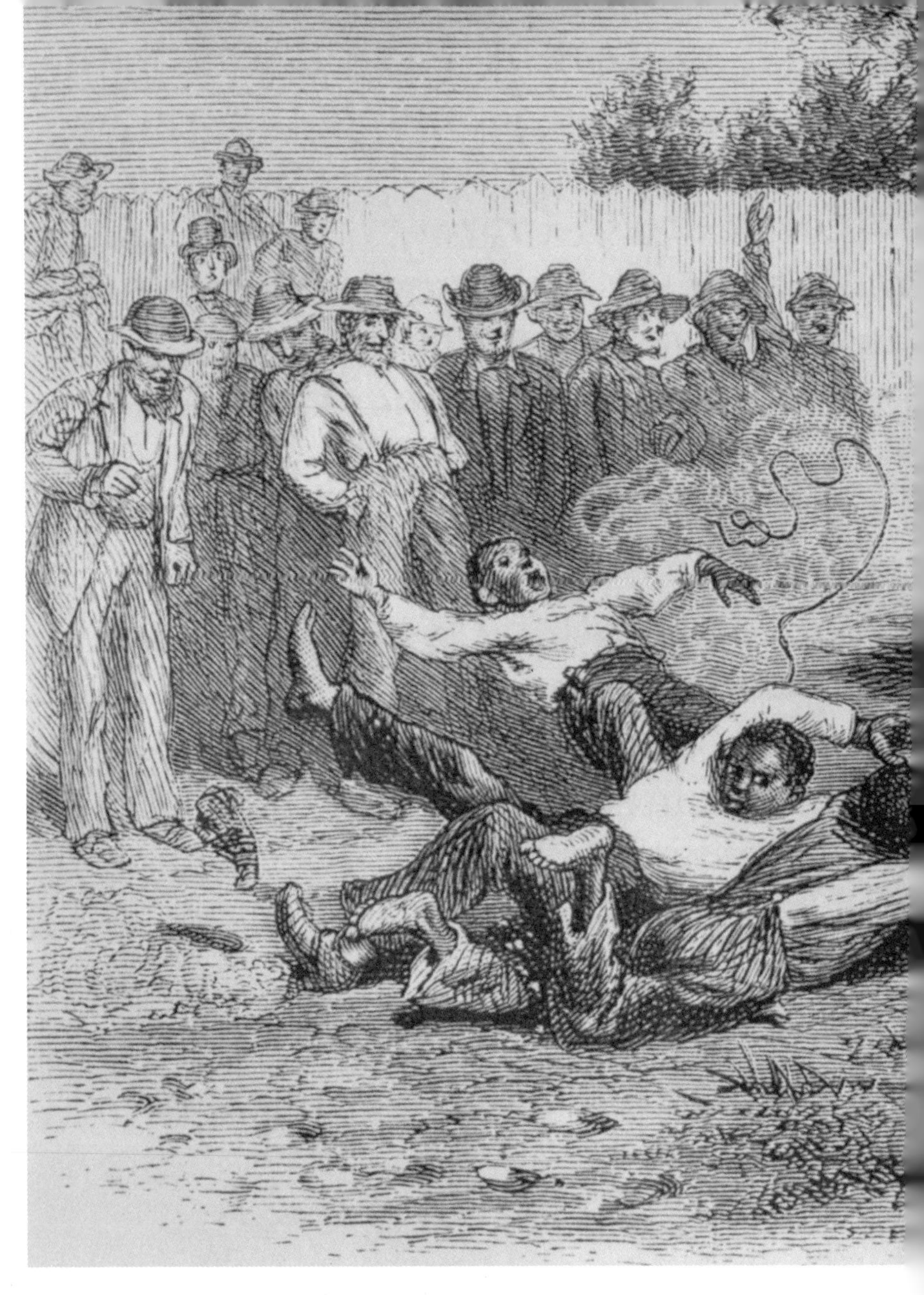

1835

Some Account of the Wild Horses of the Sea Islands of Virginia and Maryland

THOMPSON HOLMES

Today, the annual pony penning on Chincoteague Island is a formalized tourist attraction. In 1835, as the account below makes clear, the penning had long been a melding of conviviality and commerce. Thompson Holmes, a physician of middle age, lived at Pharsalia plantation on the Accomack County mainland near Chincoteague Bay. Holmes removed from the Eastern Shore to Philadelphia around 1840.

Pharsalia, (Accomac,) 30th July, 1835

To the Editor of the Farmers' Register.

The florid description which you have recently received of "wild horses" and "horse pennings" upon our Atlantic islands, was better suited to what they were thirty years ago—and indeed, before my knowledge of Virginia—than to their present appearance. The horses have been gradually diminishing in number, by neglect, until on one island, they are nearly extinct; and the rustic splendor, the crowds, and wild festivity of the Assateague horse-pennings, scarcely retain a shadow of their ancient glory. The multitudes of both sexes that formerly attended those occasions of festal mirth, were astonishing. The adjoining islands were literally emptied of their simple and frolic-loving inhabitants, and the peninsula itself contributed to swell the crowd, for fifty miles above and below the point of meeting. All the beauty and fashion of a certain order of the female population, who had funds, or favorites to command a passage, were sure to be there. All who loved wild adventure—whose hearts danced at the prospect of a distant water excursion, and a scene of no ordinary revel, where the ocean rolled his billows almost to their feet; all who had a new gown to show, or a pretty face to exhibit, who could dance well, or sing; belles that sighed for beaux and beaux that wanted sweethearts; all who loved to kiss, or to be kissed, to caress, or be caressed; all, in short, whose hearts delighted in romance, without knowing its name, hurried away to this anxiously expected scene of extravagant jollity, on the narrow thread of beach that the ocean seemed, every moment, threatening to usurp. You can scarcely imagine, sir, the extravagant enthusiasm with which this exciting sport was anticipated and enjoyed. It was a frantic carnival, without its debauchery. The young of both sexes, had their imaginations inflamed by the poetical narratives of their mothers and maiden aunts, who in their more juvenile days were wont to grace those sylvan fetes, of the mad flight of wild horses careering away along a narrow, naked, level sand-beach at the top of their speed, with manes and tails waving in the wind before a company of mounted men, upon the fleetest steeds, shouting and hallowing in the wildest notes of triumph, and forcing the affrighted animals into the angular pen of pine logs, prepared to enclose them: and then the deafening peals of loud hurras from the thousand half-frenzied spectators, crowding into a solid mass around the enclosure, to behold the beautiful wild horse, in all his native vigor subdued by man, panting in the toils, and furious with heat, rage and fright; or hear the clamorous triumphs of the adventurous riders, each of whom had performed more than one miracle of equestrian skill on that day of glorious daring—and the less discordant neighing of colts that had lost their mothers, and mothers that had lost their colts in the *melee* of the sweeping drive, with the maddened snorts and whinnying of the whole gang—all, all together, formed a scene of unrivalled noise, uproar and excitement, which few can imagine who had not witnessed it, and none can adequately describe.

But the play of spirits ended not here. The booths were soon filled, and loads of substantial provision were opened, and fish and water fowl, secured for the occasion, were fried and barbacued by hundreds, for appetites whetted to marvelous keenness by early rising, a scanty breakfast, exercise and sea air. The runlets of water and the jugs of more exhilerating liquor, were lightened of their burden. Then softer joys succeeded: and music and the dance, and love and courtship, held their undisputed empire until deep in the night, when all sought shelter and repose on board of their boats, moored by the shore, or among their island friends, who gladly entertained them with characteristic hospitality. Many a winter evening's tale did the incidents of those merry-making occasions supply, and many a peaceful young bosom of retired rural beauty was assailed with other emotions than the rough sports of an Assateague horse-penning inspired; and from one anniversary of this half-savage festivity to another, all was talk of the joys and transports of the past, and anticipations of the future.

In regard to the origin of the race of our insular horses, there is no specific difference between them and those of the main land; the smaller size and superior hardihood of the former are entirely accidental, produced by penury of sustenance through the winter, occasional scarcity of water, continual exposure to the inclemency of the seasons, and the careless practice of permitting promiscuous copulation among them, without regard to quality. These horses are, in general, neither so sure-footed or hardy, or small, or active, as the famous Shetland pony; nor are their hoofs so well formed, although there are to be found among them numerous exceptions to this remark. All this may be readily accounted for from the operation of physical agents, the difference of climate, better water, long winters, and the localities of the soil on which they subsist. The interior of

Shetland is mountainous and boggy, and abounding with wholesome water; and the more nutritive grass of the rugged mountains, inviting the little animals to feed principally upon those rough grounds, during their short summers, and occasionally in the latter part of the spring and beginning of autumn, impart greater vigor and activity to their systems, and give them, doubtless, better feet. Assateague and Chincoteague islands are flat, sandy and soft, producing abundance of excellent grass, upon which they become very fat during the summer and autumn, notwithstanding the annoyance of flies, with which those islands frequently abound. But horses and cattle suffer for good water in dry summers and hard winters. Having no springs of running water, the animals which the islands support, depend for their drink upon ponds and glades, or small excavations made for the purpose, which are filled by the rains. These soon become putrid in our burning sun, are often dry in the summer, and freeze over in the winter, so as seriously to injure the suffering creatures, that have no other resource for this indispensable article. All this might be easily remedied by a little care and trouble; but insular habits are at enmity with systematic labor, or provident industry. Fishing, and shooting, and oystering, which yield immediate profit or subsistence, agree better with their indolent, temporary habits of living, whilst the slower and more remotely profitable processes of agriculture, or rearing stock, are considered as servile drudgery.

The horses of Assateague island belonged principally to a company, most of whom resided upon the peninsula. No other care of them was required, than to brand and castrate the colts, and dispose of the marketable horses, all of which was effected at the period of their annual pennings, (June,) the whole, nearly, being joint stock. Their winter subsistence was supplied abundantly by nature. The tall, dense, and heavy grass of the rich flat lands, affording them green food nearly the whole winter, the tops of which alone are killed by the frosts, mild, as usual, so near the ocean. They never suffered for provender, except in very deep snows, with a crust upon the top, or when high tides were immediately succeeded by intense cold, which covered the marsh pastures with ice, both of which accidents were of rare occurrence, and very transient in their duration. Once or twice since my residence here (24 years,) the loose and spongy ice, formed from salt water, either lay so long as to injure the grass, or it was so entangled with the ice, that upon being suddenly carried off by a second north-easter before it had melted, it swept away, in its broken fragments, much of the food upon which the animals depended for their support. But I never heard that the scarcity thus produced, had any other effect than to reduce their flesh: no deaths occurred from that cause.

The wild gang of Assateague horses were secured by driving them into pens, made for the purpose, of pine logs. The horses seized in the pens (by islanders accustomed to such adventures, who pushed fearlessly into the midst of the crowded herd,) were brought to the main land in scows, and immediately backed, and broke to use; their wild, and apparently indomitable spirit deserting them after being haltered and once thrown, and subdued by man. More docile and tractable creatures could not be found.

The price of these horses has been greatly enhanced of late. Thirty to forty dollars were estimated high prices, until within the last few years; some may still be obtained at these prices, but not of best quality—and at a sale of part of a joint stock, a few weeks ago, on an adjoining smaller island, (Morris',) several horses, that from some peculiarity of food, or better water, or superior and more recent origin—the latter I believe the efficient cause—had attained a larger size and more elegant shape, were sold upon the spot as high as from 60 to 70 dollars each. A considerable number may still be purchased on the islands—and some tolerably handsome—at prices varying between 30 and 45 dollars. I saw this week a beautiful little animal just bought by a gentleman from Jersey, at the latter price. The only peculiarity I have ever observed in these animals, is their predilection for salt marsh grass, which never deserts them, however long they may live, and however early they may be removed from their native pastures.

I am perfectly assured that a small capital might be most profitably employed by a man of enterprize, in horses, black cattle and sheep, upon these islands, if one careful herdsman could be procured. Pasture lands are extremely low. Since I have disposed of my real estate in Virginia, preparatory to a removal north, I have sold 200 acres of first-rate pasture land—part arable, a portion of a large body which I own upon the northern end of Chincoteague island, and affording the principal winter subsistence for the stock of the island—at 100 cents per acre. The remainder is still unsold. The largest and finest work-steers of the Eastern Shore, are raised upon these islands, without any expenditure for winter support; a proof that horses of full size, might also be reared there, with judicious attention to the breed, proper selection of stallions, and care to provide water. No other attention is necessary, except to watch the winds and weather about the periods of the equinoxes, when desolating tides are threatened, and to drive the stock upon high grounds, secure against inundation. Drovers from the North, purchase their cattle, and their horses always command a good price in the neighborhood. They are hardy, rarely affected with the diseases to which the horse is subject, perform a great deal of labor, if proportioned to their strength, require much less grain than common horses, live long, and are, many of them, delightful for the saddle. I have a beautiful island pony, who for fifteen years has been my riding nag in the neighborhood and upon the farm, who has given to my daughters their first lessons in equestrian exercise, and has carried us all many thousands of miles in pleasure and safety, without having once tripped or stumbled; and he is now as elastic in his gait, and juvenile in his appearance, as he was the first day I backed him, and is fatter than any horse I own, though his labor is equal, with less than two-thirds of their grain consumption. His eye still retains its good natured animation, and to one unskilled in the indications of a horse's teeth, he would pass readily for six or seven years old. My regrets at parting with this noble little animal, are those of the friend.

Chincoteague island contains upwards of seventy families. One-third of their bread corn is raised upon the island; and the productions of the water, and occasional profits from disasters at sea, afford them an ample support. Assateague, though containing three or four times as many acres as Chincoteague, has but few inhabitants. It is unfit for the cultivation of corn, and has but little wood. Its rich, bent-growing lands, are subject to inundation during spring tides. The scenery around certain localities upon Chincoteague, are inexpressibly sublime and beautiful; and the view of the ocean and surrounding clusters of islands, from the elevated sand hills of Assateague, directly opposite my house, would enchant you. To give you some faint idea of the extent of surface upon the two principal islands near me, I will just say, that Chincoteague is perhaps seven or eight miles in length, narrow at the two ends, and gradually widening in the middle to two or two and a half miles. Assateague is vastly larger. Nothing but the total prostration of all enterprize among us has kept these islands in their present unprofitable condition. Some hundreds of horses, cattle, and sheep, might be raised here, and annually sold, without one dollar of cost, except the expense of herdsmen, whose whole care and supervision would be confined to two or three objects—a supply of water—to drive the stock to high grounds when violent north-easters were threatened—(of the approach of which, sufficient premonitions are always given—) and to attend to the branding and castration of the young stock, at the periodical June pennings. The Hebrides of Scotland, so profitable to their proprietors, do not possess the one-hundredth part of the advantages of our Atlantic islands, for all the purposes of comfortable living and extensive stock raising; and yet they are stupidly neglected.

From *Farmers' Register* 3 (November 1835): 417–19

1835

Christian Guardians of Their Little Island Home

JOHN W. A. ELLIOTT

Evangelical religion, which came to the barrier islands during the great revival at the turn of the nineteenth century, dominated the spiritual and social lives of the islanders. In 1835 John W. A. Elliott (1813–1896) reviewed the state of Methodism on Hog Island. He found at once diminishing fervor and abiding faith. A native Eastern Shoreman, Elliott was the inventor of a popular plow, a merchant who made and lost a fortune in Civil War cotton speculation, and a Methodist parson famous for the number of couples he wed. In the late 1880s and early 1890s, he published in an Accomac newspaper a series of reminiscences and historical sketches from which is taken the following account.

The remarkable revival of 1800 not only spread over most sections of the peninsula, but actually extended to the adjacent islands.

One Stephen Fletcher of Hog Island had married a lady from the main land, and these on a visit to the wife's former home attended one of the revival meetings, became converted and took back to the island the early seeds of Methodism. Not long afterwards the Rev. Thomas Smith, then in charge of the circuit, visited this sea-girt shore, beginning a revival at the house of Mr. Fletcher which soon spread to several other neighboring cabins. His visit resulted in the organization of a society of about twenty-five members, the island being made a regular appointment. Services were held here once in four weeks, the weather permitting, the appointment alternating between the cabins of Stephen Fletcher and a Mr. Floyd. This society soon developed its own class-leaders, and ultimately a local exhorter by the name of Isma Fletcher. It was remarkable that a large number of the oldest inhabitants of the island attached themselves to the church. An entire change was brought about in many ways among these simple minded people. The Sabbath became not only a day of rest, but of religious observance, and even the ruder elements of social life were brought gradually under the dominion of gospel precept.

The Hog Island of that day was nearly twice as large as it is now, the beach and even the surf having long since encroached upon much of the land then in cultivation. There were in that day several extensive lots, carefully fenced in with cedar logs said to be a hundred years old, and duly tilled by the owners. Corn, the largest and most luscious melons, figs in abundance, and any quantity of island plums and grapes, made up the yield of the sandy soil. A well-beaten pathway leading from the north to the south end of the island passed by every cabin door-step; the latter generally a fragment of flotsam brought up by the wild waves of the coast. Quite a number of families lived here too in that day. They were mostly Fletchers, Floyds, Doughtys and Kellys, names which have been handed down to the present day.

But after the termination of Mr. Smith's labors on the Eastern Shore, his successors did not manifest the same interest in this remote field, and the appointment was left in the main to the care of local ministers. Two camp-meetings were held on the island, the last in 1831, under the direction of Rev. Asa Smith. But the larger portion of the old society had died out, and the ranks had not been filled by corresponding accessions. The writer, in company with a friend, visited the island in 1835. Of the old society he found only three living—Isma Fletcher, his wife and a Mrs. Cottrill. Like the aged survivors of the Bounty, they were the Christian guardians of their little island home, the simplicity of their declining years lending grandeur to the sublime faith upon which they leaned. Services were held in the cabin of Martha Floyd on Saturday night, and on Sunday morning in that of Isma Fletcher, the larger portion of the islanders being present. After the sermon, the aged exhorter arose and addressed a few words to the island people, tears of deep feeling meanwhile coursing down his cheeks. The Gospel, he said, is God's word, and my spirit beareth witness to its truth. He was probably ninety years of age, and soon after went to his rest.

Since that period the island has been sadly neglected by the church, until at a late day by the great kindness of a noble Christian lady, a neat building has been erected there for divine worship, which is now regularly supplied by the Virginia Conference.

From *Accomac Court House Peninsula Enterprise*, 27 March 1886

1864

We All Supposed Hog Island Was a Little Paradise

GEORGE W. BONSALL

After a devastating Confederate raid on the lighthouse on Smith's Island in August 1863, the Union military periodically posted guards for the barrier island lights. In late July 1864 a company of Ohio infantry set sail from Cherrystone in Northampton County for duty on Hog Island. The soldiers anticipated a pleasurable holiday at the beach. They soon would be disabused of that notion.

George W. Bonsall survived the war to return home to Cincinnati, where he earned an enviable reputation as a finish carpenter.

July 30. Saturday. When I awoke at my usual hour of arrising (ab't 4 o'clk am) the wind was blowing very hard. The sky was over cast with dark murky clouds, which had every appearance of rain & the appearance was not lessened by occasional flashes of lightning and low rumbling thunder. The weather however soon cleared up.

We left Cherry Stone about 7 o'clock. The distance to Hog Island is about forty miles. Nothing worthy of note occured during our voyage. The vessel at times rolled considerably, but I did not at any time feel in the least sea sick. The boys were all delighted with the pleasant prospect before them. We all supposed Hog Island, notwithstanding its not very elegant name, was a little paradise and we were informed that the people were all loyal, and we were prepared to enjoy ourselves, as much as these favorable circumstances would admit. Arrived at our destination at 2.15 pm. Disembarked in small boats. Crossed the island to the Light House—a distance of about ¾ of a mile. The mosquetoes of this Island are most horrid looking "animals"—they can hardly be termed "insects" on account of their size and ferocity. They attack us in broad daylight. Had a very good supper this evening—coffee, bread & fried bacon. After supper I went down to the beach. Remained there for some time watching the immense billows which roll one after another upon the beach. Between the light house and the Ocean is a broad bare expanse of sandy beach, between one and two miles wide.

The mosquitoes attacked us in force tonight. I covered my head with my handkerchief and woolen blanket, but the "gallinippers" bit me thro' the blanket, and kept up such an uproarous noise around my head that it was some time before I could get to sleep. I lost but little rest, but some of the boys were kept awake nearly all night.

July 31. Sunday. The boys tell some very large stories this morning concerning the "skeeters," and some of them are disfigured with red, black and blue marks, swollen eyes, and other marks of the terrible charge, as to be scarcely recognizable. The gallinippers show no mercy—they go in with demonic yells, and inflict such terrible punishment on their unhappy victims that the poor fellows are hardly recoverable next day. This is our "Paradise."!! Had only a small piece of bread and a pint of coffee for breakfast this morning. After breakfast with several others, I made a general tour of observation through the Island. It is 7 miles long and about two miles wide, including the beach. It is situated 10 miles East of the mainland, in Latitude N. 57 , 28′, 16″, Longitude W. 75, 41′, 35″. There is a fine light house, which serves as a guide to coasters and for entering the Matchepungo Inlet. It is No. 195, round, white tower with a red top; fixed light, distance visible 13 miles; it is 60 feet high. Built in 1852, refitted in 1855. It has been kept since 1862 by J. G. Potts, who is to be succeeded by David Bool, a faithful and loyal Union man.

There are on the Island, I am informed, 60 persons, constituting ten families—simple, goodhearted[,] talkative people, as far as I have seen, & all very loyal. Not one of them voted for Secession except the then keeper of the light house. There are no negroes on the Island now. The houses are very small, generally having but one or two rooms, and are constructed in primitive style but are kept very neat and clean. The men fish and follow the sea; the women are very industrious. But little land is under cultivation.

Found plenty of beach plums and wild cherries and some very good blackberries. I am informed by one of the "oldest inhabitants" that the proper name of this Island is "Teach's Island," being named after a very cruel pirate chieftain of that name, whom the elderly inhabitant said had buried an immense amount of treasure somewhere on the Island, which has not yet been found. This elderly gentleman said the Island was once a pleasant abiding place but the sand has "taken possession of it." (Near the beach the sand has been blown on the hills covering them to a depth of many feet). The elderly inhabitant states that the limits of this Island are constantly becoming smaller. Nobody appears to know why the Island is called "Hog Island," but it is supposed that an immense porker—the largest ever raised in the country was raised here and the Island was named in honor of this great event. Don't know whether this story is true or not, but I don't believe there is a swine large or small on the place now. There is but very little livestock of any kind—a few sheep and cows but not half a dozen horses fit for use. There is only one cart on the whole Island. There is no road—the houses are all built along a narrow foot path which runs thro' the Island. I saw the "oldest inhabitant"—he is 98 years of age and was born on the Island which has always been his home.

Returned to "Camp" at 12.30 o'clk. I can't imagine why we were sent here—there never has been more than a Lieut. and 20 men here. And the people say there is no guard needed. The place has never been visited by guerrilas, and if it should be they would soon leave in disgust. The people are very poor. We are tormented day and night by the mosquetoes. Fish-hawks are the only game to be found. On the whole, I come to the conclusion that Hog Island would be a most excellent place to go away from!!

Murray & I pitched our tent this afternoon. Took a bath in the rolling billows of the Atlantic Ocean after supper.

August 1. Monday. Found a letter and three papers from home in my tent this morning. The papers were the *National Union* (17th July), *Enquirer* (19th), *Commercial* (18th). The letter was dated "July 21st." In the papers was a hair comb. They were brot. to camp this morning by Lieut. Timberman and several others, who went to Eastville, Sunday morning in an open row boat, and returned in the same manner. They went to request the Colonel to remove us from this wretched island. If Alexander Selkirk had been left on this island instead of Juan Fernandez, I fear poor Alex would never have returned to his native country, but what with the "skeeters" and the utter barrenness of the Island, the poor fellow would before many days have met with an inglorious death. Murray built a large fire near our tent last night after supper and the smoke from this kept the gallinippers away for a long time, but when the fuel was burnt up they attacked us. Many of the boys slept on the beach near the water's edge. They say the mosquetoes do not trouble them there.

After dinner I went out on the beach with Chas. Smith to get some shells. Did not return until about half past six. I found three very pretty small conch shells and some others. The shells are in beds near the center of the beach, and apparently have been laying there for many years undisturbed. Nearly all of them are more or less injured by the sun. My idea of an ocean shore has always been a vast sandy or pebbly beach, strewn with countless millions of beautiful shells, and a fresh supply constantly arriving. We spent over an hour in hunting crabs, which are very large and very numerous here. A cool North West wind drove the mosquetoes away tonight so I got a good night's sleep.

August 2. Tuesday. Recd. for breakfast nothing but a piece of meat, one inch wide & two inches long & coffee. I had a few small pieces of hardtack in my haversack. I got no crackers last night for supper. After breakfast I went out with several of the boys to get some shells, but I was so hungry that I returned to camp in a short time. At camp I found that the men who went to Eastville with Capt. Boyce in the yawl had returned and reported a small sailing vessel as having been ordered to take us from this horrid Island. I made a cup of coffee—after drinking which I felt much better. The captain brot. some bread, beans and pork from Eastville. We fared sumptously at dinner today. Had bean soup, soft bread and fried "hog." I am more myself again. Each man recd. ¾ of a loaf of bread.

Two messes left us this evening. They will sleep on the beach, & are ordered to be ready to embark at three o'clk to-morow morning. The sloop which was sent over for us is able to take only half the company in one trip. The "Ripraps" and "White Mice" go to-morrow morning, and wait on the mainland for the "Buckeyes" and "Gillies." Bathed in the Ocean after supper.

August 3. Wednesday. Slept very well during the night, but early in the morning I was charged upon by an army of mosquetoes, who soon drove sleep from "mine eyes." I covered my head with my blanket and listened to the angry, demoniac yells & shrieks of rage and disappointment of the baffled fiends. I think I have heard more "loud swearing" since we came to Hog Island, than I ever heard in half a year before. Each man in our mess had dealt out to him 10 day's rations of sugar. We had this luxury in our coffee this morning for the first time since Saturday.

The boys are all in good spirits. We are going to leave this Island. Since we came here we have done no duty at all, and have had no drill. The company was scattered. The Ripraps and Buckeyes were together. The "Mice" were a short distance from them. The "Gillies" were about half a mile off, in the woods. But very few tents were pitched. At two o'clock we walked about two miles across the beach, and were taken on board a small single mast sloop called the "Josephine." It was manned by a squad of infantry soldiers, under command of a Sergeant and corporal. The boys straggled to the beach one after another, and the company baggage was delayed for a considerable time, but we got off at last. We had what the Islanders here would call a "right smart" shower just after we started. As there was but little wind we progressed slowly, and sometimes came to a dead halt.

We arrived at Jacob's Landing, Matcheponga Bay, at about six o'clock. Found the other two messes there. We got supper—coffee & bread, about 8.30. At about nine o'clock we packed our knapsacks in a wagon, put on our other traps, and commensed our march to Eastville, which is variously estimated by the natives at 17 to 20 miles from the landing. Halted at three o'clock to wait for stragglers. Murray & I slept on a poncho between two rails with half a tent for covering. We made our "bed" on the road side.

From George W. Bonsall Diary, 11 July–26 August 1864, Eastern Shore Public Library, Accomac, Virginia

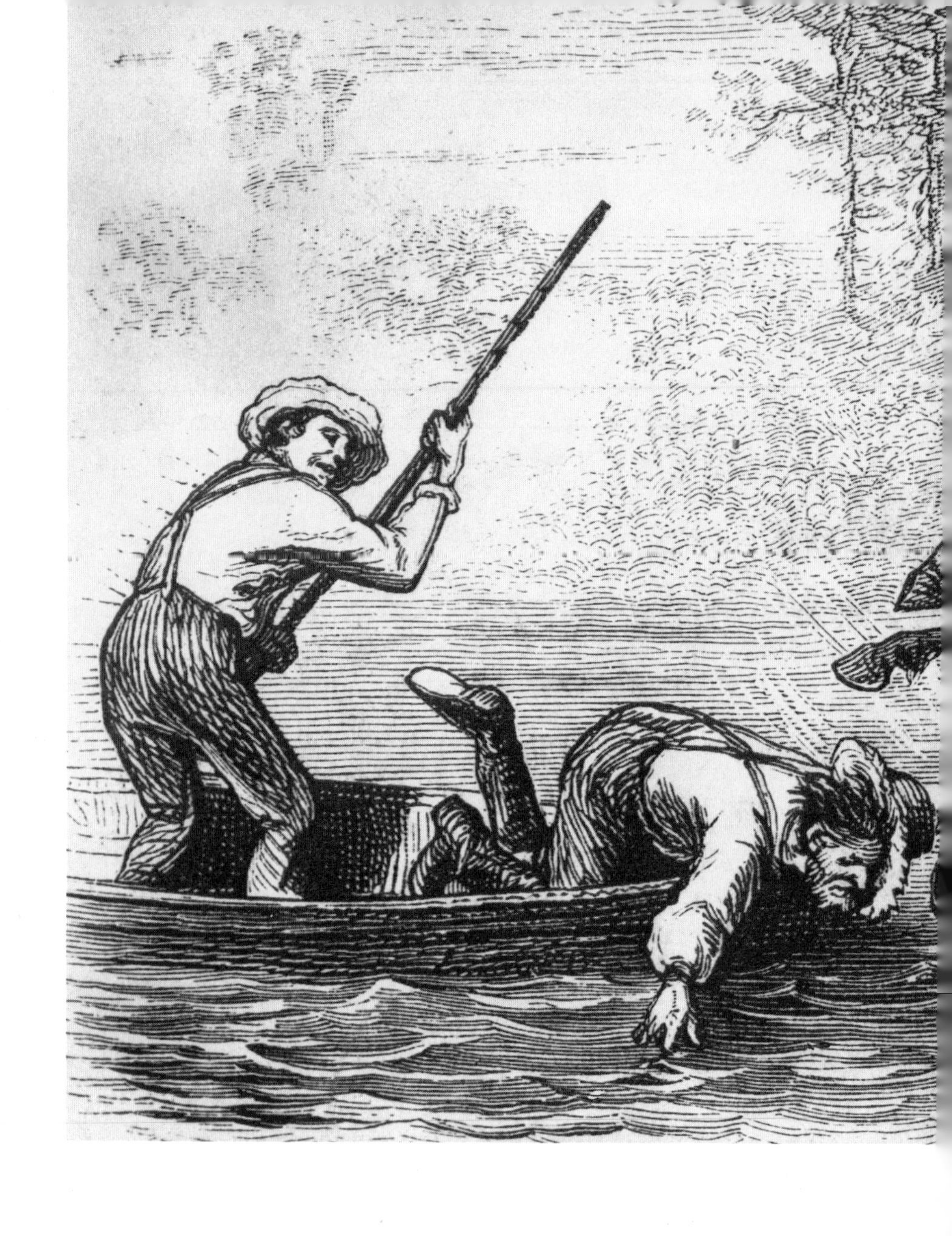

1876

Chincoteague: The Island of Ponies

HOWARD PYLE

The expansion immediately after the Civil War of the national railroad and steamboat networks brought the barrier islands within easy reach of the burgeoning northern cities. In 1876 Howard Pyle (1853–1911) became one of the first tourists to take advantage of the new rail line to Franklin City on Chincoteague Bay and of the new hotel on Chincoteague Island. Young Pyle's sojourn on Chincoteague awakened dormant artistic and literary ambitions. A distinguished career as author and illustrator ensued.

Off the north-eastern shore of Virginia, and about five miles from the main-land, lies a small island known as Chincoteague—an island possessed of peculiarities shared by no other portion of the eastern United States; for here roams, in an entirely untamed state, a breed of horses, or rather ponies, as wild as the mustangs of Texas or the Pampas.

How these ponies first came upon the island is not known except through vague tradition, for when the first settlers came there, early in the eighteenth century, they found the animals already roaming wild about its piney meadows. The tradition received from the Indians of the main-land was that a vessel loaded with horses, sailing to one of the Elizabethan settlements of Virginia, was wrecked upon the southern point of the island, where the horses escaped, while the whites were rescued by the then friendly Indians and carried to the main-land, whence they found their way to some of the early settlements. The horses, left to themselves upon their new territory, became entirely wild, and, probably through hardships endured, degenerated into a peculiar breed of ponies.

In 1670 the island was first prospected; it was subsequently granted by King James II, to a person by whom it was sold in minor sections to various others. At present it is greatly subdivided, though one land-owner, Kendall Jester by name, holds over six hundred acres of marsh and pine land, and there are other holdings scarcely less in extent. Among the earliest settlers were the Thurstones, Taylors, and Mifflins; the head of the last-named family was a well-known Quaker, who, upon the introduction of slavery to the island, removed thence to the town of Camden, in the upper part of the province of Maryland, near Delaware.

It was long before Chincoteague was fairly settled, and even as late as 1838 there were but twenty-six house there; now, however, many strangers, tempted by the exceptionally good fishing and oyster-dredging of the place, are pouring in from the main-land to settle there. To mere visitors the ponies are still a great, if not the main, attraction, and during the periods of "penning"—driving them into a corral—numerous guests arrive daily from the coast.

When one puts foot aboard the puffing, wheezing little steamboat "Alice," it is as though the narrow channel, across which he is ferried in about an hour, separates him from modern civilization, its rattling, dusty cars, its hurly-burly of business, its clatter and smoke of mills and factories, and lands him upon an enchanted island, cut loose from modern progress and left drifting some seventy-five years backward in the ocean of time. No smoke of manufactories pollutes the air of Chincoteague; no hissing steam-escape is heard except that of the "Alice;" no troublesome thought of politics, no religious dissension, no jealousy of other places, disturbs the minds of the Chincoteaguers, engrossed with whisky, their ponies and themselves.

Chincoteague is land-locked. Assateague Beach—a narrow strip of land; composed of pine woods, salt marshes and sand flats—lies between it and the ocean, separated from it by a channel about half a mile in width. Midway upon this beach stands Assateague light-house—a first-class light, and one of the finest on the coast. Between this beach or island upon the one side and the main-land on the other, in a calm, sleepy bay, lies lazy Chincoteague. There is but little agriculture; the inhabitants depend upon the sale of ponies and upon fishing for the necessaries of life, and mere necessaries suffice them. A little pork and bread, rank tobacco and whisky, in the proportion of Falstaff's sack, and the acme of the Chincoteaguer's happiness is attained.

Thick pine woods cover the island, in virgin growth, here and there opening into a glade of marshy flat, stretching off for a mile or more, called "the meadows," where one occasionally catches a glimpse of a herd of ponies, peacefully browsing at a distance.

Tramping through the island, which is barely a mile in width, one emerges suddenly from the pine woods upon the western shore, where broad extended salt marshes, rank in growth, lie weltering in the hot sunlight the whole length of the island. A fence protects this marsh from the encroachments of the ponies, which are turned out here in the winter, and find a plentiful supply of fodder in the dead sedge underneath the snow.

There are two distinct classes of inhabitants upon Chincoteague: the pony-owners—lords of the land—and the fishermen. Your pony-owner is a tough, bulbous, rough fellow, with a sponge-like capacity for absorbing liquor; bad or good, whisky, gin, or brandy, so that it have the titillating alcoholic twang, it is much the same to him. Coarse, heavy army shoes, a tattered felt hat, or a broad-brimmed straw that looks as if it had never been new; rough homespun or linen trowsers, innocent of soap and water, and patched with as many colors as Joseph's coat; a blue or checked shirt, open at the throat, and disclosing a hairy chest, these complete his costume. Your fisherman, now, though his costume is nearly similar, with the exception of shoes (which he does not wear), is in appearance quite different. A lank body, shoulders round as the bowl of a spoon, far up which clamber his tightly strapped trowsers; a thin crane-like neck, poking out at right angles from somewhere immediately between the shoulder-blades; and, finally, a leathery, expressionless, peaked face, and wiry hair and beard complete his presentment. Hospitable in the extreme are these rough people. Any one visiting them at the time of their noonday meal will find some ingenuity necessary to parry their pressing solicitations to share those nodules of fat pork fried and floating in a dead sea of black molasses, fried potatoes, and chunks of bread—the last to be dipped in the molasses, and eaten with the pork. If sickness is pleaded in excuse, equal difficulty will be found in avoiding the administration of a dose of villainous whisky.

In visiting their houses, you pick your way with some trouble through a flock of geese, over a pig, a dog, and probably a nearly naked baby rolling over the floor, and find yourself at last safely ensconced in a rickety chair. The good-woman of the house, who is smoking a very dirty pipe with a short stem, is profuse in the offices of hospitality, spanking the rolling baby with one hand and handing a tin cup of water with the other. She may then, if you are a good listener and quiet enough, recount in much detail the ins and outs of her last attack of fever'n'ager, or how our Mariar married Jim Strand; in the meantime you can be making your own observations of an interior well calculated to repay the trouble. A rusty stove, a broken pitcher, a griddle, a skillet, two tin cups, a coffee-pot, and a dirty bucket, the smaller properties deposited in a rickety wash-tub in the corner of the room, which is mounted upon a crippled chair with a broken back; walls highly ornamented with cheap prints, labeled respectively "Ellen" or "Maggie," circus bills and advertisements of patent soup; and, to crown all, a dozen or more bottles with little bits of red flannel in them hung here and there, enlivening the monotony like Turner's daub of red in his gray sea picture. Then, lastly, the bed! We of the North have no conception of such beds—rising, a voluminous mountain of feathers, five feet in height, and bedecked with a gorgeous patch-work quilt, the valance slats at the top of the narrow spindle posts hung here and there with parti-colored worsted bobs. Let the family be ever so poor, the bed is the glory, the soul of their cottage. It is the pride of the good-woman's heart, and in it she will swelter and suffocate in the hottest day of summer. Visiting, one day, a house where the woman was sick with bilious fever (quite a common complaint in Chincoteague), we saw nothing of her upon first entering, but a smell of tobacco-smoke stung our nostrils like vapor of oil of vitriol. Looking toward the bed, we saw a thin column of smoke ascending, and, approaching, saw the patient peacefully reposing and smoking in the midst of a feathery Yosemite.

Quaint and unique are the characters one meets. Kendall Jester, more popularly known as "Uncle Ken," the beau-ideal of a Chincoteague pony-penner: one need have no fear of failing to make his acquaintance. An old fellow approaches, his face good-humored and redolent of innumerable potations of the favorite beverage. His daily life is comprised in three stages of existence: morning, when he is sober; noon, when if his thoughts are steady, his tongue is thick; night, when his thoughts are wool-gathering, and his stumbling tongue in vain tries to overtake them, like a man pursuing one of his own ponies in the dark. He approaches with "My name's Kenneljester" (pronounced all in one word), " 's no harm in me."

We assure him we know that.

"I drink a little whisky now an' then."

We know that too.

"Doctor says got's drink quart 'er whisky day—keep away bilious. Drink quart an' pint—never have bilious."

To do Uncle Ken justice, he implicitly follows the advice of his physician.

Should you imagine that when Uncle Ken is drunk he no longer has his wits about him, you will be vastly mistaken. A man who came over from the main-land to buy ponies from him thought that by making him drunk he could "skin him out of a bargain," but his horror was unbounded when upon every drink that Uncle Ken took he increased his original price by ten dollars.

Here, too, is old Dan Tucker, boot-black and white-washer, with his pock-marked face and rich guttural "ki-he!" of a laugh. The artist wanted to make a sketch of this worthy, and ten cents were offered as an inducement for him to stand.

"See yeh, mars'! Guess I'se ugly 'nough 'out puttin' on me on paper."

"But we only want you as a—ah—memento,—a remembrance of our trip to Chincoteague."

"Ke-he! Can't fool me, wa-wat you want me fo'?" (A sudden burst of righteous indignation.) "Go long, sketch some o' de gals, dey's heap puttier 'n me. Black yo' boots fo' ten cents. An' I wants money, too. Money takes a man anyways—'cept to Hebben!"

Here, too, is old Uncle Benny, ex-slave and now boot-black, freighted with glorious reminiscences of by-gone plantation days, possum and coon hunts, pumpkin pie and turkeys.

"Thankye, Mars'; sarvent:" says the poor old cripple, as he takes our ten cents, little knowing that we had made a hasty sketch of him as he bent over our shoes putting on the old-fashioned gloss he had acquired as a "boy" on the plantation.

Many more rise to memory: old Aunt Sally Jones, with her great scoop bonnet, her blue yarn stockings and her manifold complaints; old Mrs. Grant, who charms away cancers; and scores of others, the enumeration of whom would tire the patience of the reader.

Once or twice a year the ponies of the island are driven together in a pen or corral for the purpose of branding the foals or for sale. Then is there excitement in Chincoteague. The natives are all agog. Rose and Hannah in the hotel kitchen are hard at work broiling, baking and stewing, preparing a brisk campaign against the appetites of the guests that assemble at such periods. Every now and then, above the frizzling of mutton-chops and frying of potatoes, arises a sudden burst of that rich minor hymn music heard only at its best among the southern plantation negroes—the wild music holding something half savage in its cadences—a music one might imagine their barbaric ancestors sang at some secret sacrificial feast.

And so on *ad infinitum,* now rising full and lusty, now sinking into the sputtering of the frying pan.

It is still morning and the broad white sand beach stretches far up the island. Here and there lies a pool of salt water glassily reflecting the clear sky.

Suddenly some one cries, "Here they come." Down the beach come the ponies, pattering over the moist sand and dashing the placid salt pools into a myriad sparkling drops. Close behind ride the drivers, men and boys, gesticulating wildly. For saddles most of them have tanned sheep-skins, the woolly side out, strapped around the bodies of their ponies. Now a driver, bending almost level with his pony's back, dashes on to head off some fractious animal. At length they approach the pen into which, after some trouble, they are headed, a tumultuous crowd, kicking, biting and squealing; then a rush and they are in! Now comes the tug of war, the lassoing and haltering; but that is left till the afternoon. It is well; for there goes the dinner-bell and we are ready for the summons.

Merciful Providence! What a crowd of hungry excursionists are coming from the main-land in the little steamer to attend the sales! From upper deck to lower the vessel is crowded with passengers. Can ever Rose and Hannah's labors suffice to stay the appetites of all these hungry wights? But to look at the face of Mr. English, the hotel keeper, re-assures one. He is as calm and courageous as Napoleon at Austerlitz, or Nelson at Trafalgar. But we hasten into the dining-room and are seated by the time the boat touches the wharf, and then the rush begins. Meal tickets are given, and Captain Caulk (pronounced Cork) stands at the door and collects them.

"Sir," cries he to one old man, as the crowd pushes tumultuously against him, "for the love of Heaven, do not tread on my cork foot!"

"Have you a cork foot, sir?"

"Two of 'em."

"Tut, tut, tut! Well, I'm sorry!" cries the sympathetic old gentleman from Snow Hill.

At length dinner is completed, and we start at once for the pony pen. The momentous time arrives for casting the lasso; not as they do in the West, but by hanging it on the end of a long pole, and then dropping it skillfully over the pony's head. Uncle Ken takes the pole. Holding the noose well aloft on the top of it, so as not to frighten the intended prey upon which he has fixed his eye, he cautiously approaches the herd, around which the crowd has gathered. One of the ponies takes a sudden fright and a stampede follows, the spectators scattering right and left. For a moment the intended captive is wedged in the midst of the rest of the herd. Uncle Ken sees his advantage. He rushes forward, the noose is dropped and settles around the pony's neck. Immediately six lusty negroes, with glistening teeth, perspiring faces and glittering eyes, are at the other end of the rope.

The animal makes a gallant fight. This way and that he hauls his assailants, rearing and squealing. Now he makes a sudden side dash and sends them rolling over and over, plowing their heads through the shifting sand till their wool is fairly powdered; still, however, "the boys" hold on to the rope. At length the choking halter commences to tell; the pony, with rolling eyes and quivering flanks, wheezes audibly. Now is the moment! In rush the negroes, clutching the animal legs and tail. A wrestle and a heave, a struggle on the pony's part, a kick that sends Ned hopping with a barked shin like a crazy monkey, and Sambo plowing through the sand and stinkweed in among the spectators, and then over goes the pony with four or five lusty shouting negroes sprawling around him. The work is done: a running noose is slipped around the pony's nose, his forelock is tied to this by a bit of string, and soon his tantrums cease as he realizes that he is indeed a captive.

Many of the ponies are taken over the narrow channel that separates Chincoteague from Assateague, to run wild upon the latter island, which is largely unclaimed land. We were so fortunate as to witness the lively scene of the swimming of a number of ponies across this channel or inlet. For a mile we tramped through salt meadows rank with sedge, while everywhere from beneath our feet scattered innumerable ridiculous little fiddler-crabs about the size of a silver quarter of a dollar, one claw of enormous magnitude and conspicuousness and the other preposterously small and insignificant, like the candidates for President and Vice-President. At length we arrived at the edge of the channel, the ponies whickering as their nostrils fill with the salt air. One man enters the boat and poles it along, the channel being very shallow, while another with a rope in his hand drags at a pony. The pony is stubborn and will not enter. Kicks and blows rain freely upon him, the negroes running up to give him a kick and then rushing frantically away in mortal terror of the returning kick of the animal. Presently, with a splash the pony is in, and then all goes smoothly until his feet touch the sheltering bank on the other side, when the plunging recommences, and one poor wretch who has hold of the halter and whose thoughts are wandering, awakes to find himself where he has not been for a long time—in cold water.

Among the visitors to the island we made some pleasant acquaintances, chief among whom was a learned naturalist from the Baltimore Academy of Natural Sciences. The professor was puzzling the natives greatly by his strange proceedings, his butterfly nets and insect-collecting, his seines, dredges, and deep-sea fishing. During a trip we took together through brake and thicket,—the professor wide-awake for specimens,—we made, unknown to ourselves, some very unpleasant acquaintances. As we returned to the shore and seated ourselves leisurely upon a stranded boat to smoke and chat, we suddenly discovered that we were literally covered with seed-ticks, minute insects that burrow beneath the skin, causing a maddening irritation. After vain endeavors to pick them off, we started in haste for the hotel, there to scrub, in the secrecy of one's chamber, in a tub of salt water.

Everything at Chincoteague seems conducted in unique and unconventional fashion. The only butcher-shop is no shop at all, but only a spot in the woods, where from two cross-pieces between the trees cattle are strung up by a block and tackle and slaughtered, after which their skins are stretched and dyed. It is a wild, gloomy place, surrounded by towering pines of a century's growth, straight as arrows. The piney needles have sung to the wind many a dirge of slaughtered cattle.

The chief restaurant of Chincoteague is a piece of sail elegantly draped over a few upright posts, with a canvas streamer above it bearing conspicuously the sign, "Stewed Oysters."

Upon the western side of the island is a bluff that overlooks the Atlantic toward the south. It is a barren, sandy spot; here and there a cactus crawls along half hidden in the shifting sand or a clump of coarse grass shivers and whispers in the breeze. It is called the Old Grave-yard, and in this lonely, desolate, silent spot a few rounded stones and pieces of carved wood without letter or sign mark the last resting-places. There is something touching in the sentiment that impelled those rough, uncultured people to lay the weary, fever-burnt bones of their companions here in this lonely spot, facing the ocean they knew so well. Every year, as from the south the tumultuous waves of the Atlantic roll up the shore, the bluff washes away, the bones of the departed are brought to a premature resurrection. The burial-ground now in use is farther up the island and in the interior; a ridge dotted with head-stones runs up beneath the shelter of aged pines, with branches crooked as the cedars of Lebanon and draped with pall-like festoons of gray Florida moss.

Upon "Uncle Ken's" estate of six hundred and sixty-five acres, valued at about four thousand dollars and called Wild-Cat Marsh, numerous flocks of domesticated wild geese are feeding. Every year numbers of those birds are shot in their passage south. The natives sink a barrel into the ground close to the beach in which they hide, and when the geese swimming far out at sea approach the beach to "gravel" they fall an easy prey to the gunners. Those that are only winged are saved and subsequently domesticated. One frequently hears the peculiar resonant "hank" of the wild geese, and, looking in the direction from which it came, sees the black head and neck of a bird stretching above the surrounding sedge. These birds cross freely with the ordinary domesticated geese, producing a hybrid which is called a "mule goose."

The fishing and gunning of Chincoteague are excellent. Innumerable snipe are shot and sea trout caught, some of the latter weighing as much as two pounds. The bathing would be excellent were it not for numerous neighboring sharks, some of them twenty or twenty-five feet long. When one sees a triangular fin cutting the glassy surface of the water near at hand, much of the pleasure of bathing is taken away.

Sharing the interest with the pony penning is an occasional camp-meeting in the woods, occurring once in a year or so. In among the great pines of Chincoteague is a noble place for such a gathering, when at night their huge trunks are illuminated by the light of the "pine chunk" bonfires, in the gleam of which the distant trees flash forth for a moment and then vanish into obscurity again,—and when the solemn measured chant of the Methodist hymns is heard and the congregation sways with the mighty religious passion that stirs them, while over all hang lurid wreathings of resinous smoke.

So far as one sees, geese, dogs, children and pigs compose the chief population of Chincoteague. The last thing to be heard in the evening and at intervals during the night is the cackling of geese, and when ones wakes in the morning the geese are cackling still. Pigs are almost as much a feature of the place. The natural born Chincoteague porker is a thin, scrawny animal like his owner, the fisherman. He has a meditative air of curiosity and will watch a stranger askance, at the same time grunting in a low tone to himself, as though making his own observations. Quite a different character is the porcine nobleman from the main-land. He is regarded with affectionate reverence by his owner and grows fat upon fish and succulent mollusks, taking his *siesta* in undisturbed possession of the softest sand-bank.

It is difficult to say to what extent the law may be exercised in Chincoteague, for certainly there is not a place of confinement upon the whole island. We witnessed, however, what we imagine must have been a sample of the enforcement of the law. Two negro "boys" were fighting, rolling over the ground and biting at each other, when up rushed the magistrate of the island, seized a heavy barrel stave and delivered such blows right and left upon the heads of the belligerent blacks as would have stunned any ordinary white man.

Many traditions of the island are handed down from mouth to mouth by the natives, but few of them being able to read or write. It is thus we receive a full account of the great storm and accompanying tidal wave of the year 1821; telling how the black wrack gathered all one dreadful day to the southeast; how all night the breathless air, inky black, was full of strange moaning sounds, and pine needles quivered at the forecasting hurricane that lay in wait in the southward offing; how sea-mews and gulls hurtled screaming through the midnight air; how in the early morning the terrified inhabitants, looking from their windows facing the ocean, saw an awful sight: the waters had receded toward the southward, and where the Atlantic had rolled the night before, miles of sand-bars lay bare to the gloomy light, as the bottom of the Red Sea to the Israelites; then how a dull roar came near and nearer, and suddenly a solid mass of wind and rain and salt spray leaped upon the devoted island with a scream. Great pines bent for a moment, and then, groaning and shrieking, were torn from their centuried growth like wisps of straw and hurled one against another; houses were cut from their foundations and thrown headlong; and then a deeper roar swelled the noise of the tempest, and a monstrous wall of inky waters rushed with the speed of lightning toward the island. It struck Assateague, and in a moment half the land was a waste of seething foam and tossing pine trunks; and the next instant it struck Chincoteague, and in an unbroken mass swept away men and ponies like insects; rushing up the island, tearing its way through the stricken pine woods.

Many a time by the side of his bright crackling fire, the aged Chincoteaguer, removing his pipe from the toothless gums where he has been sucking its bitter sweetness, will tell, as the winter wind roars up from the ocean, how Hickman, with his little grandson clinging to his neck, was swept by the great wave to King's Bush marsh, far up on the main-land six miles away, and caught in the tough branches of its bushes; or how Andrews, with wife and family swept away in his sight, was borne up the island on the waters, and the next morning, was discovered hanging in a pine-tree, by his waistband twenty feet from the ground.

Chincoteague, united by no ties of interest to the rest of East Virginia, and depending for its necessaries, its flour, tobacco, whisky, and calicoes, upon Philadelphia and New York, claims to have been during the war the only loyal portion of the eastern coast of Virginia. When the ratification of secession was returned to the votes of the people, only one man in Chincoteague, Joseph Hill, by name, cast his vote for it—and then died. An immense Bell and Everett flagpole, one hundred and twenty feet in height, was erected,—chiefly through the instrumentality of Mr. J. A. M. Whealton, one of the most prominent of the present inhabitants of Chincoteague,—and to the top of the pole was raised a great bell and a United States flag. It was distinctly seen from the main-land, and a deputation soon visited Mr. Whealton, demanding its removal.

"Gentlemen," said the gallant little Unionist. "I erected that flag and bell, and when they go down I go down with them; but so long as I have a dram of powder and an ounce of lead, and am able to use them, there they stay." And there they staid.

But when the northern ports were closed to southern trade, Chincoteague suffered much. No flour, calico, or tobacco, and, what was worse, no whisky, could be obtained from the North. As to the South, it was more bitter against the so-called renegades than against the Yankees proper. A boat was loaded with oysters and sent to Philadelphia, only to be immediately captured. Another was started, and met with a similar fate. Then Mr. Whealton went himself, and, after much difficulty, secured the desired articles and conveyed them in triumph to Chincoteague. He then employed Dr. Snow of Snow Hill to plead the cause of the loyalists in Washington, and so well did the Doctor fulfill his mission, that the gun-boat "Louisiana" was sent to lie in Chincoteague Bay for the protection of the inhabitants. For two or three days the Secessionists, some two or three hundred in number, stood upon the main-land, about half a mile from the

"Louisiana," upon which they kept up a running fire, without, however, doing any damage. Soon General Lockwood was stationed upon the eastern shore, and then, with the protecting arm of the Federal Government around her, Chincoteague enjoyed her hominy-pots and whisky in unbroken felicity.

From *Scribner's Monthly* 13 (1877): 737–45

1877

Trip to Cobb's Island

JOSEPH F. MORGAN

In the late nineteenth century the Cobb's Island Hotel attracted guests from all over the eastern United States. Excursionists and vacationing families frolicked in the surf and enjoyed the delights of the resort's famous table and bar, while harried professional men found relaxation in gunning and angling. Representative of the latter were Joseph F. Morgan and seventeen convivial friends from Leonardtown, St. Marys County, Maryland, who aboard the schooner Father and Sons visited the island around 1880.

Friday, July 13th. At 10 o'clock, a.m., we cleared Capes Charles and Henry and were gliding over the waters of the mighty Atlantic. Now we see for the first time the majestic waste of waters spread out before us.

An apparent awe took possession of the party in presence of such majesty. All seemed to feel the power of the Infinite and for sometime we were silent trying to conceive the grand glorious waste before us. We felt the nearness of danger but knew that "He who marks the sparrow's fall" would hear us, when the face of the waters began to frown upon us. At 12 o'clock, we were about 10 miles outside the Capes and off Smith's Island Light.

Our party began to get sea-sick, with some exceptions. Those who could, tried to pass the time by fishing from the side of the vessel. Very soon, two of the party captured dog sharks, which created great excitement and seemed to rouse up the sick ones. Our cooks, for a long time, refused to touch them, calling them *wild* fish, but after some persuasion, they were induced to dress and serve one for dinner. We thought the fish delicious, and many were the praises lavished upon the dish. After dinner, however, some suggestions were made as to the man eating propensities of the shark. Anyhow, "Sport" had to eat the other one. All that we could get out of any of the party, when asked how he liked shark, was, that "he could eat it, but didn't hanker after it." We discovered, however, after arriving at Cobb's Island, that this species of shark was considered delicious, and commanded a high price in the Norfolk market. In this way we floated along slowly until 4 o'clock in the evening, when a slight breeze came up from the South West, and at six o'clock we passed between the breakers, and cast our anchor in the harbor of Cobb's Island.

We had now arrived at the *ultima thule* of our voyage, and when the rattling of the chains told us that the anchor was cast, our hearts gave vent to pent-up emotions with which danger and the sea had filled them, and while some gave thanks to the Giver, others showed their appreciation by "here's to Cobb's Island"! Having arrived about 6 o'clock on Friday evening, and as yet there was time to take a cursory glance of the "Mysterious Island," our party availed themselves of it and disembarked. We were met on the wharf by Warren Cobb, a son of Nathan Cobb, the owner of the Island, who gave us a kind welcome, and invited us to the Hotel. Our commissary was busily engaged in laying in a stock of "spots" for our supper. After taking a hasty view, darkness overtook us, and we returned to our vessel.

Supper was soon served, and next came an order from the Commissary, Albert Fenwick, that while at the Island the party should be self-supporting, accordingly, he assigned to each member of the party a certain duty to be performed on the morrow. The following was the composition of the several divisions so assigned. Gunners—Edelen, Freeman, Simms Fenwick, Neal Henry Combs. Fishermen—Albert Fenwick, R. C. Combs, Capts. Tyler and Sol and Ben Foxwell. *Hard* crabbers, King and Wile. Shell pickers and Egg hunters—Drury and Morgan. The said duties having been understood and acquiesced in, we retired, and fell asleep.

Saturday, July 14. A cloudless sunrise sprung out of the Ocean, and all were on deck at an early hour, eager to enjoy the pleasures of the day. An early breakfast was enjoyed, and then came the stationing of the several divisions in their places on land and water. The gunners, after having hired a set of decoys, were carried over to Bone Island, a small barren place to the south of Cobb's Island, at a distance of about two miles. The shell pickers and egg hunters were carried to Cobb's Island, the fishermen went to the fishing ground, and the crabbers were left on the boat, plentifully supplied with bait, lines, nets, &c. While all the others were engaged in performing their several duties, your correspondent was stationed on Cobb's Island, and as it was understood that each party should report at night, concerning the pleasure and sights enjoyed, he will now give his impressions of the wonders and sights seen by him. First, after landing we went to the Hotel, where we met a pleasant party of young men from Northampton county, Va. We enjoyed a social talk with them for an hour or two, after which we called on Nathan Cobb, the owner of the Island, for the purpose of gathering some points of the early history of the place. Mr. Cobb is an old man, about 85 years of age, but time seems not to have conquered him, and with a clear mind, and in a strong voice, he gave us a history of this wild and wonderful Island.

The island at low water is seven miles long, and not over 400 yards wide at the widest part. It contains about 1000 acres of land, mostly in marsh and uncultivated. Not over 20 acres are under cultivation. At high water there is not over 100 acres dry land, upon which are built the Hotel and buildings. The Hotel and buildings are situated about half way between the wharf, which is on the inlet side, and the ocean, being about 150 yards from each. The buildings consist of two rows of houses running from East to West, and could easily accommodate 200 guests. There are other smaller buildings erected by parties who, in former years, frequented the Island. One building, called the "Baltimore Building," was erected by citizens of Baltimore, and another, called the "Virginia House" erected by Virginians. All the buildings, from some cause, seem to be neglected and undergoing decay. But one thing holds out, as of old, and that is the Bar Room. It seems that no matter what adverses overtake men or places, this institution is still in full blast. We patronized it pretty extensively, and should be excused, as the atmosphere of Cobb's Island leads to exhilaration. Midway between the two main buildings is the skeleton of a whale which floated up on the beach many years ago. Many of the party brought home relics of this leviathan. Nathan F. Cobb purchased the Island in 1840 from Elizabeth Fitchett, paying therefore one hundred and fifty dollars in money, and fifty bushels of salt. In 1840, there was not five acres of the Island that the sea did not wash over at high tide. A greater part of the Island has been reclaimed by Mr. Cobb, by bringing boat loads of earth from the main land of Virginia. The first house erected by him was pointed out to us, through which the sea washed at high tide. Mr. Cobb, being originally from Massachusetts, called this place Cape Cod. He has been married three times, and should his last wife, who is still living, happen to die, we are very sure he would make the number *even.* We regretted very much to see this renowned Summer Resort not open for the accommodation of visitors this season. With some outlay and judicious management, it could be made one of the most desirable places on the Atlantic Coast. A line of steamers could easily, in the summer season, be ran between the Island and Norfolk for the convenience of travelers. We fear that there is a little too much contention between the parties in interest. They should relinquish their claims to some company, for a limited number of years, receiving, of course, a share of the profits annually. Where people can't agree, some one should agree for them. Cobb's Island is a grand place, and should be the Summer Resort of the Atlantic Coast. With a little more concord, and with some outlay of money, there would be in the language of "Col. Sellers," "Millions in it."

Through with our gleanings of the early history of the Island, we sailed forth, basket on arm, to perform the duty assigned us, that of shell picking and egg hunting along the Ocean side of the Island. The main or common beach, over which the sea ordinarily washes, is about 50 feet wide, of hard and compact sand. Beyond this seems to be another beach of pure white sand about 100 feet wide. Upon this beach is found the beautiful shells, which it was our duty to gather. Very soon our eyes were attracted by some, half buried in the sand, which we picked, only to be thrown down by finding prettier ones as we advanced. The most beautiful were the conchs and whelk shells.

We soon gathered as many shells as we could carry and lugged them along to the vessel, where we arrived just in time for dinner, and after the others had come aboard. Our gaze was greeted by innumerable specimens of the feathery and finny tribe, piled up in abundance on the deck of the vessel, but as each party has to give its own account we will wait until after dinner before we call upon them for their reports. To dinner we go, and enjoyed some things of the morning's sport, which were the splendid Trout and "Spots" caught by the fishermen—together with some of the spoils of the gunners. Dinner over, each division was called on for a report. The gunners came first and showed their lot of birds—Willets, Gray-backs, laughing Gulls, barking Gulls and Curlews. Of these birds, the two first named and the last are worth eating, being in fact delicious. The gunners reported fine sport and incessant shooting. Two of the party, Col. Fenwick and Henry Combs, seemed to take a mortal antipathy to the Gulls—one towards the barking and the other the laughing Gulls. We can't imagine the cause of this, as they are not considered good to eat. We suppose it was because they barked at one and laughed at the other. Anyhow, such a goodly number of each was killed that the barking Gulls had begun to *growl* and those left of the laughing Gulls were filled with sighing. These two varieties followed our boat to the Capes on our return to bid these two gentlemen farewell. The fishermen were called next, who *reported* excellent sport, but had some trouble in finding the fishing ground. They at last employed one of the native fishermen, who soon carried them to the right place. In a short time they had caught two or three dozen fine trout, when they pulled up stakes and came on board in time for dinner. Our fisherman-guide rather got to us as he charged the party fifty cents a head for showing them. We could not see the fairness of this, as he said that he only charged fifty cents for one, but if there were twenty in the boat, he would charge fifty cents for each. He never lumped anything. He was not up to the lumping business. So much for the fishermen. How about the crabbers? It was amusing to see the faces of the "crabbers" when they were called upon to report. Before they had spoken, we knew that they had not done "the task assigned." We were confident, however, that excuses would be as thick as the birds. King was spokesman, and in an humble voice stated that as his companion was opposed to performing servile work on Saturday, the Jewish Sabbath, and as it required two men to capture one crab, one to pull up the line and the other to use the net, he begged to be excused for this dereliction of duty. The ingenuity of this excuse was accepted, coupled with promises of a better performance the next day. We were then called to the dinner of dinners—trout, birds, clams, oysters, and all things common to this region. One of our party, not content with the bill of fare, enjoyed a few mussels, which he pronounced very good. The oysters are too salt, but after being soaked a short time in fresh water and stewed are very fine. We noticed too a reversal of the order of nature, or, at least, our order of nature at home. With us the mussel is a parasite to the oyster, while there the oyster is such to the mussel. The mussel is very large, sometimes over four inches in length, and serves as an excellent bait for trout. After dinner our party again divided up for operations, with some slight changes. A party of clammers took the water, while others went for birds and fish. The clams are caught by wading in water about three feet deep. Your feet pressing upon the bottom comes in contact with the clam, which is buried in the sand or mud at the depth of about three inches. The clam is then easily caught with the hand. In a very short time they had caught two or three bushels. We were assigned to the fishermen and didn't get a bite. The party were not so successful as in the morning; owing possibly to not being able to find the fishing ground, although two Captains, who fished in the morning, had a contention about it. The trouble is, that at flood tide the Inlet is all water, while at ebb tide it is all land or nearly so—and then the tides are so rapid in the ebb and flow. The winds are hardly ever taken into consideration for the purposes of navigation. No matter how favorable the wind is, no boat can make headway against the tides if they happen to be unfavorable. This was a great detriment to our fishing, as it required so much lead to sink the line you could not tell when the fish had taken the bait. We returned to the vessel about sundown with but poor success. The gunners and clammers had arrived before us and were awaiting supper. Freeman had agreed to give us a bird supper cooked in wine, and was busily engaged on the task. We had grown impatient, but at last the summons came and no man was out of place. Long live our friend Freeman for the dainty dish fit for a King. Whether we ate one or ten birds we don't remember. We know we consumed birds enough to make us *tight.* Of course nothing but taking a smoke and sleeping could be done after such a supper. So, accordingly, after enjoying the one, we indulged in the other.

Sunday, July 15th. Another pretty day, the Christian Sabbath, but as we must live, we determined to go foraging again. Some slight changes were made in the divisions—but the crabbers remained intact. Great things were expected from them this day. Up to this time crabs had been the only thing we had missed. Early in the morning breakfast was served, a new feature of which being an omelet of bird's eggs which had been found the day before, and which was pronounced excellent. After breakfast, a small party of us again went ashore to see the remaining sights—being the flock of wild geese and the Life Saving Station. We thought the geese a great curiosity. The flock numbers about 25 or 30, among which are two of a smaller size than the ordinary wild goose, called *Brants.* We were struck with their intelligence. Old Mr. Cobb seems to have them under his especial charge, and in answer to his stentorian and broad accent "manners to master," we could see them bowing and chattering in their language, especially the Brants. There were several goslings in the flock. We were told that during the winter season they were sometimes away from home several days, but invariably returned, bringing with them new companions, who in their turn became domesticated. We regretted very much our failure in not seeing the Life Saving Station, which was owing to the absence of the officer in charge. The object is to rescue the crews of the ships that have been wrecked on the breakers off this coast. We understood that some good service has already been performed in saving ship wrecked crews. We noticed in many places along the beach remains of wrecks, which, we suppose, made a station on this part of the coast a necessity. In this way the day wore away until about dinner, when the party again met on the boat. Each division gave a favorable report with the exception of the crabbers. When called upon this time Wile acted as spokesman and had about the same excuse, saying that he was ready, but that Sunday being the Christian's Sabbath, his companion was opposed to working. Thus, as two Sabbaths came on consecutive days, we were debarred the pleasure of eating crabs. Our pleasure ended at Cobb's Island, we concluded to weigh anchor, which we did about 5 o'clock, and steered our vessel South, down the Inlet, towards the Capes.

We bade farewell to the Mysterious Island, and the swelling sails gave life again to our little boat. Owing to the shallowness of the water in the Inlet and the irregularity of the channel, it became a necessity for us to employ a pilot. We soon secured one by the name of Richardson, who came on board and undertook this employment.

The wind was unfavorable, but the tide was fair, which made our sail down the Inlet tolerably easy. Our pilot was in charge, and about dark, when the tide changed, we came to anchor in Magothy Bay—between Prout's Island and the main land of Virginia. Early the next morning we made sail and passed out of Magothy Bay into "Fisherman's," between Smith's Island and Cape Charles. At this junction, our pilot informed us that this was as far as it was necessary for him to pilot us—that the balance of the way to the Capes was easy to navigate—informing us at the same time that where we then were was a great place for fishing. We believed his representations about the navigation, and cast our anchor for the purpose of indulging in the fishing sport. Our commissary paid him five dollars and he soon left in a small boat and we saw him no more.

We determined to spend the morning here, leaving time enough in the evening to make our run to the Capes. Everybody now felt a desire to fish, crabbers and all. Lines and bait were soon in readiness, and while the expert fishermen boarded the Magnet, the amateurs fished from the side of the vessel. In a very short time we had taken two or three dozen of a species of fish called "Mullet." The spoils were served for dinner and enjoyed. After dinner lounging was in order, as it now became necessary that we should wait for the tide, which we had lost by turning to our pleasure. Some time in the evening, the tide changed and we again made sail towards the Capes, certain, at least, of arriving there before nightfall. On we sped—on we tacked. At each length of our boat the water became more shallow, until it became so shallow, that in the opinion of our Captain, the navigation became dangerous. It was then for the first time that some of our party felt an interest in the throwing of the *lead.* After a consultation between the sailors on board, they determined to anchor and wait until the beginning of the next flood tide, which would not occur until the next morning, as at that time there would be more water over the shallows, Captain Ben insisting that, as the rise and fall of the tides were six feet, that any part which was covered with water at low tide certainly could float us at high tide, as our boat only drew 3 1/2 feet of water. Here we were pent up, strangers on a strange water. Many were the maledictions we put on our pilot, who had left us in the lurch in this manner. We accused him of deceiving us, and we really think that he should return us our money, as it will be seen hereafter that we had to employ another to relieve us from this greatest trouble. We *blessed* our luck, but made the best of matters. We were here for another night, and we patronized the "comfort." Having come to this conclusion, we cast anchor in a little harbor on the South Western extremity of Smith's Island.

Smith's Island is about 10 miles from Cape Charles, in the Atlantic Ocean, and is about 5 miles in length by a half mile in width. It presents a better appearance from the Ocean than any of the small Islands on this part of the coast, being covered by a thick growth of *live* oaks, and apparently of a soil which could be cultivated. We heard that it takes its name from Capt. John Smith of Pocahontas fame, and originally belonged to the Lee family of Virginia. Nothing better to do, and as we were booked for Fisherman's for another day and night, we determined to go on shore and take a survey, and to fill to completion our collection of shells. For some time fears were entertained whether or not the yawl boat could make headway against the tide which was making out towards the Ocean. Reckless John "Pump," however, dared the attempt and satisfied our minds. We then went on shore. On landing, we were struck with the beautiful sand, and so firm and compact that a buggy and pair could easily be driven the circuit of the Island without making an impression. Between this first beach and the second is a natural moat, which, we were told, encircles the Island. Beyond the moat is the second beach, upon which we found some very pretty shells, although the shells are not as abundant or as pretty as those at Cobb's Island. We gave our cooks the privilege of going on shore for the purpose of getting some shells for "Mary." They seemed to be delighted and filled their baskets, coat sleeves and breeches. The Light House at Smith's Island is the highest in the United States. We could see it towering above the trees and could easily see it from Cobb's Island, a distance of 30 miles. The surf at Smith's Island rolled in to the shore more majestically than at Cobb's Island, but we accounted for this by knowing that the wind, which was blowing pretty high, was beating in directly on that part of the beach contiguous to our harbor. Then the breakers are not so plentiful along the line of the beach, and are further out in the Ocean, giving the sea more space to renew its strength before dashing its force against the beach. The Light House was situated on a part of the Island distant from our harbor, and none of our party was able to visit and inspect it. We regretted this very much, as from the top of it we could have had a commanding view of the Ocean on one side and Virginia on the other, or a *radii* of 50 miles. During the excursion of some of our party on shore, Captains Sol Foxwell and Tyler and R. C. Combs went out in the Magnet on a *sounding* expedition for the purpose of discovering an outlet to our watery prison. We thought this party somewhat reckless, and many were the eyes that watched anxiously the course of the little waif upon the waters of the Ocean. We watched her until nearly invisible, on account of the distance and the heavy sea. They explored nearly ten miles out and returned with doleful news, that no channel could be discovered. They had gone nearly to the "Dry Isaacs," about midway between the two Capes. They succeeded, however, in discovering a new Island, to which no name had been given. Like Captain Nemo, they planted their standard upon it and called it Combs' Island. We hope the next geographer will take notice of this. The Island lies about half way between the South Western extremity of Smith's Island and the "Dry Isaacs." The party found some live whelks, which they brought on board with them. The evening came, and still we were imprisoned. Like criminals we rested that night.

Tuesday, July 17th. The sunrise was beautiful and betokened a pleasant day. Our thoughts were, alone, concerning our escape from the jail of waters. We were waiting for the last of flood, to take the highest tide to get over the shallows, Our Captains having attained this or nearly so, hoisted sail and we commenced to tack about. On the first tack we make about an inch. We kept on tacking, and after about twenty tacks, we lost about five inches. We soon found out that in this way we would return to Cobb's Island, and as we were going towards home, we thought it advisable to keep what we already had, and our sails were again lowered and anchor cast. We were in a terrible fix. We were penned up, and neither wind nor tide would carry us out. We thought at one time of writing home and telling our friends to expect us no more, but there was no postoffice through which the news of our imprisonment could be sent. We had settled down to the inevitable, and were having hearts for any fate when we discovered in the distance a little boat making for us. Very soon she crossed our bows, and we saw a man and a boy on board of her. Having been once deceived by these Inlet pilots, we were very particular in approaching or employing another.

We determined, however, through necessity, to speak with this man. A consultation was held as to the mode of questioning him, which resulted in the conclusion that Captain Ben should be the spokesman of the party. This decided upon, we hailed him and he came on board. We will report, as far as we can recollect, the conversation between them.

Captain Ben. "What is the price of butter down here?"
Fisherman. "Twenty-five cents."
Captain Ben. "Do you know Mr. Cobb?"
Fisherman. "Oh! Yes, very well."
Captain Ben. "Are you going fishing?"
Fisherman. "No—I am going over to the fish house at Cape Charles to get a load of fish."
Captain Ben. "What do you do with them?"
Fisherman. "I sell them on the mainland for fertilizing purposes."
Captain Ben. "Which is the best channel out of this place?"
Fisherman. "Well, you go a short distance towards the Capes, then turn a short distance towards the Ocean, then pass by a stake about half way between the "Dry Isaacs" and Cape Charles—."

Captain Ben, for the first time, was put out, and we determined to employ this man to pilot us out of the place. As we thought him one of the most original characters we ever saw, we must devote some space to an account of him. He represented himself by the name of John Half. Half, apparently, was a man of about 28 years of age. At first he seemed to be bashful and reserved, and only answered in monosyllables. He succeeded at last, however, in breaking the ice of reserve and became very communicative. He first assured us, that he had never taken a glass of whiskey, sworn an oath, played a game of cards or used tobacco in any way. His boast seemed to be—his strength. We inquired about his weight, thinking that to be about 150 or 160 pounds, but were surprised when he told us that his weight was 214 pounds. We at first doubted this, but believed it when he showed us his muscular limbs. He certainly had been just wound up when he came on board of us, as there was no end to him when he commenced talking. We believed his other virtues as above enumerated, but this we do know, that he can tell as many *questionable* stories as the next one—and could laugh enough for his audience. Among other things, he stated, in speaking of his strength, that he could crush a clam shell in one hand. Now, this we were disposed to doubt, and that doubt was confirmed by hearing him say, when a clam was offered him, that once before he had attempted the same feat, and had injured his hand very seriously. Of course the party insisted then on his not doing it. Subsequently Capt. Sol got him up in the bow of the boat and secretly gave him a clam, which he crushed with all possible ease, and without doing any injury to himself. A clam is much harder to crush or open than an oyster. His next feat was placing a small button on the deck of the vessel, and then leaning over backwards, picked it up with his teeth. Many other things he did which were marvellous to us. The little boy who accompanied him was another curiosity in his way. Equally reserved, which reserve he sustained through the whole time he was on board. He refused to eat, or say anything, and sat apart from the party with a downcast expression of countenance.

The tide now being favorable, we made sail and steered under the direction of our new pilot. Just at this time, our first Squall came up, and our hearts kept time to the muttering of the thunder. Our pilot, undismayed, stationed himself out on the extreme end of the jib-boom, and, when the storm burst over us, seemed to enjoy it as if it was his natural element. We did not feel exactly at ease but were amused at the alacrity with which the different orders were obeyed. Our party, who had been laying around loose, and as sluggards, now awakened to the danger, and stationed themselves where wished, their only concern being that the man at the helm should hear and understand the orders of the pilot on the jib-boom. This was our first squall and except for the fury of it, we would have enjoyed it. It broke at last upon us, and in silence, except the raging of the storm, we passed over the shallows, and were off Cape Charles, and once more in our native waters. Our pilot here left us with his little boy, and we steered our course South West, towards Hampton Roads.

From *Chronicles of St. Mary's* 17 (1969): 286–94, 301

1878

A Peninsular Canaan

HOWARD PYLE

Howard Pyle also visited Hog and Cedar islands. Pyle fully appreciated the romantic and picturesque, but he also had a good eye for the more mundane details of island life. His descriptions of sheep shearing and drum fishing indicate that he made his trip in the spring of the year.

Outlying along the Atlantic coast reaching from Cape Charles to Cape Henlopen, from the Chesapeake to the Delaware Bay, is a continuous chain of islands, corresponding to the Sea Islands of the Carolinas, separated from the main-land by a sheet of water varying in width from a quarter of a mile to seven or eight miles, bearing different names in its more considerable portions, such as Chincoteague Sound, the Broadwater, Sinepuxent Bay, and so forth. These islands, varying in length from less than a mile to two or three leagues, are of two characters, either low and marsh, covered with a thick growth of rank sedge, the refuge of countless millions of fiddler-crabs, the brooding-place of numberless gulls, marsh-hens (Virginia rail), and willits (a variety of snipe), or sandy, and covered with alternate strips of pine glade and salt-meadows, on some of which run wild a peculiar breed of ponies, called "beach hosses" by the natives. Off-lying from Northampton County, and separated from it by the Broadwater, is one of the most considerable of these islands, rejoicing in the not very euphonious name of Hog Island, a favorite resort of thousands of fish-hawks, which mate, brood, and rear their young at this spot, finding ample means of sustenance in the treacherous shallows of Broadwater shoals. Stretching here and there through this sound are numerous reefs of "oyster rocks," spots whereon oysters have lived, propagated, and died for ages, until the accumulated mass of shells and live oysters has grown into a reef nearly as hard as a rock close to the surface of the water.

We who proposed making a trip to this island found ourselves on our way thither in a small open boat, under the care of an experienced guide, following the tortuous windings of one of the many creeks that intersect the off-lying marsh along the shore. North and south, as far as the eye could see, extended the broad salt-marshes, here and there relieved by a so-called island—a patch of ground somewhat elevated above the surrounding marsh, clustered with a growth of pines or cedars, mostly scrubby and stunted. Overhead sea-gulls and forked-tail terns wheeled clamourously, while flocks of snipe and curlew swept in rapid flight along the more distant marsh. Along the banks of the creek numberless absurd little fiddler-crabs stood erect, waving each his one preposterously large claw at the intruder, or went popping into their holes that riddled the marsh in all directions. Here and there a column of oysters called "cat's tongues," grown into an irregular, consolidated mass, thin, bitterly salt, and useless, stood in black clumps, tangled with weed and drift. So we passed out through the crooked windings of the creek, past a long low marsh called "Gull's Island," on account of the numberless gulls, terns, marsh-hens, and willits that build their nests at this spot, and so into the Broadwater. The fishermen take innumerable eggs here during the season. One can see their black figures, stooping with baskets, gathering the eggs, while in the sunny air above them a cloud of clamorous gulls hovers with anxious cries.

Indeed, these marshes are plentifully stocked with Nature's dainties. None but those who have tasted can judge what a delicate morsel a spotted marsh-hen's egg is, or how savory that of the gull—surprisingly large for the size of the bird—or the sharp-pointed egg of the willit. The nest of the marsh-hen is built in a clump of sedge above high-water mark, that of the willit on the ground beneath an overshadowing knot of grass, and the gull's upon a few sticks or drift, open to the air. Besides these dainties, wild fowl and snipe abound in their season, growing surprisingly fat. The waters are plentifully stocked with fish, and numerous terrapins—the most sought after of all delicacies—abound. These latter are generally caught in the autumn, when they commence digging down into the mud, where they lie torpid during the winter. The hunter, walking slowly along the bank, looking closely with practiced eye, presently sees a round spot of mud softer than the surrounding marsh. Into this he thrusts a long pointed stick until he strikes the back of Master Terrapin, when nothing remains but to dig him up from where he lies, as he thought, so securely. In the spring and early fall they are caught with nets in the deeper pools where they abound.

Leaving the creek and the marshes, we sailed across the beautiful Broadwater, just rough enough to make the boat dance merrily, passing numerous fishermen in little cockle-shells of skiffs on their way to spear drum-fish on the shoals. The drum somewhat resembles a large black-fish, and receives its name from a peculiar drumming noise it makes under the water, probably caused by the sudden expulsion of air from the air-sac or bladder.

On a calm day their smothered thum! thum! can be distinctly heard in all directions. They are taken with a harpoon, which the fishermen throw with the greatest accuracy, striking the fish at a considerable distance below the water. When the fish is struck, the pole comes loose from the gaff of the harpoon, to which it is attached by a cord some six or eight feet long; this then serves as a float, constantly drawing the fish to the surface until it is exhausted. The drum, strong and lusty, sometimes runs for a mile or more, dragging the pole through the water with surprising velocity. Away goes fish, and fisherman in pursuit, up and down the channel, until at length, fairly tired out, the victim is captured and hauled into the boat. We were told that these fish are sometimes taken weighing over a hundred pounds.

The inhabitants of Hog Island are nearly all fishermen and their families, the exceptions comprising one or two store-keepers and the United States light-keeper's family, the light-house standing on a little sand-knoll in the eastern part of the island. At the time of this visit the fish-hawks were mating, and as they circled overhead the air was filled with their peculiar note, sounding like the cry of a half-grown chicken. The party struck across the island to the sand-dunes, about a mile away to the eastward. Nothing could be drearier than these hillocks of bare sand, rolling in undulations of whiteness; yet withal it is a picturesque dreariness. In some places the sand-hills were eighty feet high, covering every vestige of trees they have buried, except at the sloping sides, where the occasional skeleton top of some dead pine protrudes through the surrounding whiteness. Beyond the hillocks, to the eastward, stretches a barren waste of flat sand resembling the ripples in water known to sailors as "cats'-paws." On the distant eastern shore the surf of the Atlantic breaks with perpetual rumble and roar, now loud and angry as the sound is borne down on the salt breeze, now a muffled and distant thunder as the wind dies away.

The wooded portions of the island are in many cases swampy, and tangled with a thick growth of vines and underbrush—excellent harborage for that most abominable of nuisances the wood-tick, as we found from personal experience.

On almost every tree on the borders of this swamp, standing stark and solitary, is seen a huge mass of twigs, indicating a fish-hawk's nest. Some of these are of enormous size, the interstices between the sticks in some cases being occupied by families of grackle, or common crow-blackbirds. The small, solitary, stunted trees that stand at the feet of the sand-dunes are also frequently burdened by one and sometimes two of these huge, unwieldy nests, and in some cases they are perched on the bare sand atop of some bald melancholy knoll.

The light-house stands at the southern extremity of these hillocks, which are continually shifting their position, moving ever inland and southward, destroying every thing in their way. Even the light-house seems in some danger of submersion by this rolling sea of grit, and already fences and trees appear half drowned by it. Below the light the level waste of sand extends far away southward to the sea, the life-saving station looking like a speck in the extreme distance.

In the afternoon we took a stroll across the intervening sand-flats to the Atlantic coast, where a number of fishermen were drum-fishing with strong lines heavily loaded with lead, which they cast far out beyond the breakers.

Nothing could be more spirited than this scene. The day was windy, and the breakers roared thundering up the beach, filling the air with salt spray. Little sandpipers ran up and down at the edge of the water, following the under-tow down until it met the on-coming wave again. In the offing the dark and troubled Atlantic cut sharp against the horizon. In the foreground stood the fishermen, clad in a motley of water-proofs, sou-westers, and huge rubber boots reaching to the hips, standing thigh-deep in the water. Presently one of them hooked a fish. He threw his line over his shoulder, and turning, splashed through the surf up the beach, dragging his flouncing captive after him and landing it bodily.

These fishermen live in small cottages on the westward of the island, standing back each in a little yard, some with a row of fig-trees in front, their outward appearance poorly indicating the sumptuousness of the bill of fare of the meal the visitor will receive within—ham and eggs, hot corn bread, drum-fish steaks, clam stew, coffee, and preserves. No matter how poor these people are, they always manage to live well, having for their every meal what people of the outside world consider dainties.

Perhaps the reader has never seen a Virginia bed; the huge pile of feathers, mattress upon mattress five feet high, Pelion upon Ossa, in the depths of which one sinks as into a valley, a mountain of feathers rising high upon either hand; the gorgeous counterpane resembling Joseph's coat in point of motley, the valance of snowy linen. The best bed in a poor Virginian's house is as the apple of the housekeeper's eye. It stands conspicuous, the first object that catches the visitor's glance. In such a bed we (compelled to a night's stay upon the island by a coming storm and the unseaworthiness of our boat) found our weary frame recumbent, somewhat to the disturbance of the original inhabitants, who took a bloody vengeance upon us. This bed stood not in the main room of the house, but in a large apartment in the second story, haunted by a ghostly spinning-wheel, two or three old sea-chests, and some bonnet boxes. Immediately above it was the roof, sloping on either side to the eaves close to the floor. The storm soon broke in all its fury, but we only dimly heard it as we floated away into the fathomless sea of sleep.

In some of the off-lying Atlantic islands owned by private individuals, numbers of cattle and sheep are raised, running nearly wild, and requiring but little attention, finding ample sustenance in the rank salt sedge or in the scrub bushes that cover the more elevated sandy portions. It was sheep-shearing time, and as we were curious to see not only these island sheep, but the manner of shearing them, we had an excellent opportunity of examining both the one and the other under the pilotage of the owner of one of these islands—one of those many temporary friends whose open-handed hospitality we have so much cause to remember.

[Orris A.] B[rowne] keeps bachelor's hall on the main-land, under the strict supervision of a self-relying, self-asserting, kind-hearted colored woman, Aunt Saber, an ex-slave of the B[rowne] family, to whom she seems to have attached herself with all that faithful, uncompromising affection sometimes attending the old "patriarchal institution." After many vicissitudes subsequent to the war, during which B[rowne] had served in the Confederate navy, he returned once more to settle in Virginia, and Aunt Saber, who had nursed him when a child, came to keep house for him. She calls him "honey," scolds him vigorously, and oversees his household economy with the strictest attention.

B[rowne]'s lawn slopes gently down to the shore of a salt creek or inlet from the Broadwater, along the bed of which lie quantities of delicious oysters, which can be raked up not fifty yards from the house—fat and delicious bivalves, not flaccid as those in a city restaurant, but plump, firm, and sweet, as they never are but when fresh from their native beds. At the shore of this creek, its bow on the gravelly beach, lay a large flatboat, with a leg-of-mutton sail, in which B[rowne] and his guest proposed to cross to the island of sheep-shearing. The crew consisted of B[rowne], the writer, four men, and a small negro boy; the freight of two baskets of "grub," sheep-shears, and a demijohn of water, for rarely any thing but rain-water can be obtained at these islands.

They reached the island about night-fall, and after wading about a quarter of a mile through five inches of salt-water across an overflowed marsh, finally arrived at their destination—the overseer's cabin. It was a little log-built hut, containing but two small rooms. The lower one, half filled by a gigantic bedstead, is used for kitchen, sitting-room, bedroom, and dining-room all in one; the upper, for some mysterious purpose that man knows not of.

Luckily a warm fire awaited the bedraggled travellers, and a hearty meal of the food Aunt Saber had put up for us, eked out with a dozen or two of delicate marsh-hens' eggs—tidbits for a king. The overseer had carried a bushel or so of these beautiful little eggs over to the main-land to sell, but had luckily left enough for our consumption.

The night passed comfortably enough, except for the requisitions of the native occupants of the bed, a heavy smell of damp clothes in a close room, an occasional feeble grumbling of the men on the floor (where the overseer's wife had wrapped them up like four babes), and once the frantic yells of the little darky, who had the nightmare, and scrambled over the recumbent men amid muttered execrations. Beyond these little inconveniences, the night passed as comfortably as could be expected.

At dawn the next morning the men started to scour the island over and collect the stray sheep in a flock. They were scattered in all directions, some along the Atlantic surf, some across the marsh, some in the thickets in the southern part of the island. At length the sound of distant bleating was heard, and soon the drove—constantly augmented by the stragglers that joined it from all directions—slowly and reluctantly moved toward the sheep-pen; a moment more and they rushed tumultuously into it.

The shearing was done on a long table, a carpenter's work-bench, the small negro being sent into the pen to catch the sheep for the shearers. It was amusing to watch him—the cautious way in which he would approach the frightened drove huddled in a corner, he scarcely less frightened himself. Suddenly he makes a dive, misses his sheep, stumbles, and the whole flock gallops over his prostrate body. Another rush is more fortunate, and he fastens his black little hands in the shaggy wool on the back of some old ram, which drags him, grinning, yelling, and with gleaming eyeballs, half around the pen before the animal acknowledges itself conquered. In the afternoon the wind blew up from the northeast and rain set in; the poor denuded sheep, shivering in the cold wind, looked so miserable that B[rowne] in very pity stopped the shearing.

It was a cold passage across the water to the main-land. All were wet to the skin, silent, and grim, the little darky's teeth rolling like ivory castanets. Aunt Saber scolded when we arrived, of course.

"What yo' come across fo' in dis kine o' weather, anyway?" But she presently provided a roaring fire and warm clothes; then, seated in easy-chairs, with feet stretched to the grateful blaze, with a bottle of claret and our pipes of tobacco, we rather enjoyed than otherwise our late experience.

From *Harper's New Monthly Magazine* 148 (1879): 808–15

1894

The Robb's Island Wreck

LYNN ROBY MEEKINS

In the early 1870s, Congress, acknowledging the immense loss of life and property resulting from shipwrecks, created the United States Life-Saving Service. By the end of the decade, a half-dozen life-saving stations had opened on the Virginia barriers, including one on Cobb's Island. Each station was manned by a keeper and

six or eight surfmen who for miserably low wages risked life and health in winter storms to rescue endangered mariners and to refloat stranded vessels. Between 1875 and 1915, the Life-Saving Service on the barrier islands came to the aid of 383 vessels of which 174 became total losses.

Lynn Roby Meekins (1862–1933) was a Maryland newspaperman who at the turn of the century briefly edited the Saturday Evening Post. When his short story "The Robb's Island Wreck" first appeared in 1894, Meekins had worked for a dozen years as editor of the Baltimore American.

They began by having great fun with the captain. Ten minutes before they arrived the captain came out and took his usual chair in the usual spot under the shadow of the station. He was not a handsome man. He was strong, rugged, picturesque, but not handsome. Six feet high and two hundred pounds in weight, he was an epic in hardened flesh and muscle. His face was as full of lines as an etched portrait. His general appearance offered a contrast to every rule of a fashion-plate, and he appeared like some big shaggy animal that was particularly lazy because it was especially strong.

On this occasion the captain's eyes were half-reefed, and they looked over an expanse of sand on which low houses were built, and saw the smoke of passing steamers that crept along the horizon. It was peaceful, but it wasn't much of a view.

In fact Robb's Island wasn't much of a place; simply a few hundred acres of sand in a wilderness of salt water. But it had its fascinations. For instance, in summer, people—some of them of such good family stock that they didn't have to talk about it—left their best clothes and formalities at home and went there. They lived in rough sheds, by courtesy collectively called a hotel, fished in the inlets, tumbled around in the surf, waded through the ever-shifting sand, and gathered flesh and tan and strength and freckles on the worst food that a summer resort could possibly offer. At first Robb's Island was deeply disappointing. You reached the place in a stuffy little boat, after a sail of ten miles from the mainland. The commonness and glare of everything disgusted you. You firmly resolved to return the next morning. But the boat didn't go for two days, and there you were! In those two days you got into the surf, and pulled up more fish than you ever saw before, caught a shark or two, became the owner of a wonderful appetite, and when the boat was ready to start, you were on the other side of the island. In a week you were a confirmed victim to the repose of the place, and you remained a hopeless islander until your conscience or your finances drove you across the ten miles of marsh and water to the world and its cares.

After the summer visitors went away in September, parties of men with canvas clothes and big guns arrived to kill ducks and geese; and when they departed, the island, with its hundred people, was left alone in the solitude of the waters. There was not much to do then, and the inhabitants did it. It was a dull life and a dull place. Everybody was well, and the only way to break the monotony was for the women folks to imagine a few complaints to fit the descriptions in the patent-medicine almanacs. A small community without sick people to gossip about is stupid, but the best that Robb's Island could do was to manufacture petty aches, and doctor them on home-made remedies. The idea of a resident physician was preposterous. He wouldn't make enough in a year to feed a cat on bread-crumbs and water, much less milk.

The most interesting place on the island was the life-saving station,—a fine house of two stories, with a broad gable roof, a flagstaff, a veranda, and a liberal decoration of red paint, whose contagion had spread over the neighborhood, and given the settlement a sanguinary hue. The keeper of the station and the captain of the life-saving crew, who, according to the authorities, are two gentlemen at once, at four hundred dollars a year for the total, was, and is, Captain Zebedee Graves; and on this afternoon he had eaten his dinner, and was trying to smoke and sleep and keep his eyes open at the same time. He almost succeeded, but he was losing himself in furtive naps when other men began to come out. At first they didn't disturb him. They took seats, quietly stretched their limbs, and gazed across the expanse of sand and sea. The captain dozed; then the six surfmen looked at one another and smiled.

The smallest man struck a match and lighted his pipe. He puffed twice, threw his hands over his knees, rocked backwards and forwards several times, and began to speak. "Gentlemen," he said, "this life's getting too slow. I think I'll go ashore, and let some nice girl with a farm marry me,—a girl or a widder; I guess I'll take a widder."

There was a pause. The captain's eyes opened one-thousandth part of an inch. The other men looked into vacancy. The captain said nothing.

"You'd better be quick about it, then," advised the long man. "From what I hear, widders is mighty popular now, and somebody might cut you out."

"Oh, I guess not," said the short man. "Good goods come in little bundles, and widders know quality. Don't they, captain?"

The captain's eyes opened another fraction, and he took his pipe from his mouth and growled, "What are you up to now?"

"Oh, nothing. I just thought of going ashore and getting some things, and calling on a widder."

"Then why don't you go?"

"I'm afraid somebody's got ahead of me."

The men laughed, and the captain scowled, and took an extra puff from his pipe.

The long man spoke up: "You needn't try to deny it, captain. We've got the dead wood on you this time."

And then followed volleys of questions from all the six men. They wanted to know when the marriage was to take place, when he was going to bring his bride over, and whether or not they would receive invitations to the ceremony. The captain puffed away at his pipe, but behind the smoke was an increasing exasperation. The boys welcomed the signs with undisguised glee. The truth of the matter was that the captain aroused was one of their greatest delights. They often said that they would rather hear him swear than the church choir sing; and they never thought it a sin, because the oaths—which, of course, cannot get their natural glow in repetition—seemed to be an inevitable part of the man. He stood their prodding longer than they expected, but finally he blurted out something which, considerably expurgated, amounted to this:—

"What if I did go to see the widder? Is it any of your business? If people would attend to their own affairs this here world would be a heap better off. I'd get married if I wanted to; but, thunderation! Who wants to get married? I wouldn't marry a angel if she was to come down and ask me, 'specially if I had to introduce her to some good-for-nothing loafers that I know of."

"We're not talking about angels, captain, but widders, which is altogether different."

"You jaw about marriage as if it was a joke," continued the captain, ignoring the interruption. "It ain't a joke, it's serious; and it ruins more men than whiskey. Men don't know their own minds till they are forty, and then they mostly stay single; but if one does marry, he generally picks out the right sort of wife. What's the matter with the world now? What caused all this hard work and this starvation pay? What but an early marriage? If

Adam had had the sense to wait for another woman, he'd 'a done something in the world a little better than stealing apples."

"But, captain," put in the long man, who had married when he was eighteen, "there are—"

"Of course there is. I don't say nothing about present company. There's a few married men who's all right, and there's a big lot who ain't worth a cupful of salt water. And yonder's one of 'em."

The men turned, and about four hundred yards away saw a heavily built young fellow with hatchet and nails mending the fence that enclosed a small and neatly kept two-story house. The countenance of every one in the party fell—every one except the captain. He ground his teeth and sneered.

"That's a nice married man for you; a nice land-lubberly piece of dough and fresh water he is!"

"Now, captain, you've no right to talk against Henry that way. You know that he resigned because he had the heart-disease. You know—"

"Tom Thorpe, I know more about Henry Dane in a minute than you do in a year, and I say he's a lazy loafer. Who brought that boy up? I did, d—n him! Who taught him to be the strongest helmsman and the best all-around life-saver on the island? Who got him a place in this crew? I did, and you all know it. When he wanted to get married, I said no; not that I had nothing agin the woman, but she was a woman, and if Tom was to take my place, he had no right to get married. But married he got; and what come of it? Why, pretty soon he had the heart-disease. Bah!"

"Be fair, captain. There ain't a braver man on the island than Henry," said the tall surfman. "We all saw him keel over out there in the surf no less than four times."

"What if he did?" growled the captain. "Hain't I been knocked out a dozen times? That don't show nothing. He passed the examination, didn't he?"

"But it wasn't very strict in his case," answered the long man.

"It was strict enough. There ain't no sickness on this island—you know that—and Henry was the soundest boy here till he got married, and then his wife and that doctor who was down here last summer made him believe that something ailed his heart, and told him he had to get out of the service or die. And he got out, d— him! he got out. And I hain't spoke to him since, and I wouldn't if he was on his dying bed. Every hope I had was wrapped up in that boy. He'd 'a'been keeper of this station; and look at him now, a big calf yoked to two apron strings! Heart failure, is it? I tell you it's nerve failure—that's what it is."

Never were six men more miserable. They tried to defend their comrade, but it was useless. Each word increased the captain's anger. Presently there was silence. He puffed at his pipe; they tried to look at ease.

"Now I guess you want to know why I went to see the Widder Marling," resumed the captain, with something like contempt in his voice. "She's a cousin of Joe Black, who happens to be at the head of things over in the county just now, and the doctor says she must come to Robb's Island for her health, and she wants something to do while she is here. So she's going to teach the school."

The miserable men were no longer quiet. They started as if a bomb-shell had dropped in their midst.

"You don't mean to say, captain, that she's goin to take the place of Henry's wife?" stammered Tom.

"That's exactly what I mean."

Every man had something to say in indignant protest.

"It's no use to kick," answered the captain to them all. "The thing's settled. We done enough for Henry in giving him the place here, and he throwed it up. His wife don't belong to the island, and as he married her, let him support her. I've got no hard feelings agin her, but the bosses over in the county say Mrs. Marling must have the place, and she's got it, and I've been to see her about moving over."

It was an ill ending to the joke of the jokers. They were too depressed to talk, and gradually they got up and moved away.

II

Some people still talk about the November storm of that year. It sent more than forty boats ashore, and for hours it kept many of the one hundred and sixty-five life-saving stations along the Atlantic coast in constant readiness and apprehension. Had it not been for the work of the life-savers, more than a hundred souls would have perished; but in the face of cold and death these brave fellows risked everything, and played the roles of heroes with as splendid a courage and as honest a purpose as ever the world saw. The great public, with its twelve-hour memory, read the brief reports in the newspapers the next morning, and then promptly forgot all about it by dinner-time.

On Robb's Island the day began queerly. A yellowish sunshine disfigured the morning. By nine o'clock thick, deep, dark clouds were rolling along the horizon, and by noon a heavy wind, uncertain in its direction was beating the waves into whiteness, and piling up the blackness of the heavens. Rain poured down in big drops, and fell faster than the porous sand could receive it. Then there was a lull, and by and by came a deluge from above, driven by the wind into every crevice, and forcing everything animate to a refuge. In the life-saving station the men looked out of the windows and smoked—and smoked and looked out of the windows. The first regular watch was at sunset, but the sun was behind an ocean of ink, and by the time it got below the horizon, twilight changed to night, and the rain turned into a bombardment of hail, that rattled on the roof like a fusillade of infantry bullets.

Just about that time the small man came into the room in oil-skins and rubbers.

"Rough night, Tom," said the captain.

"Yes, captain. I don't think it'll be very dusty on the sands to-night. Perhaps some of you fellows would like to take the walk?"

"Glad you think so," said the long man.

"Well, never mind. I'm rather thinking you'll all get baptized before morning. The shoals look ugly, and if any boat gets in too close, may the good Lord help her! Good night, gentlemen."

"Good-night, Tom."

The patrol on Robb's Island was different from that of the ordinary coast station. The stretch of beach being less than two miles, only one patrolman was needed during a watch. Tom was the first man out. He carried his lantern and the Coston signals. The hail having turned to snow, the light of the lantern reached but a short distance, and beyond that was utter darkness. In ordinary weather the walk was not bad, but that night it was a sorry journey. The violence of the wind increased enormously. It was as if the storm god was using the air as a herculean lash to whip nature into chaos, and was wielding it right and left, backward and forward, with gigantic recklessness. More than once the poor fellow fell, but he was soon up again, fighting his way along the sands. You, my dear sir, with your comfortable bank account, wouldn't have stayed out there for forty dollars an hour. This surfman—thanks to the munificence of the richest government on the earth—was doing it for forty dollars a month.

In four hours he was back at the station, and another unfortunate was sent forth to make the round. After four hours he came back, half-drowned and exhausted. Then another set out in the face of the storm, and a weary time he had of it; but he stumbled along against the tempest, going down frequently, but soon rising, and all the time gazing seawards, with his Coston signal ready to warn any ill-starred mariner.

As calculated afterwards, it was sixty-five minutes before the break of day when this patrolman thought he saw the glimmer of a light a half-mile beyond the shoals. He climbed on a bluff of sand and looked again, but the snow fell thick and fast, and he could see nothing. Suddenly he heard a cry. He was sure of it, and then, settling all doubt, came the report of a gun. Before its echo had answered the sound, he ignited the Coston signal.

For two minutes its brilliant red flame illuminated the storm. And then he struck another, and for two minutes more the warning glare burned forth, and from the dark water came a second report of the gun.

The patrolman turned at once, and ran as fast as he could towards the station.

Somehow the captain had not slept that night. His thoughts were on the sea. His eyes were looking towards the window. He heard the muffled echo of the gun, and thought he saw the glare of the signal.

He jumped up and shouted, in a voice louder than the roar of the angry surf, "Get out, everybody!"

There was a stampede, a rush down the steps, a swinging open of the big doors, and in a twinkling the surf-boat, resting gracefully on its four-wheeled carriage and drawn by the six men, had rumbled down the incline, and was on its way towards the beach.

The snow was deep and the sand was deeper, and the work was hard, but the six men had muscles of iron and wills of steel, and they pulled the load of nearly a thousand pounds as if they were horses trained for the work. No one spoke except the captain, and his vociferous tones rose above the storm and urged the men to their best endeavor.

The same tones reached the houses on the island, and in a short time the whole population was aroused. No one thought of cold, or of the snow, or of pneumonia; there was a wreck, and a wreck would call a dying Robb's-Islander from the portals of the grave. So out the people came, with untied shoes and unbuttoned garments, running pell-mell across the sands, and trying to overtake the life-saving crew.

The crew were several hundred yards ahead, and were making good progress. By that time, too, the patrolman had met his comrades, and was pulling with them at the ropes of the carriage. They needed his assistance, for the sand dunes were getting larger, and the work was growing heavier, and the captain was swearing harder. A hundred yards more, and the half-dressed islanders caught up with the crew, and lent their willing aid to the men.

Day was just breaking when they reached the point opposite the wreck. In the uncertain light they saw a schooner stuck fast on the shoals. The heavy seas were pounding her sides and throwing cataracts of water across her decks. No vessel could long endure such violence, and already pieces of the wreckage were reaching the shore, showing that she was breaking up. She was too far out for the guns and the breeches buoy. The only hope was the surf-boat, and between her and the crew were the great shoals covered with prodigious breakers, whipped into whiteness by the fury of the wind, and full of uncertain currents and death-sweeping undertows.

"The boat can't live in that sea," said a voice in the crowd.

"Live?" roared the captain. "She's got to live!"

The half-dressed islanders shivered. Some of the women, whose husbands or sons were surfmen, sobbed aloud. The captain turned his head a second to look at them, and as he did so his eyes fell on Henry Dane, who, pale but calm, was standing with this wife watching the crew fix the carriage for the launching of the boat. Across the captain's face swept a wave of indignant disgust. Henry saw it and felt it.

But minutes were hours then, and there was not time for anything but the work of rescue.

"Ready, captain," said Tom.

The captain leaped into the stern, and grabbed the long steering-oar. The six surfmen, obedient and watchful, waited for the sign. A great wave rolled in, and on its recession the boat glided into the turbulent surf. Down she dropped and up she came, again she fell and again she rose, but as she rested on the wave's crest, another breaker, driven diagonally by the uncertain wind, slashed her side, hid her in its spray, and turned her prow from its course. With magnificent skill the Hercules in the stern sought to swing her back, but the forces of hell itself were in those breakers, and the vantage lost, human skill was not enough. Before the oar could get a second hold on the water, a great maddening cascade, larger and stronger than all the rest, picked up the boat as if she were a child's plaything, and tossed her angrily towards the shore.

The men on land ran forward and helped the surfmen get the boat back on the sand. And they brought with her the form of the captain, his right arm powerless, and blood streaming from a deep gash across his temple.

Henry Dane saw all this. He saw what the broken wrist meant. He saw the grounded vessel giving way to the pounding of the waves. He saw that the lives upon her had to be saved at any cost. There in the stern he would be at home,—he whom the captain had taught, whom the boys had trusted. So intent were his thoughts that he scarcely felt the clinging of the woman at his side—of her who was more to him than all the world—scarcely heard her words imploring him not to go.

"We need another man," hallooed Tom.

Henry looked at the trembling form of his wife, and unclasped her hands from his arm.

"It's my duty; I must," he said.

"Then go," she replied; "and may God keep you!"

He sprang forward. In an instant he was in the stern, with the steering-oar balanced for its work. There were no cheers, no demonstrations from the islanders. It was Henry's place to go, and he went; that was all. And, moreover, most of the folks were around the prostrate captain, binding up his wounds, and holding him down.

The surfmen and their new captain saw nothing, knew nothing, but the work ahead of them. As Henry stood at his post the whiteness left his face, and all the old earnestness rushed back to warm his blood, to strengthen his muscle.

It seemed like the old days to the surfmen to hear him sing out: "Steady now, boys. Here comes a bully one. One, two, three, *let her go!*"

She went. Into the seething turbulence she fell, and on the snowy crest she rose. Henry held her true and straight. He profited by the captain's failure; calculated for the diagonal waves, and with firm nerve and splendid strength guided her through the dangers of the breakers. His loud voice rose above the storm.

"Strong there, Tom. There's a whopper. All together, boys. That's past. Now we're all right."

The men never pulled more magnificently, and the boat, obedient to the helmsman's touch, leaped from wave to wave, carrying the prayers of those on shore, the hopes of the freezing wretches on the wreck.

And yet she seemed to go slowly—oh, so slowly! The captain, his left eye hid by the rough cloths which were bound around his wound, arose and looked.

"God bless the boy!" he said.

And the people thought the boy needed it, for the boat was often hidden by the spray, and it looked as if she could not live through the trip. But when they saw Henry standing steadfastly at his post, the men working the oars like machines, and the whole crew fighting the storm inch by inch towards the vessel, they took hope, and believed that he would conquer. It was a half-hour of indescribable suspense, a half-hour that seemed a whole day, but at the end of it the surfboat was nearer the vessel's side.

Three times she tried to approach the wreck, and three times the waves swept her away; and as failure followed failure, the five men and the boy on the vessel seemed to give up hope. But not so Henry. The fourth time success came, and in a minute the six castaways jumped aboard, and nestled there in speechless joy.

All knew the perils of the trip ashore. Progress was easier, but the dangers were greater. Henry was exuberant no longer. His face was grim, not boyish, and the paleness came back. For a while the boat cut swiftly through the sea, leaping from breaker to breaker with splendid speed. But when she reached the cut-off channel that ran between the shore and the shoals the serious work began. The beach seemed only a few yards away, but between it and the boat more than one tragedy had ended the hopes of sailors in bygone years. Henry knew it well. Just as the boat plunged into it, a hidden current tried to pull her to her death; but he was quick, and the boat was brought back to her course. A minute more and they were in the thick of the eddies, and the thundering breakers hammered the boat with titanic force. They were over more than half the channel now. A few more pulls meant land and safety.

"Pull, boys; pull for your lives!"

They did so, but there was a monster breaker chasing them like a wild beast after its prey. With lips set, the man in the stern concentrated every muscle upon the work: but, just as he seemed to be getting ready to beach the boat and clasp his wife in his arms, his hand relaxed, and he fell.

As Tom jumped to the oar, the big breaker took the boat and tossed her near enough in for the captain and the men, who were waist-deep in the surf, to grab her side. There was a turbulence of whirling water, of rapid movement, of strange words and anxious cries, and the boat and her crew and her passengers were safe on the beach.

All safe save one. His unconscious form rested listlessly on the boat's bottom. The men bore it tenderly to a place where the women had spread their shawls. The big captain knelt in the snow and tried to bring life from death.

"He must be taken home," said Tom. "We'll do it, captain. Your wrist is broken."

"Wrist be d——!" and the rugged old fellow lifted him in his big arms and carried him through the storm, followed by the woman who had asked God to keep him.

III

"Like everything else, this marrying business is pretty much a matter of circumstances," explained the captain to me two years ago.

We had arrived on the island after a long absence. The old fellow was changed—greatly changed. His beard and his speech and his dress were all better trimmed, and he bore an air of intense respectability.

"Now, for instance," he went on, "take a man who's got his notions set. He goes on through life without finding anybody to fit them notions. You can't blame him for staying single. But suppose that a man is put on a island, and he finds a woman there,—a fine woman, too,—and the circumstances throw them at each other every day in the week, why what's to be done, notions or no notions, but to call in the first preacher that comes along?"

"Captain, your logic is beneath respect, and, what's more, I'd like to know if an old woman-hater like you has any right to talk about marriage? Has an infidel a right to preach from a pulpit?"

"Yes, he has—when he's converted. Haven't you heard?"

"You don't mean to say—"

Yes, I do. I'm converted. Oh, I'm married. You needn't laugh. It wasn't my fault; it was circumstances. You see, after Henry's death from heart-disease in that wreck, we all said the widder should have the school back; but there was another widder in the way, and she said she was going to stay on the island on account of her health, and there we were. Talk about your circumstances, two widders is a whole boatload. Well, I had to go to see the second widder about the school and so on, and I found out she wasn't going to budge, and the only way to get her out of the school was for somebody to marry her. I swore to myself that Henry's wife should get back in that school, if I had to turn Mormon, and marry a whole county full of widders. So I kept on going to see her, and pretty soon we dropped school, and began to talk about other things, and so on, and such like, all of which was a d—d—draggled—"

"'Draggled,' captain?"

The captain gave a sigh of infinite pathos, and continued: "Yes, draggled! That's one of the drawbacks of marriage—she won't let me swear; won't let me say anything worse than draggled. Now don't you listen to the yarns the boys'll tell you about the hard time I had giving it up. It was hard; but, as I was saying, that going to see the widder got to be a draggled sight pleasanter than I ever imagined, and inside of a month we called in a preacher. And so Henry's widder got the school, and she's got it yet; and we built her that new house over yonder; and if there's anything she wants on this island or anywhere else, the boys will get it for her, and thank her for letting 'em do it."

"I suppose, captain, that you like married life?"

"Like it? Young man, I was here on earth fifty-one years, and when I was fifty-two—the day the preacher came—I commenced to live. I've got the best wife in the world. She's the best woman in the world except Henry's widder, who is the best woman in the world except my wife. But here we are at the station. You'll stay for dinner, and after we eat, we'll go over and look at the boy's grave."

It was delightful to be welcomed by such a woman as Mrs. Graves, but it was strange, very strange, to see the captain bow his head with real reverence, and hear him say grace with genuine unction.

Late in the afternoon we strolled over to the little cemetery. We stood together by the carefully kept grave, and read this inscription:—

> Here Lies the Body of Henry Dane,
> Aged 25 Years.
> Who Gave his Life, November 19, for Six
> Souls on the Wrecked Schooner
> Ocean View.
> He Was a Hero and a Christian.
> Erected by his Comrades of the Robb's Island
> Station.
> "Greater love hath no man than this, that a
> man lay down his life for his friends."

From *The Robb's Island Wreck and other Stories,* 2d ed. (Baltimore, 1894), pp. 1–26

1895
Along Shining Shores
THOMAS DIXON JR.

Thomas Dixon Jr. (1864–1946) experienced a varied career as journalist, actor, legislator, lawyer, clergyman, and novelist. He is best remembered for The Clansman *(1905), a vitriolic indictment of Reconstruction upon which D. W. Griffith based his landmark motion picture* The Birth of a Nation *(1915). In the mid-1890s Dixon maintained a home in Cape Charles City and a cottage on Cobb's Island. An avid hunter and fisherman, his best writing is found in his outdoor memoir* The Life Worth Living. *Dixon's experience of hunting transcended the mere killing of game for table or sport. It involved a deeper awareness of the beauty and prodigality of nature.*

I hold that Old Tidewater Virginia is the most fascinating spot on our planet. I can prove it by the shorebirds, anyhow.

When the migrating snipe have raised their young in the far South, they come north to spend the summer. Far up in the sky, flying V-shaped, as the wild goose, the curlew leads the way in April. With his keen eye surveying from the heavens the glories of the world, he sweeps over the wild beauty of the tropics, calling now and then his silver trumpet-note of command to his flock.

But when he looks down from the clouds and sees the thousand rivers, creeks, channels and solemn marshes of Old Tidewater Virginia, his voice rings with joy, his wings droop with ecstasy, and the whole flock break their long silence with such a shout as the Greeks of old raised when, homeward bound, they first beheld the sea.

Gracefully they circle downward, chattering, calling, screaming their delight. They stop and spend six weeks. They know a good thing when they see it, and they see the world from pole to pole.

The curlew is to the shore what the ruffled grouse is to the woods, has about the same weight of body, and carries the same dark brown-and-black-spotted plumage, until sunburnt on his return in August. His bill is about four inches long, unless he is a sickle-bill, when it measures from five to nine inches. The jack-curlew is now the only variety seen in Virginia, though an occasional marlin or sickle-bill make the exception to the rule.

The jack-curlew is the wildest, shrewdest and most tantalizing bird with a snipe's bill that ever worried and fascinated a hunter. His eye is as keen as a wild duck's, and his ways past finding out. I have hunted them for ten years in Virginia, and many an evening have I gone home with but two or three birds for supper, while the sky above me rang with their shouts of derision.

I have watched them for days and weeks going in thousands to a certain spot on a marsh at a certain tide. I mark the spot and wait ten days for the tides to get back to the appointed hour. Then, all in readiness, I sneak away an hour ahead of my rival, whom I half suspect of knowing my secret.

Everything depends on the tides. By the calendar, the tide should make high water at sundown. If it does, and doesn't make too high or too low, and the birds don't find out I'm on the marsh by hearing the gun, or from the report of a scout—why then, I'll get some of them. The hunting ground is nine miles wide and eighty miles long, and a curlew thinks nothing of a ten-mile flight.

Two hours before sundown, I reach the ground. I've marked the spot on a marsh a mile wide and seven miles long, surrounded by a stretch of mud-bars and channels at low tide, which melt into a beautiful silvery bay at high tide.

I go in my naptha launch, following the winding channels, from twelve to fifteen miles, to get two miles as the crow flies. But I must get to the marsh, put out my decoys on the exact spot on that seven-mile stretch to which the birds are coming, and hide before the first bird appears, and this must be done before the tide rises. The curlew are now scattered over the vast reaches of this eighty-mile bay, eating bugs, worms and sand-fiddlers on the mud-bars and on the creek banks.

I leave the launch at the head of the channel and drag the hunting dink with guns and decoys over the mud-bar to the marsh.

I take an hour to locate the right spot. I'm dead sure of the place they went the last run of tides, but, if the conditions of weather differ, they may change their notion with the change of wind and stop a mile below or go a mile farther on, and to miss their track five hundred yards is to miss them five hundred miles. They will not listen to a call in their great flock flights on this run of tides.

At length I select the place in which to cast the fate of the day. I set the decoys in the short grass of a bald high place on the marsh, exactly where I believe they will assemble in grand conclave to sit out the high water. A hole is dug with a spade just deep enough to lie flat on one's back and hide below the surface of the ground, and tall green grass is cut and stuck carefully around the hole until it looks like a hundred other clumps of grass.

The calico birds begin to come in long before a curlew is seen or heard. I take a crack at them to get my hand in for Mr. Jack Curlew. The calico plover is a fine practice shot, for he is swift as lightning unless he sees fit to decoy perfectly.

At last the mud-flats are all covered and the hour has come for the flight to begin. I am on the lookout for a scout. The curlew send out a scout to survey the ground to which the great flocks are coming. If things look suspicious, he goes back and reports, and they change their flight ten or twenty miles in another direction.

No scout appears. I wait an hour and begin to grow uneasy. The tide is slow, a westerly wind has spoiled the flow, and not a curlew comes within five miles of me.

I try the next afternoon, and the wind jumps around to the east, the tide covers all creation and runs me out of my hole before I get a shot, even at a calico.

Again, not a curlew came to the marsh. They all went to the sand-dunes on Myrtle Island, fifteen miles below. I watched them for an hour. The heavens were streaked with them as far as the eye could reach—north, south, east and west. I ground my teeth and vowed vengeance. I have but one more day of this run of tides. If they don't come to the marsh the next night, they will not come till the tide gets around again in two weeks.

Again I've baled out my hole and rebuilt my grass blind, and snugly resting on the rubber blanket, I gaze up at the southern sky, or away over the endless marsh and bay, and wait. My guide has gone a mile with the launch and hidden in the tall grass of the creek.

How still the world!

To the east, I see the dim white line of the ocean beaches, but the wind is from the south and I cannot hear the surf. North, south and west of me sweeps the dark green marsh, until it kisses the sky-line and fades into eternity. I begin to dream of great things. Nothing small disturbs my vision—not a house or man or woman is in sight.

I begin to feel pity for the feathered life I've come to take, when my eye rests on a mother fiddler in the mud beside me, peeping out of her hole to make sure no curlew is near before venturing out for food for her children. I clutch my gun and determine to take sides with the fiddlers.

"A curlew's a mean bird, anyhow," I muttered. "Confound 'em! Let 'em come here and I'll burn 'em up! Besides, I've promised my wife enough birds for the table this week."

Suddenly the shrill call of a curlew scout rang over the marsh, and old Mrs. Fiddler cut a somersault to get into her cyclone cellar.

I slipped the safety-lock of my gun and tried to get under my hole in the ground.

I must either kill that scout or let him go back without seeing me. I tremble with excitement, afraid to answer his call lest I reveal my position. I know he has seen my decoys and determine to keep silent and still as death.

He came high, circled around me twice, and then came straight up behind, about a hundred yards in the air. Just over the decoys he poised, cocked his long-billed head to one side and peered down at me.

I knew he was coming no closer and it was a long chance shot, but I determined to make it before he could jump. Lying flat on my back, I snatched up my number ten and let him have a snap-shot.

He quivered a moment, and down he came, softly, without a struggle, and fell with his wings spread out three feet on the grass, so close to where I lay that I could reach him without rising.

I picked him up and found a tiny scarlet spot on his big fat brown breast. A single shot had taken effect.

He fell just at Mrs. Fiddler's door, and left a drop of blood in her front yard. When I lifted him, the fiddler emerged, with three trembling little fiddlers clinging to her skirts, smiled and thanked me. And then, seeing a baby snail toddling slowly along the road in front of her house, she ran out, grabbed him by the throat, broke his neck, tore him into bits with her big cruel claw, and handed the pieces to her hungry children.

"It's the way of life," I thought, grimly. "Life feeds on life; the man on fish and animal; the bird on fiddler; the fiddler on snail; the snail on worm; the worm on cabbage, and the cabbage on the vegetarian!"

And, when we get down to the last cell-life, no eye can tell the difference between the germ that will grow into a vegetarian and the one that will grown into a cabbage.

And yet the vegetarians put on holy airs, and say mean things about hunters and meat-eaters. I've often wondered what the cabbages, beets, turnips, peas and beans whisper to one another about these people in the still moonlit nights of the spring, when they are struggling to reproduce their kind.

I reloaded my gun and lay for another curlew. In about half an hour they began to come. I found I had missed the spot they had selected for their meeting by about three hundred yards. They were going just beyond my blind, three hundred yards farther up the marsh across a creek. But they were leading so close to my decoys that by vigorous whistling I enticed in a dozen large flocks and scores of small groups. When the sun sank I had bagged seventeen. I went home with a song of victory. I felt I could look my wife and children in the face once more. Only once in ten years did I break this record. Then I had the remarkable luck of having the wind and tide just right and I got to the right place. Then I carried home twenty-six. Fully fifty thousand curlew came on the marsh that afternoon.

We get a few curlew when shooting grayback, willet and plover on the marshes from blinds. But this can be done only in the early part of the season. One shot from a blind is all that is necessary to educate every curlew who sees the performance. No amount of whistle-calling will get him to come in range of a blind again.

At ebb-tide we shoot the grayback, blackbreast, yellow-legs and curlew on the mud-bars, where they come to feed on fiddlers and bugs as the tide ebbs off. I have killed a dozen curlew sometimes from an ebb-tide blind.

One never-to-be-forgotten day the grayback came like chickens, and I made a bag of eighty-two on the first of the summer season. The grayback snipe decoys beautifully and is the toothsome quail of the shore and marsh.

But by far the most interesting sport of the shore is when the red-breasted snipe come suddenly trooping in from the mists of the southern seas about the middle of May. They feed almost exclusively on the mussels of the ocean beaches at ebb-tide. They usually appear about May 15, though their advent varies by a week or so, according to conditions of the spring weather.

I have walked along the surf in the spring on one day without seeing a single red-breast, and have gone back the next morning and found flocks of ten thousand chattering and feeding. They came in the night out of darkness and mystery, and they will go in two weeks, as they came, into silence and mystery.

Where they go the Virginia hunter does not know. Unlike the curlew and grayback, they do not stop on their return flight from the North Pole in August. The curlew and grayback come in April and leave the last of May. They spend five weeks in the far North and return to Virginia about July 15, and remain till the latter part of August, or middle of September.

Not so the red-breast. He comes in a night in May, gets fat in two weeks and leaves suddenly. He is not seen again until next spring.

May 17 we reached the Life Saving Station of Smith's Island, by the invitation of its genial captain, George Hitchens. It was blowing a furious gale and raining in blinding sheets, with the wind hanging steadily on to the northeast.

The birds had not come, the crew told us, but Captain George said they would come in on the wings of the storm that night. At daylight we caught the old plug of a horse from the stable and hitched him to the cart. The Smith's Island light, just over our heads, the greatest light of the Atlantic coast, was still flashing its gleaming message, "45," over the storm-clouded sea.

Within an hour we had reached the bend of the beach, five miles above the station. The tide had just begun to ebb as the sun burst from the ocean through the cloud-banks of the passing storm.

The Captain was right. The birds had come on its black wings. The beach was literally covered with them. We were in rare luck. We were the first on the beach, the first day of their season, and the wind was blowing a steady gale from sea, just the way we wished it.

Hastily gathering some dead bushes and grass from the sand-dunes, we build a scraggy blind, place our decoys on the edge of the receding surf, and are ready for them!

How beautifully they come!

Sometimes they pitch among the decoys.

First they come in little bunches of two or three, when we take one with each barrel; then the big flocks begin to streak along the magnificent surf and decoy like chickens.

They require no calling. The moment they see our decoys they set their wings in all sorts of fancy shapes and sweep into the happy hunting-ground to share the mussels with our fat wooden birds, whose round shapes no doubt excite their hunger and envy.

Some set their wings in a beautiful bow-shaped curve, some drop them gracefully downward, some swing them gracefully upward and drop their legs as they descend.

Sometimes the sky is black with them, their wings set at every conceivable angle. Then it was impossible to choose a good shot in the confusion of a hundred challenging groups. We generally take the poorest chance on such occasions, and perhaps get one bird out of five hundred.

The ideal flock has from ten to fifteen birds. We wait for the critical moment when they double in their flight after they swing past the decoys. A shot just at this second will often kill a dozen.

At the end of three hours the tide has ebbed off, and the sport is over for the day.

I lie down on the sands, and wait for the flood tide to catch a drum, loath to leave the glorious spot. North and south stretches the long white strip of sand as far as the eye can reach. In front rolls and curls and thunders the surf. Behind me lies in shimmering beauty the mirror of the Broadwater bay, nine miles wide and eighty miles long. There is not a human habitation in sight. Above me the infinite space, flecked now with white, swift-flying clouds—I dream of a world without railroads, or mail—the happy hunting-ground the red man saw in visions of the olden time.

From *The Life Worth Living: A Personal Experience* (New York: Doubleday, Page, 1905), pp. 72–88

1895

Cobb's Island

ALEXANDER HUNTER

Few sportsmen knew the Virginia barrier islands as well as Alexander Hunter (1843–1914). In the decades from the end of the Civil War through the turn of the century, he came to the island resorts frequently and in all seasons to hunt shorebirds and waterfowl. Confederate veteran, Civil War historian, Virginia state legislator, and chronicler of the outdoor life, Hunter wrote charmingly of island history (in which, regrettably, he was sometimes careless of the details), wildlife conservation, and the experience of hunting.

"There's nothing new under the sun," they say, yet the history of Cobb's Island, off the coast of Virginia, differs from any romance ever told.

The story of a lone island in the ocean has ever been an enthralling one, both to the old and the young alike, whether the island is peopled by savages, castaways, or buccaneers; and its buried treasures have ever been the favorite theme of the historian, dramatist and story-teller. Yet what romancer has ever told of a speck of land in mid-ocean that grew day by day, until it became a broad domain, and produced more wealth than any pirate's hoard ever contained? Furthermore, when this lone isle in the sea passed from the possession of the sons of Neptune, the ocean recalled its gift, the island sank from whence it rose, and now the heaving billows sweep unchecked over the place where but a few years ago there flourished a large village, with its hotel and sportsmen's lodges.

Some time between 1825 and 1830 there lived on the eastern shore of Virginia an old man named Cobb, who had emigrated from Marblehead, Massachusetts, and who gained a living by fishing and oystering.

The fisherman was a shrewd old fellow, and after much cogitation he conceived the idea that if he could find a good, solid piece of land near the source of supplies it would save him time and money. So keeping his eyes open, he came across a small sandbank a few acres in extent, about sixteen miles from the mainland, off the Virginia coast, that evidently had risen directly out of the ocean by some convulsion of Nature. This solitary spot was already occupied by a lone fisherman who spent the spring and summer in catching fish and gathering oysters. A bargain was soon struck between the two, and for and in consideration of the sum of thirty dollars and a sack of salt the fisherman transferred all his rights to the sand dunes to his rival, no doubt congratulating himself that he had gotten rid of a doubtful piece of property, inasmuch as it was likely to be swallowed up by the waves. Probably, like many an unlucky fellow, he deplored to the day of his death the fact that his fore-sight was not equal to his hind-sight, for he lived to see the time when old man Cobb refused a cash offer of one hundred thousand dollars for the property.

The new owner was a man of great nerve, and coolly took all the chances of having his family name extinguished, by moving his family, bag and baggage, to the sandbank and making the place his permanent home, though the ground was by no means secure, and would tremble, so the story goes, like a bowlful of jelly whenever an unusually large and heavy billow struck it. It is said that many seasons passed before the women of the island could sleep quietly in their beds when a storm was raging along the coast.

Day by day the island grew in area and solidity, and in about two score years there was a substantial piece of land, of fully fifty acres, and sea meadows of several thousand more.

Old man Cobb and his sons formed a wrecking company, and fortune smiled upon them. A ship loaded with coffee from Brazil went ashore, and the Cobbs saved the cargo, and received $10,000. Another ship panned out $5000 for salvage, and their last windfall was a three-masted bark of $4000. Had old man Cobb and his three stalwart sons been content to remain in their humble sphere, they would have been kings of fishermen, the emperors of sportsmen, and Rothschilds among the toilers of the sea.

Then the United States Government built a station, and manned it with a picked crew, and the Cobbs found their salvage fees gone. They had more money than they could spend, but when is man ever content?

So the Cobbs, who received a steady income from visiting sportsmen, determined to make Cobb's Island a summer resort. Just here it may be well to say that this place was then by far the finest shooting-grounds on the Atlantic coast for wild fowl and bay-birds. It was not only the feeding-grounds of enormous numbers of brant, geese, and snipe, but, being so far out in the ocean, it attracted, as a resting-place, vast flocks of migrating birds, and it was literally the paradise of sportsmen.

The Cobbs erected a long, rambling structure of boards along the line of architecture of the inns of Virginia and North Carolina, which have been built in the same style since the memory of man. Several cottages were also added, and the season opened auspiciously with two hundred guests.

I happened to be there at the opening, and it made a greater impression upon me than any seaside resort I ever visited. The attempt of three simple-minded, honest fishermen to run a watering-place, without the remotest idea of anything outside of their storm-tossed isle, was certainly unique and rare.

Warren Cobb, the eldest son, was a rough and ready mariner, with a voice like a fog-horn, and an insatiate thirst. He was a typical ruddy-faced, good-natured, weather-beaten, ocean fisherman. He never refused an invitation to "splice the main brace," and each succeeding drink only made him happier than the one before.

Nathan, the second son, was a very tall, angular man, of powerful build, and withal as gentle and tender as a child. He was the only sportsman in the family, and was, without exception, the finest shot I ever met. He probably killed more wild fowl for market than any other gunner in America. With all his simplicity, he had strong horse sense, and refused to join the hotel syndicate. "Here I is, and here I stays," was his ultimatum, as he pointed to his neat house and fine garden. So he stuck to his business, and in the course of time he owned nearly the whole island.

Albert, the youngest, was the bright one of the family; he was a sport, too, but his game was draw-poker.

Well, the opening was a great success. However, a young, inexperienced fellow from the mainland, a friend of the family, was installed as clerk at the hotel. But he kept no books; he carried the current sheet and ledger in his head, and at the end of the season he "skipped," and left nothing behind save his conscience, and that was probably of small value.

It was truly ludicrous, these untutored, unimaginative wreckers catering to the wants of the delicate, refined pleasure-seekers. Well, the balance was about even; these Norsemen did not understand their guests, and the guests certainly did not comprehend their landlords.

The guests were, for the most part, fashionable people. When the hotel and cottages were filled at the opening of the season the Cobbs were simply dumbfounded that there were people in the world who could want so much. Livery, telegrams, drainage, laundries, waterpipes were as Sanscrit to these simple-minded men, and they were as much out of place as was Christopher Sly in the lord's palace.

The fare was plentiful, most profuse; in fact, it was served in wholesale quantities. For example, a guest would call for fish, and a huge sea-trout, some two feet long, enough for a whole family on Good Friday, would be placed on the table. Bread—a corn-pone the size of a Belgian curbstone would be handed up. Beef—and a collop that would satisfy a Pawnee Indian would arrive. Soft crabs—six at a time would be brought. Such things as sauces, pickles, condiments, preserves, were unthought of there—simply because they were unheard of. Indeed, the weather-beaten wreckers who had lived, as it were, in a world of their own, must have felt as did our savage Saxon ancestors, when the witching *dames par de la monde,* of the French Court, following in the wake of William of Normandy, appeared before the eyes of the uncultured Britons.

These wreckers, like the old Norsemen, were children of Nature; they ate when they were hungry, drank when thirsty, rose with the dawn, and retired to their rest at the end of the day. So, the rich and fastidious sportsmen brought their wives, sisters, cousins, and aunts to the island on a kind of lark—and they had it.

It must be confessed that some of the sportsmen, for the sake of a practical joke, inveigled their people to Cobb's, and many of the visitors expected to find on the island a modern hotel with gas and electric lights, splendid band (alas for that one fiddle and harp!), superb bar, wine vaults, tonsorial accommodations, billiard saloon, telegraph facilities, and many other things considered by many the necessaries of life; and when they saw the meager establishment, a few actually returned home, but the majority remained, and many declared it to be the best time of their lives. There was no conventionality at Cobb's, no grades of social position; every one was on an equal footing, and as one of the Cobbs was heard to remark, "If they didn't like it, they could lump it."

But it was in the ballroom, where the *"band"* was waving and weaving a "voluptuous swell," that the proprietors would saunter through the room clad in their usual costumes of an oilcloth hat, Guernsey jacket, canvas breeches, and rubber boots reaching to the hip. But withal, there were no bonifaces in America that were so popular, for the Cobbs were so sincere, so true, so democratic that they treated all alike. Whether you were noble or serf, rich or poor, famous or unknown, it was all the same to them; and when the visitors left the island it was with regret at the parting.

Old man Cobb took no part in the new deal; none ever saw him at the hotel. He had a fine plot of ground, and a snug, comfortable house, and there he stayed with his tame brants, as isolated as if he were a lone fisherman on a lone isle, as in days of yore.

For many years Cobb's Island was the most famous resort in America for the combined attraction of hunting and fishing; and a week's stay at that place was like taking an ocean trip abroad. It possessed a peculiar fascination for the sportsman, and many of us went to the island year after year.

We went in the spring for the robin-snipe; in the summer for the baybirds, and in the winter for that king of salt-water birds, the brant.

Cobb's Island was a favorite rendezvous for the American Yacht squadron, and in the summer all sorts of craft filled with pleasure-seekers would anchor off the place, and there would be feast, fun and frolic.

Warren Cobb was a favorite guide for the sportsmen, as nothing could ever disturb his good nature or exhaust his patience. He used to tell a tale of a dude huntsman and his valet, whom he once took out snipe-shooting. Warren said all the girls gathered on the porch to see them off. The valet had to get a cart to carry his traps down to the landing, where a boat lay.

Arriving at the blind just off Wreck Island, Warren set the decoys, and if the sportsman was not made comfortable, it was not the fault of the valet. A large camp-chair was placed within the blind, and then the valet held an umbrella over the master's head to keep off the torrid rays of the August sun, and actually fanned him as the heat grew more intense. A big block of ice had been brought along, and with it a half dozen bottles of champagne, a few bottles of beer and a quantity of old rye. Then the fun commenced.

A few young birds came up to the decoys, in spite of the strange appearance of the place, and Warren Cobb swears that after the sportsman fired he would hand his gun to his Jeems Yellowplush to be reloaded. "And," said Warren, "bust my breeches if we didn't have a drink around over every bird he kilt! And when the water riz and come in the blind, he makes me take him on my back and carry him to the boat."

I asked Warren how many birds the dude killed? He replied that he counted ten, and then his memory "done give out."

Bill Johns, another guide, more like Warren in looks and temperament than any of his brothers, swore that Warren did not let out all the details of the dude's eventful hunt. He avers that he had to bring the whole crowd home, and that the mixture of beer, champagne, and whiskey was a sure knockout for them all; the valet was as helpless as his master. However, Bill said he got them all onto the wharf save Warren, who, in attempting to jump from the boat to the wharf, went head-first in the water, which was about three feet deep, and that the shock only half sobered him, for when he arose, and spit about a bucket of the briny from his mouth, he hiccoughed out, "Doggone it, Bill Johns, how your boat do leak!"

A few years later, under modern management, Cobb's Island became a popular watering-place, and was known as the sportsmen's heaven. The bay-birds were killed by the thousands every summer, and the fishing was a revelation to many of the guests. The islanders were making money, and when affairs were at high tide, old ocean gave them a high tide of Neptune's.

On the 19th of October 1879, a steady rain commenced falling, which continued for two days, and on the night of the 21st the north winds shifted to the southeast, and by nine o'clock was blowing a hurricane; the windows rattled, shutters banged, and the pine board hotel shivered in the force of the wintry blast. The Storm King let loose, careened at pleasure across the wide waste of waters, and shrieked in its mad glee as it swept resistlessly over the broad Atlantic.

"A bad night for vessels," remarked some one, and then all retired for the night; for the islanders were used to hard blows, and could slumber quietly in a tempest that would cause a landsman to say his prayers and keep on praying the night through.

All were asleep except the coastguardsmen, who kept watch, ever and anon looking through the window, trying to pierce through the darkness, it being impossible to patrol the beach; the wind was so violent it would carry them off their legs.

About midnight the different inmates of the cottage were aroused, one by one, by the coastguard with the startling information that the tide was rising and bursting over its high-water mark, and was advancing in angry charges that would sweep the island away.

Like the dreadful cry of fire in dreaming ears, it woke the slumbering inmates, who started up affrighted, in such garments as they could hastily snatch in the darkness. They all ran for safety to the hotel, which occupied the highest point of ground on the island.

The angry roar of the waves was now heard, mingled with the scream of the blast, and surely and slowly the black billows advanced; the bath-houses were swept away; next the coastguards' house was torn from its place, and drifted inland. The crowd assembled in the ballroom of the hotel. The women cried and moaned; the men cursed and prayed alternately. They could do nothing; and stout wreckers as they were, inured to the dangers of the deep, they shrank appalled as the treacherous waves closed in around them. No boat could live in such a sea; and, like caged rats, they could only wait and hope for the coming day and the subsidence of the waters.

About four o'clock in the morning a dreadful sound smote their listening ears. Above the noise of the warring elements they heard the crash of a building, the splitting of timbers, and the falling in of beams and planking. It was the New York house, within fifty yards of the hotel, that had caved in, the supports having washed away, and the whole fabric sank in an unsightly ruin.

Old man Cobb sat stoically waiting for death. His son Nathan was bidding his wife farewell, and Albert sat with his head buried in his hands. But

Warren, jovial-hearted son of Neptune, seeing all hope gone, waded across to the bar-room, and, lighting a tallow candle, which cast a ghastly light over the scene, he and Bill Johns drank until they grew recklessly happy, and began playing seven-up on the counter, where they both sat cross-legged, for fifty cents a game, while the water was two feet deep on the floor and the chairs and tables were swimming around the room.

At half-past four o'clock the waves lapped the porch; at a quarter to five the steps were washed away, and the beat of the charging rollers thundering on, made the island tremble and rock as if it were in the throes of an earthquake. At five the fluid in a thin stream trickled through the cracks of the closed door, and then they all thought their time had come. But the storm had reached its height; in a few minutes the water began to recede, and every one drew a long breath. By eight o'clock the ocean was in its usual place.

Daylight showed that the topography of the island was much changed. Immense sand lines were thrown up, looking like miniature mountains; the ground was covered with driftwood, spars, shells and marine vegetation. All the fences were washed away, as were several cottages.

A most singular circumstance of this flood was that all of old man Cobb's tame brant were swept away. Many of them drifted into Chesapeake Bay, and some of them found refuge on Hog Island, twelve miles distant; but they every one returned, and their show of delight at again meeting one another seemed almost human.

It was several years before Cobb's Island recovered from the blow; but at last patrons were assured that floods, like the eruption of Vesuvius, never happen twice in a lifetime, so the old place was regaining its former prestige.

I will long remember one Christmas I spent on the island all alone. My two companions had business engagements compelling their presence at home, and they left on Christmas Eve.

The morning of Christmas was warm, bright and sunny. The ocean lay in all its majestic beauty, as calm, still and smooth as a lake hid away in some mountain fastness; stately ships decorated with bunting appeared motionless on the surface, and earth, air and water harmonized in one grand anthem in honor of the Nativity.

"It's too calm for ducks," said Nathan, whose opinion on all matters pertaining to hunting was as irrefutable as the laws of the Medes and the Persians, "but it's a perfect day for snipe."

"Why?" we asked.

"Because bad weather scatters the large flocks in every direction, and they are very shy; but on a calm, warm day they unite and become lazy and will let a man walk almost up to them. I'll make the boy get the cart and carry you where there are acres of them."

In a short time we were on our way along the beach toward Hog Island.

After going about five miles, our island gradually contracted, until a narrow strip of sand some fifty yards wide, over which the waves at high tide dashed, showed where the possessions of the Cobbs ended.

On this sandbank the snipe were feeding in countless numbers, and I am not exaggerating when I say that the bar running into the sea was so thick with them that there was not a bare spot discernible. Creeping up on my hands and knees to within forty yards, I sighted along the fluttering mosaic-looking ground and pulled trigger. A long swath of dead and dying marked the track of the shot.

For every one killed there were two wounded, and I had a lively chase in the water after them. Many escaped, for the tide was rising and the crippled birds can swim like a duck. They soon reached deep water and were safe from me, but not from sea hawks, who came out in force and swooped down on the wounded.

I gathered up the dead and piled them in great heaps. I had nearly gotten through when I stopped work for further sport. A flight of snipe fully a hundred yards long and thick were performing the most beautiful evolutions possible to conceive. A leader marked the way, and with unerring precision each bird followed, and kept his proper distance. There was no confusion, no jostling, as they spun through the air with the speed of the wind. Now skimming along the surface of the water, then in a second up in the blue vault with the suddenness of a rocket, next a slanting curve, a concentric circle to turn its body, and the bright sun shining on the mass that shifted in color every moment made the result indescribable.

I was brought back to earth by Bill Johns, my guide, who grasped my arm, and said we had better hurry back home.

"It's going to be a splendid day for brant. See, the northwest wind is rising."

I looked around; it was true; the surface of the ocean was ruffled by the breeze, and what sportsman does not feel his pulse thrill at the thought of a perfect day with the brant.

There must be three elements, all favorable, before one can have any luck over decoys. The tide must be just right,—that is, falling on the ebb at daybreak,—the sun must come out brightly, and the wind must be blowing. During all of our stay these three things did not conjointly appear. If a wind was blowing, the tide was wrong. If the tide was right, there was a perfect calm. If the sun was shining and the wind blowing, the tide was on the flood; or if not on the flood and the wind was just right, then the clouds were banked up in the sky. In fact, these three uncertainties making one harmony was as risky a thing to count on as a call in faro, and all sportsmen know how uncertain a thing that is.

Arriving at the hotel the guide left the cart, and we hurried to the wharf where the boats, loaded with decoys, always floated. I only stopped long enough to change my box of No. 8 shot for No. 4's, and filled my flask.

We were soon under weigh, and reached the blind off Gull Island about noon. Bill scattered about a hundred decoys around the blind, and left me in a little flat-bottomed boat inside the blind. He with the large boat put back to Gull Island, about a half mile distant.

Now it must be understood that the deep ocean did not surround Cobb's Island. On the south side was what is known as the Broadwater; that is, sea-meadows, sand-bars and mud-flats, with deep channels running through them. These flats were covered at high tide with from four to six feet of water; at low tide they were bare, and it is here that the brant have their haunts, feeding on the young mussels, clams, and the like.

The blind was built of long, slim cedar trees, about six feet by four, just wide enough to enclose a small flat-bottom boat.

The wind had freshened, and, as it came from the north, it was piercing and cold. The tide was falling. It would probably be an hour or two before the birds would flock to the flats to feed.

Shades of Aeolus, how old Boreas was spreading himself! I cowered in a corner of the blind, lit my pipe, tied an old glove over the bowl to save the tobacco from being blown out, humped my shoulders, and gave free rein to my imagination.

Here was the one day in the year when every man feels his heart softened and touched, and "good will toward man," for twenty-four hours at least, is something more than a mere sentiment. Here was the day which the whole civilized world celebrated, when reunion of family and friends is the universal custom. What mortal would voluntarily leave home, relatives, or boon companions to sit out in the ocean, in a driving wind, solitary and alone? "Surely, no sane man would do such a thing," is what nine-tenths of the people would say; but the fraternity of sportsmen would, almost to a unit, agree that he would leave everything his heart held most dear for a shy at the royal brant, even though the day be Christmas, Thanksgiving and Fourth of July rolled into one.

The silent, solitary figure in the blind, who smokes his pipe and waits motionless hour after hour, has a keen and vivid sense of enjoyment incomprehensible to those who have no sporting instincts in their make-up. What do they know of the thrilling pleasure which comes with the sight of game, or at a neat, quick shot?

What do they know of the quiet, meditative happiness of watching the distant flight of birds, and speculating upon their possible movements? What do they know of the delight of strained expectancy that a sportsman feels as, with finger on the trigger, he watches with keen eye the rapidly fluttering wings which bring the game within shot?

But my meditations were cut short by a brant—a brant is about the size and weight of a Muscovy duck—darting by; evidently he was a scout sent to learn if the flats were visible.

I knew by the signs that the birds would soon appear, and I prepared for action.

The tops of the sandbars now began to be visible among the waves, or rather the surf, for the wind was simply howling over the ocean, and it drove all the brant from the ocean into the Broadwater, and tore the big flocks all to pieces.

I had expected good sport, but I never dreamed that it would rain brant; for when they did appear, they came with a rush, and from all points of the compass. I fired at least fifty shells loaded with No. 4 shot, as fast as I could slip the shells in, and my gun-barrel became so hot that I had to immerse it in the water.

The brant must have seen the decoys glistening in the sunlight for miles, for I could see the birds high in the sky, coming to the blind with wings set on a gentle decline. Many of them actually settled among their wooden prototypes, a rare thing for them to do. There were so many birds that I could pick the shots, and let the ones going with the wind alone, and blaze away at the brant that approached beating against the gale.

The water was about two feet deep when the birds began to fly, but the waves made the boat rock so that it was impossible to take certain aim. I had to make snap-shots, and scored many a miss; but when the water receded a foot, and the boat settled upon the sand, then it was that the shooting was simply perfect, and I would not have changed position with any man on earth, Czar, Sultan or King.

I did not stop to count the birds that fell; it was the living, not the dead, I was after.

It was warm work! I discarded my coat, then the woolen jacket, and worked in my vest. Oh! It was glorious while it lasted; it was the very summit of a sportsman's dream, and repaid me for the long weary days on the island, the fruitless waits at the blinds. It is the hope deferred that maketh the heart of the sportsman sick.

I had carried only one box containing one hundred shells, and I fired the last when the sun was low in the west, then I drew a long breath, took an equally long drink from my flask, and looked around. I saw Bill Johns picking up the dead and shooting the cripples—a very easy task, for the brant never dives, but swims straight on.

Nobody but a born and bred waterman could have managed a sailboat in such a fierce breeze, and I sat there and watched Bill with the keenest interest. In about an hour he anchored his boat in deep water and waded out to where I sat.

"What's the matter?" he shouted.

"I have fired my last shell," I replied, "and I have had enough."

"All right, we will stow the decoys away."

On our way to the island I counted my game. Fifty-eight birds was the total; the finest day's work among the brant in all my thirty years' shooting.

"There were some cripples I could not reach," said Bill. "They were on the flats, but I hadn't any time to waste."

The next day I strolled over to Nathan Cobb's, and found him packing his game in barrels to send to New York.

"How many have you, Nathan?" I asked.

"I killed one hundred and eighteen," he replied, "and a good day's work, as I get forty cents apiece for them."

I asked him what was the greatest number he ever killed in one day, and he replied, "One hundred and eighty-six."

Nathan was the best wild-fowl shot I ever met. He used a No. 8 Greener, very heavy, using brass shells which he loaded himself. But few men could stand the jar of continued shooting from such a gun.

In the summer of 1890 it looked as if Cobb's Island was destined to become one of the finest watering-places on the Atlantic Coast. A rich syndicate commenced negotiations for the property, intending to erect costly buildings and improvements strictly up to date. An engineer examined the island and found that the front was slowly crumbling into the sea; so he advised the prospective purchasers to wait another year. At the end of that time he made another examination, and found that ten feet of the entire beach had disappeared; this discovery stopped the deal.

The hotel as originally built was fully five hundred yards from the beach, but steadily and surely the ocean had encroached until, in 1896, it was within fifty feet of the hotel; then the end came.

On the evening of October 4, 1896, the sun set in a blaze of golden splendor. The sea was unruffled, the air balmy, and there was not a cloud in the sky. The islanders pursued their ordinary occupations; some were mending their nets, others were gathering their harvest of fish from the boats. The life-guardsmen were told off, and those on duty had started on their rounds along the beach. The housewives were busy getting supper, and from each chimney there arose a light cloud of smoke.

Sunday morning dawned clear, with a fitful breeze from the northeast, which increased as the hours wore on, and the surf began rolling inward with increasing power, dashing beyond the high-water mark. Still no alarm was felt until the wind changed into a gale, which soon became a hurricane. Then the islanders were moved to sudden action. All the furniture was moved from the lower floors and crowded into the rooms above. The life-savers manned their boats and watched the beach.

The breakers were now driven by the wind with inconceivable force, and rolled up around the hotel, and as the wind increased in velocity some tremendous billows swept clear across the island. Then there was "hurrying to and fro," and most of the people sought the houses that were on the elevated ground, which was generally the crest of some sand dune, over which the coarse grass had grown.

Soon, instead of an occasional vagrant wave, the whole line of breakers were chasing each other like race horses on a steeplechase, and breaking with a roar against the different dwellings.

It was a scene of grandeur; even the stolid islanders were moved to admiration. The island was invisible, and immense waves came charging from the ocean at their homes, as if they were serried lines of cavalry. The sand dunes broke the force of the mighty surges, otherwise the houses would have disappeared in the clutch of the ravening waters.

Whilst the people were safely housed in their second stories, the stock and cattle were swimming around the houses, uttering cries of distress and fear; but no Noah's Ark was there to afford protection. Horses, cows, goats and dogs were all mingled together, and every now and then some wave, overtopping its fellow, would catch up some animal and bear it across the mainland and drown it in the deep channel at the rear of the island.

Soon even the highest points were under the water. Then the life-guardsmen went from house to house and rescued the inmates one by one, and carried them to the life-saving station.

It was a heroic task these brave men had, for the wind had risen to a velocity of sixty miles an hour, and it required strength, courage and skill to face the dreadful storm.

There happened to be several large oyster sloops in the vicinity, and in these many of the islanders took refuge, where from the decks they watched the homes of their childhood being washed away; not the houses alone, but the very earth was swept away, and all their belongings were engulfed in the insatiable maw of the angry ocean. Where thousands once had walked was now a barren waste of foam. The island had for the most part disappeared like the fabled Atlantis; and instead of the sound of babbling children and voices of men, the notes of accordeon, or the song of the village girl, is now heard but the whistling of the blast, the beat of the breakers, and the shriek of the gull and the sea mew.

From *The Huntsman in the South*, vol. 1, *Virginia and North Carolina* (New York and Washington, D.C.: Neale, 1908), pp. 139–60

1896

The Extinction of Cobb's Island

THE *BALTIMORE SUN*

The hurricane of October 11, 1896, marked the end of an era on the Virginia coast. In the following account a correspondent of the Baltimore Sun *describes the destruction and demoralization on Cobb's Island, site of the oldest and most famous of the barrier island resorts.*

Cape Charles, Va., Oct. 19—After quite an adventurous trip *The Sun's* correspondent succeeded in reaching Cobb's Island yesterday by means of a small sailboat, in company with several other visitors, to ascertain as near as possible the actual damage received by the island in the recent hurricane which prevailed along the entire Atlantic coast with such a destruction to life and property. Our boat was the first one to carry a party to the island since the storm, and as yet the seas in the vicinity of Cobb's Island are running so very high that it is really perilous for a boat of small dimensions to attempt the trip. The reports of the damage done to Cobb's Island have been so conflicting, coming as they did from unauthentic sources, *The Sun's* correspondent thought a trip to the island would be necessary to render entirely authentic reports. Owing to the blowing down of the telephone connecting with the island and the inability of the islanders to leave their homes, correct reports have not previous to this been rendered.

We found about twenty persons on the island, including the members of the life-saving station, all of whom were in a very sorrowful mood on account of the almost entire destruction of the island and the property thereon. One of the most prominent citizens of the island took his loss in the most philosophical manner. He believes that this, as well as the previous storms encountered on the island during the past few years, are only Divine warning for them to vacate the island entirely, and he thought it would not be long before Cobb's Island would be many feet under the surface of the broad Atlantic ocean. While only a few of the houses were washed entirely away, all of them suffered more or less damage. The water was fully a foot deep over the entire island, and the seas which rolled were from 40 to 50 feet in height.

The Baltimore Cottage, a very prominent building on the island and which was occupied generally by Marylanders, and which was previous to the storm seventy-five yards from the beach, is now a total wreck, being pounded to pieces by the immense seas which swept the island. Several other cottages were about half buried in the sand. In one of these your correspondent found tacked on the wall a well-preserved copy of *The Sun* dated June 12, 1895. The room was almost full of sand; barely room enough to admit a person. The hotel is a complete wreck; the floors, porches, wall and windows are all broken up. About three feet of sand stands in the dancing pavilion on the first floor. The bar room, billiard room, bowling alley and several other small buildings were tumbled down in one heap and broken up so they were of no use whatever. There are several wells of fresh water now covered by the ocean that were previously to the storm in the barn-yard of Mr. Cobb, used for watering his stock. The island was reduced fifty acres, leaving only about twenty-five in sight at low water.

The government officials about four weeks ago moved the life saving station two hundred and fifty yards further inland, which undoubtedly saved the building, as the water stood six feet deep at the former site of the building. The Methodist church and the cottages belonging to Mr. Thomas Smith (recently purchased of the Rev. Thomas Dixon, of this city,) and Mr. Ashby Jones, of Richmond, Va., were not seriously damaged on account of their elevation from the ground. The loss is estimated at many thousands of dollars and probably the extinction of Cobb's Island as a summer resort. Quite a number of boats of considerable size are now in the middle of the island, on dry land.

Cobb's Island is situated about nine miles from the mainland, out in the Atlantic ocean. It has been inhabited for about fifty years and is unexcelled in its game products, being visited annually in the winter and spring by the sporting men of the Northern and Southern cities. It has also been quite a prominent summer resort. It had for a long time been owned by the Cobbs, of Northampton county. About five years ago a Lynchburg syndicate purchased about twenty-five acres, including the hotel and a number of cottages, for the sum of $20,000, and but for this the recent damage would have resulted very disastrously to its former owners, Messrs. Nathan and Warren Cobb. Already several families have moved from the island and others declare their intention of doing likewise.

From the *Baltimore Sun*, 20 October 1896

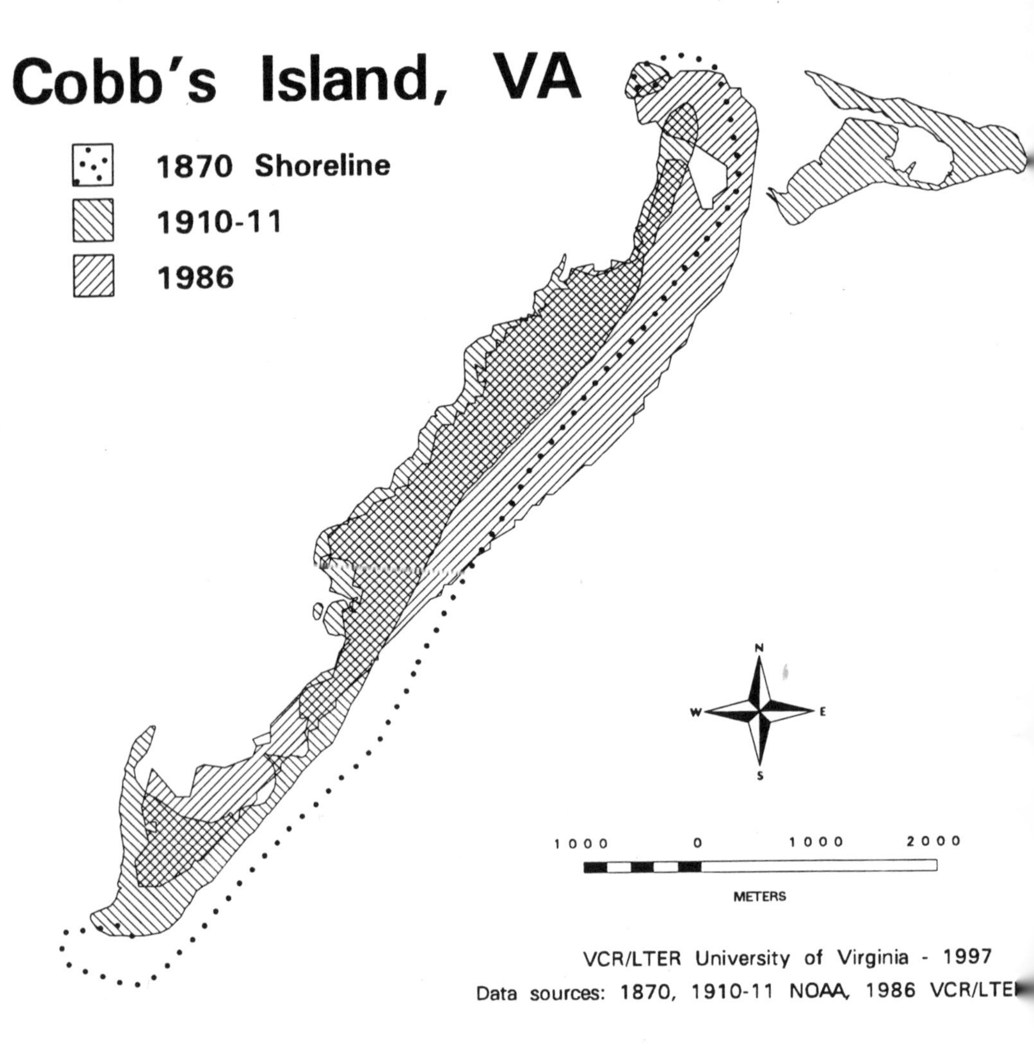

Cobb's Island, VA
1870 Shoreline
1910-11
1986
N
W
E
S
1000
0
1000
2000
METERS
VCR/LTER University of Virginia - 1997
Data sources: 1870, 1910-11 NOAA, 1986 VCR/LTE

1897

Cobb's Island

JOSEPH R. STURGIS

In 1897, the Rev. Joseph Rodgers Sturgis (1844–1921), a native of Baltimore, served as pastor of a circuit of Methodist churches in Accomack County. Learned and sensitive, Sturgis loved music and flowers and wrote poetry. A contemporary aptly described him as "a student not only of men and books, but of nature." Sturgis's analysis of the destruction of the Cobb's Island resort is a pioneer account of the phenomenon of shoreline migration.

Why is it that the sea has never washed Cobb's Island destructively, until, within the past six years?

As that question is being asked by everybody interested in Cobb's I modestly venture an answer—as no one else seems ready or willing to do so.

The question itself misleads.

It assumes what is not true. For the sea has been washing the island destructively, probably for hundreds of years; certainly and rapidly year by year during the past sixty years.

The misconception originated in the picture called up by the mind, when we say or think of "Cobb's Island." We think and speak of a mere little fraction of the Island; its south end or inhabited part. Now it is true that this part has changed, but very little during the past sixty years. Mr. Nathan Cobb, now past seventy-two years, spent sixty of those years on Cobb's. The storm of last October wrecked his cherished home and drove him from the island.

He had noted that for fifty years, on average of about every seven years, a destructive storm had washed away a bit of the outer margin of beach at this south end, but the sea had always replaced it shortly after.

Look Seaward

A great breakwater north of it is diminished and almost demolished. If the reader will take an imaginary trip with me (take the real trip if you go there this summer) I will explain and illustrate my meaning as we journey. This is the extreme north end of the island, seven miles from the inhabited part that you always think of when you speak of "Cobb's." Mounting the sand hills and looking southward, you can see the distant buildings, towards which we shall leisurely journey, over this seven miles stretch of sandy seabeach.

For our purpose it is necessary to have the tide at low ebb, as you now see it.

Before we start look seaward.

That tiny islet of marsh, crowning those reefs, was once a comparatively large island itself. Cargoes from stranded vessels have been landed and stored on its high ridges. At that time its reefs were shoaler, and they stretched their protecting barriers much, very much farther seaward than they do to-day.

That outlying island, with its system of shoals, protected this upper part of Cobb's Island. And the upper length of Cobb's, with that outer island and its shoals, constituted the breakwater that protected lower Cobb's with its inhabitants.

Now let us journey southward.

Notice how rapidly the island begins to narrow. We have now traveled several miles, and are really at what used to be the end of Prout's Island. Years ago, an inlet flowed through here, dividing Prout's from Cobb's. The inlet filled with sand, and thus united the two islands. Not far from this inlet, about forty years ago, a hotel was built. Today its site is under the sea, at least half a mile from shore. Observe how narrow our ribbon has become.

Fifty Years Ago

At high water a strong arm can throw a shell from the sea that will almost fall into the broadwater or bay inside. Fifty years ago, it would have required a musket or rifle to have sent a missile from surf to bay at this very place that is now so narrow.

When Mr. Nathan Cobb, Sr., purchased the island in 1837, a wide marsh extended itself along this inner side. One of its creeks ran directly from the broadwater towards the sea. Mr. Nathan Cobb, Jr. will tell you to day that he often sailed up this creek, fastened his boat and then, well—for awhile, Izaak Walton himself might have envied "Uncle Nathan," for the head of this creek was a famous fishing place, known as "The Deep Hole."

Now picture to yourself that wide meadow of marsh with its creeks, then the high extensive sandy stretch between the marsh and the sea, and you get an idea of the width of the island at this place of fifty years ago.

We are about at the place now and as you see it is less than two hundred yards wide. Just think of it, the sea has removed the whole width of the island here except the inmost edge of that old marsh and this is fast going daily. And remember it was the breakwater of lower Cobb's undergoing destruction.

Little by little so that you would not miss it at the time, the sea bit off and swirled away the whole breadth of that wide sandy frontage. Then it began on the marsh. Here its destructive invasions were most insidious and deceptive. Pushing a belt of sand ahead of it on the marsh it hid both the marsh and its destructive work. Some who frequented that beach from childhood, growing old as imperceptibly as the island was being destroyed, have stood on this beach recently in their old age, without realizing that the belt of sand beach had moved inland, until they were now standing over the very inner marshes that they had stood on and tramped and gunned in their boyhood days. That is they did not realize it until their attention was called to it.

Murder Will Out

Step down to the verge of the sea at this point, and I will show you the turfy edge of the marsh. Just as you would peel a banana before eating it, so the sea has uncovered this edge, before devouring it.

But you must catch the crafty sea at the disadvantage of low water—as we do now, to see this.

It hides its ravages well, but as murder will out, so this denuded turf and broken sods tell their story and tell it well. And notice all along these sands the unimpeachible testimony of the shells. Mute, but eloquent accusers and witnesses are these wave-worn, sun-bleached shells. Growing in the quiet waters of the sheltered creeks inside the island, far away from the noisy beach with its hungry sea, no dream of such doom for the bivalves entered the minds of those who knew these oyster beds—less than a century ago. But destroying as it came, the sea crept closer, closer, until the belt of its advancing sands was near enough for the willing winds to drift these sands into every creek and stream, filling and overshadowing them, and destroying the bivalves they contained. These shells remained thus buried until the sea, soon reaching them, uncovered them, tore them from their cozy beds, and rudely hurled them upon the beach, as trophies of its conquest.

Defenceless

But we are nearly at "Cobb's," with its wrecked and its remaining buildings. Pause and cast a glance backward over the six and a half miles that we have travelled. Put an imaginary front to the island. Extend it out to sea, all the way along. Put it from a half to three fourths of a mile from shore. This gives you the shore line of a half century ago. At that time, and until recently, lower Cobb's curved inward. It resembled the horn of a crescent, and was protected by the convexity about it. All that convexity, that last protecting breakwater is gone, leaving a straight shore only, above the crescent end of Cobb's. If a little washing took place at the lower end there was always a plenty of sand above for the sea to bring down to repair damages with. But taking away the breakwater, it took away this means of repairing damages. Lower Cobb's is now subjected to washings without any extra protection, just as other parts of the island have been all the time that this part was protected.

When the end will come, and what it will be, no one can predict. The island will first be cut in two. Then, as lower Cobb's will be on the south side of the new inlet, it may be built up by the shifting sands, instead of being destroyed. When we first started on this saunter down the beach I asked you to look seaward. Now that we are about to separate, I again ask you to look seaward. Miles away, you see the white breakers on the distant shoals. Those shoals are the old foundations of the island. There it uplifted its forests of cedar and pine. And, as we do now, so then, its aborigines fished its waters and trod its shelving shores.

From *Accomac Court House Peninsula Enterprise*, 13 November 1897

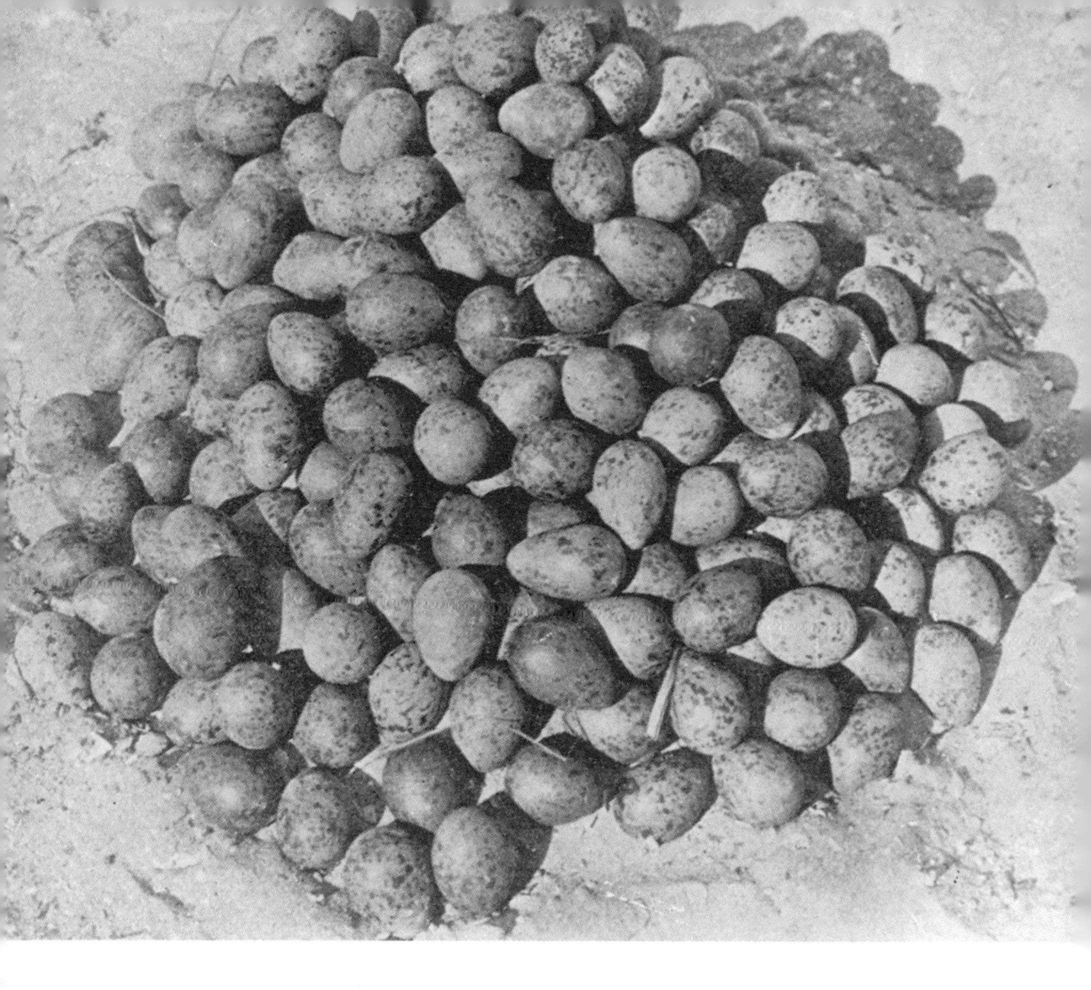

1900

Visits to Revel's Island

GEORGE SHIRAS III

Many years spent afield observing and photographing wildlife convinced the Pennsylvania lawyer, hunter, and naturalist George Shiras III (1859–1942) of the need for conservation. As a member of Congress (1903–5), Shiras introduced the original Federal Migratory Bird Bill, which prohibited spring shooting and market hunting and set seasons and bag limits for the sportsman.

In 1894 Shiras joined the gunning club on Revel's Island and remained an active member well into the twentieth century. His observations of the island's wildlife extend from the period of unrestricted hunting and egging to that of conservation legislation and the creation of national refuges and parks.

Earlier Visits to Revels Island

Revels Island, partly marsh and partly a low ridge overgrown with pines and cedars, is surrounded by extensive salt marshes and shallow bays. It lies about a mile to the southward of Little Machipongo Inlet, and the same distance inland from the sand dunes along Parramore Beach, on the Atlantic Coast.

Revels Island, owned by the Revels Island Shooting Club, of which I became a member in 1894, comprises several thousand acres. It contains two large, nearly land-locked bays, sufficiently shallow to form feeding-places for ducks, geese, and brant; a few fresh-water ponds which are visited by black ducks; and many mud flats and sandy beaches attractive to shore birds. Several navigable channels give access by motor boat to most of the property, and at time of high tides many creeklike waterways penetrate other parts of the island otherwise inaccessible by boat.

Just south of the clubhouse is a long, broad, sandy beach, extending a mile west, and terminating in a sandy point. Across the water a similar point on Sandy Island combines with it nearly to enclose Revels Island Bay, which is the best feeding-place for ducks, geese, and brant in this region.

Nearly a mile north of the clubhouse is a long narrow ridge covered with yellow pines, cedars, and several kinds of bushes. At intervals of two or three years a very high spring tide occurs, and all the property except the ridge is covered with a foot or two of water. Once when I visited the island, the clubhouse and cottages were surrounded by the tidewaters, and no land was visible for many miles except the pine ridge and the distant main shore.

Because of these occasional floods, predatory animals, as a rule, avoided the area, although once or twice a pair of foxes appeared and made a den on the ridge, from which place they were easily dug out by fox hunters. The ground-breeding birds, therefore, had no four-footed enemies, and those nesting in the trees apparently were rarely disturbed by owls. The only resident hawk was the osprey, which always lives on friendly terms with its neighbors. Bald eagles were not uncommon, but they lived mainly on fish taken from the ospreys, or on dead fish and dead or wounded ducks.

To the southward lies the long, ocean-washed Hog Island, which helps to enclose Broadwaters, a part of the eastern shore of a wide bay or sound that was once the favored shooting resort of Grover Cleveland.

The nesting birds had, however, one enemy that was present throughout the breeding season, and caused great havoc by destroying thousands of eggs and many of the nestlings. This was the fish crow. Members of the species apparently timed their coming to arrive on the island at the beginning of the period when food of this kind became abundant.

In May, under one tall pine, I found about 500 eggshells, most of them having a large puncture in one end. They were chiefly the eggs of the laughing, or black-headed gull, and the marsh hen, or clapper rail, but included, also, those of the green heron, grackle, red-winged blackbird, skimmer, and willet.

Other enemies of some of the breeding birds were the "eggers," including a large proportion of the natives of the Eastern Shore. Under local law it was permissible to collect newly laid eggs at the beginning of the nesting season. The eggs so taken were largely those of the laughing gull and the marsh hen. Gull nests were often closely grouped over several acres; consequently the eggs were easily collected.

One day I spoke to Jonah, the colored chore boy at the clubhouse, about a breeding colony of laughing gulls, and was surprised at the interest he displayed. I understood this a week later, when, on visiting the back yard at his request, I found a rounded heap of gulls' eggs, some four hundred in number. Dismayed at this sight, I voiced my disapproval.

Whether or not such annual pillage has any serious effect on the number of young raised each season, the Federal bird law has outlawed the practice, although I do not doubt that eggs in considerable numbers are still collected each year.

When Jonah saw how annoyed I was by his raid on the gull colony, he sought to turn my thoughts elsewhere by asking if I had seen the big whale that was stranded on Sandy Island. I told him that I had not seen it, but that I thought it would afford a good opportunity for a modern version of Jonah and the whale, and that if he would sit in its mouth this could be accomplished.

Jonah replied: "Excuse me, boss, I don't want to go within 100 feet of that critter, for the smell is awful. Jes' wait till the wind comes from the west and you'll want to leave here and go home."

The clapper rails, called locally marsh hens, were abundant on Revels Island, but they lived such secretive lives in the tall grasses that, despite their harsh, cackling notes, they were rarely seen except when one made a painstaking search for them. Each spring they returned from the South in extraordinary numbers, and skulked about among the grasses, rising and flying only a short distance when startled. At such times their weak flight makes them an easy target for the hunter. Their nests, neatly hidden under the overarching grasses, contain from 10 to 18 pale eggs that are comparatively large for so small a bird.

As was the case with the black-headed gulls, thousands of the eggs of these rails were taken when they were freshly laid. Trained dogs were sometimes used to help find the artfully concealed nests. In seasons when heavy tides raised the water level of the marshes, an enormous number of eggs of the clapper rail floated from the nests and formed a drift line along the shores of the marshy areas. After the tide had receded, the birds lost no time in laying new clutches, and their great numbers appeared to continue undiminished.

The eggers argued with apparently demonstrated justification that a general robbery of the nests of the rails and the black-headed gulls for a short period under local regulation had no effect upon the numbers of the young birds reared each year. The robbed parents promptly proceeded to lay new sets of eggs. If the nests were repeatedly despoiled, the effect would unquestionably be harmful.

The wild-fowl shooting in the tidal waters close to Revels Island never equaled that in the sounds farther south. The peculiar shortage was due largely to the absence of fresh-water ducks, the black duck being the only one in this class found in abundance.

When I first visited Revels Island, many geese, brant, and broadbills (scaups), with occasional flocks of redheads, and a fair number of goldeneyes and buffleheads, or butter balls, frequented the region. This club was the first, I believe, to introduce floating blinds made of green cedar boughs stuck in buoyant wooden frames large enough to admit a ducking boat. Within these floating blinds a narrow, flat-bottomed scow was sometimes left during the shooting season for the use of the sportsmen.

Such a contrivance, when anchored, was always headed up wind, so that the decoys could be placed out to advantage. The hunter needed to watch only for the approaching birds, which, according to their habit, came in against the wind. Moreover, these floating blinds rose and fell with the tide; whereas it was difficult to shoot from stuck blinds at low tide, and an exceptionally high one exposed the boat and hunter. The floating blinds were set out before the arrival of the birds, which, in consequence, regarded the clump of cedars as a part of the landscape.

In those days no baiting was done, and it was essential to have the blinds located on good feeding-grounds or along narrow flyways. At first the shooting was satisfactory, but it gradually became poorer as the shallow bays were leased for oyster planting, and the near-by guardhouses, which were continuously occupied by watchmen in the fall and winter, became nuisances.

When naphtha launches, and later those propelled by gasoline, displaced the sailboats, these bays were kept in a state of continual disturbance, for with motor craft the lack of wind was no obstacle, but tended to increase activities.

On the eastern shore marshes of Virginia, many of the black ducks have learned the danger of going to their feeding-places in fresh-water ponds by day, and seek them as the shades of night are falling. Taking advantage of this, the hunters have devised an unusual method of outwitting the wary birds. They make a high mound of marsh grass or seaweed near the side of the pond toward which the ducks usually come. Before the evening flight begins, the hunter, dressed in dark clothing, takes his place in front of the blind instead of behind it, for the approaching birds would see his projecting head if he were looking over the blind from behind. Sitting in front, he blends into it and is invisible.

For many years some market hunters on the marshes of the eastern shore of Virginia have used the destructive method of netting black ducks at night. Both the netting of the birds and their sale have long been outlawed, but persistent efforts to break up this nefarious practice have not yet become entirely successful.

Nets have about a two-inch mesh, large enough to permit a duck's head to pass through, but not to be withdrawn easily, since the feathers catch on the sides of the mesh. The nets are staked horizontally along the surface of the shallow water of natural or artificial channels, leading out from ponds frequented by the birds. Corn is then scattered in front and under the nets. The ducks, following the bait heads down, swim slowly under the nets as they feed. When their heads are raised they slip through the meshes and are held fast. Sometimes almost an entire flock will be taken by this means. The outlaws who do this are so well acquainted with the marshes and work so slyly that they are difficult to apprehend.

The marshes and mud flats about Revels Island were famous for the number and variety of shore birds that visited them during migration. Even when an alarming decrease in the numbers of these birds was noticed along the greater part of the Atlantic coast, these marshes were apparently the stopping place of all the survivors.

It is not strange that eventually a tremendous decrease in shore birds was observed during migrations; for in the spring when the local shore birds were either nesting or mating every clubhouse from Virginia to New Jersey was filled with members intent on hunting shore birds at a season when all other shooting was prohibited.

Day after day I have seen otherwise reputable sportsmen bring in 200 birds, and when the weather was warm it was practically impossible to keep such birds from spoiling. In the later years, convinced of its wastefulness, I gave up spring shooting, but, having substituted the camera for the gun, I was doubtless less tempted than some of the others.

After watching for many years the shore birds in their daily flight along the beaches and mud flats or about marshy ponds, I often wondered how they passed the night. Undoubtedly in the breeding season most of these little waders are more or less concealed about the nests, but during their migrations they remain near the open water.

To test this question on Revels Island, I made two trips with a jacklight to the places much frequented by these birds in the daytime. The Hudsonian curlews I found massed in considerable flocks on flats just above high tide, where at one time they were shot by natives with the aid of a kerosene torch or lantern. Flocks of sandpipers, turnstones, robin-snipe, and a few black-breasted plovers were seen squatting on the sandy shore, or on mud banks, while dowitchers were in the scanty grass a few yards farther back. Species that did not gather in large flocks by day, such as the yellow-legs, willet, ring-necked and semipalmated plover, were not seen. Being more or less solitary in habits, they were probably concealed in the vegetation back from the shore or about marshy ponds.

In the course of my visit to Revels Island a marked transition took place in the oyster industry. In the early years I saw oysters dredged from the deeper waters of the small bays and channels, but these shell fish gradually decreased until the business was threatened. The wild oysters varied greatly in size, and it became increasingly difficult to find a sufficient quantity of the standard sizes to meet the requirements of the market.

Finally the State of Virginia leased the best oyster grounds to individuals, although some of the beds were barren of oysters at the time. An abundance of old shells and some living oysters were strewn on the bottom to afford attachments for the oyster spawn, and this method of water farming soon proved so successful in producing desirable shell fish that a state of warfare developed between the lease holders protecting their property and those called "oyster pirates," who believed they had an inalienable right to anything produced by the sea. In order to protect the planted oyster beds it finally became necessary to station guards armed with rifles along the shore during fall and winter. Small houses were built near by for their accommodation.

The establishment of the guards in all the best bays of the region had a disastrous effect upon the wild-fowl shooting. Geese, brant, and ducks were accustomed to feed and rest in the bays, especially in rough weather. No sooner did a flock of birds settle on the water, however, than the nearest guards would send rifle balls into their midst, driving them out to sea or into the big bays, where they would remain until darkness enabled them to return in safety. In the same period the few sailboats were displaced by many noisy motor boats that kept the birds in constant alarm.

On the Eastern Shore there was as a rule no noticeable increased migratory flight on the approach of cold weather, but the birds arrived in easy stages from the North, as the waters there were gradually chilled. This was in contrast to the movement in spring when the wild fowl passed in almost continuous flights to their northern breeding grounds.

One afternoon in November, 1896, I was occupying a floating blind in Revels Island Bay. A strong, cold north wind, the first of the season, foretold the coming of freezing weather. Looking toward the north, I saw what appeared like a cloud in the otherwise clear sky. Soon it was apparent that an immense flock of ducks numbering thousands was approaching high in the air.

When the travelers sighted the broad shallow waters ahead, they swooped downward with a roar almost like that of a western cyclone. From a great height the birds descended in a graceful spiral. Three times this vast flock of scaups, for such they were, hurtled over the blind, dropping several hundred yards at each turn, making a sound with their wings resembling the sighing of a high wind in the treetops. Finally the visitors passed low over my decoys and alighted all about me with a tumultuous splashing, some almost striking the brush blind in which I sat.

Although tempted to shoot into the crowded ranks, with the prospect of dropping half a dozen birds, I restrained the impulse in order that the hungry and tired ducks could enjoy a period of rest, and thereby be induced to remain a day or two longer. It was a delightful experience to sit concealed in their midst. Some of the scaups splashed about vigorously, taking refreshing baths, some immediately began diving in search of food, and some faced the wind in little groups with heads drawn down on their shoulders, weary from the long flight.

No doubt among this flock were many ducks that were familiar with the attractions of this locality through visits during former seasons. They guided in the inexperienced youngsters of a new generation, even though they may previously have seen many a companion fall before the gun, an inevitable peril that these migrants must face wherever may be located their winter quarters.

As the wind and the tide forced the flock toward the opposite shore, I quietly withdrew, content in not having collected any toll from these newly arrived wanderers.

Aunt Caroline, a faithful and proficient colored cook, had charge of the club kitchen for more than a generation. She was always appreciated and was regarded as one of the club's valuable assets. Living in a State famous for its culinary art, she had few equals. The making of delicious clam chowder was one of her greatest accomplishments, and large clams were always available on a sandspit only about 100 yards away.

Early in the fall a goodly supply of oysters would be gathered from distant bays and placed in the shallow water on both sides of the long dock. Sometimes between meals a guide would wade out and get a basketful of them, which would be opened and eaten by us on the sunny side of the boathouse. Aunt Caroline served the oysters in several ways.

In the winter months, eels speared in their hibernating places in the mud at the heads of creeks were another delicacy on the bill of fare. In the hunting season Aunt Caroline produced the most appetizing dishes of perfectly cooked ducks and shore birds, besides stewed terrapin and snipe potpies. The memory of her pastries, including apple and pumpkin pies, puddings, doughnuts, and other tasty products of her skill, still remains with me. Even the little tin lunch pails that were sent out to the blinds with us were like little Christmas boxes with their varied assortment of good things to allay the hearty appetites we had sharpened by hours in the open air.

One resident on Revels Island familiar to all the club members for many years was Jerry the ox. Although he was almost a dwarf of his kind, his black and white figure was considered an ornament to the flat landscape.

He served us in many useful ways, and his doings afforded both exasperation and interest. Harnessed to a little cart, he hauled coal and wood from the dock and building material for new structures. He carted decoys and other material to ponds inaccessible by boat, and brought such produce as pumpkins, beets, turnips, and sweet potatoes from our productive garden on the higher ground to the roothouse under the kitchen.

None of these duties was to Jerry's liking, and whenever he saw the scow tie up to the dock, or noted any other occurrences that he had learned to associate with distasteful chores, he would quietly disappear. Later he would usually be found ensconced in a brushy thicket on the wooded ridge farther inland. Once the search for him seemed fruitless, and it was thought that he had probably crossed the channel to another island.

He was eventually discovered hiding behind the timbers of a wrecked schooner half a mile down the beach, from which point of vantage he was able to view the prolonged search with apparent enjoyment. When once harnessed to the cart, however, he was docile and energetic enough, so that his elusive ways were looked upon with tolerant amusement.

Because of the mild climate, no special shelter was provided for Jerry. When a cold wind blew, he would take refuge behind one of the buildings or mid the thickets of the little pine woods on the ridge. His four-footed companions were the half dozen young hogs that each season grew fat on the swamp roots and other food they could gather in the marsh or along the shore until the time arrived when they were converted into ham and bacon in the smokehouse.

When the day of slaughter came, Jerry always looked on complacently as if approving such disposal of the grunting creatures, which had never appeared to pay the slightest attention to him. For a long time Jerry was regarded as one of the odd characters of the locality.

Last Days at Revels Island

Like many other members of the Revels Island Club, in the middle nineties, I visited the shore in the spring not so much for shooting at a time when other game was protected as for enjoying the beauty of Nature throwing off her drab winter garment and replacing it with green, swelling buds and unfolding leaves. This beauty, the gentle warmth of the sun, and the soft spring breezes constituted a welcome change to residents of more northern latitudes who loved the out-of-doors.

To Revels Island during these balmy days came nearly all the species of shore birds that inhabit our Atlantic coast. Some were en route from their winter homes in South America to their breeding grounds beyond the Arctic Circle. There were others that nest in less distant places, as well as those that remain to rear their young along the Eastern Shore. Though the different species arrived at different times, each form had its special schedule of arrival and departure.

First to appear were the jacksnipes, or grass snipes, which usually kept to the mainland, for the fresh-water meadows were to their liking. These were followed successively by Hudsonian curlews (many of which had wintered in South Carolina), willets, greater and lesser yellowlegs, numerous species of sandpipers, plovers (ring-necked, Wilson's, and black-breasted), turnstones, dowitchers, and knots or robin snipe.

In those days the wastefulness and cruelty of shooting birds that were already mating, or those that were actually in the midst of their nesting activities among the broken shells of the seashore or in tussocks of grass in the marshes, were not appreciated until several species were approaching extinction.

Because of the large number of species, each with its peculiar habits, shore-bird shooting at the island afforded a far pleasanter and more varied form of sport than did the wildfowling in the adjacent bays, where the salt water appeared to have attractions mainly for scaups, golden-eyes, geese, and brant. Comparatively few kinds of waterfowl were to be found in the vicinity of the island.

An ample supply of wooden and tin decoys, shaped and painted to resemble the larger or more desirable species of shore birds, was available at the club. In a catboat with a large leg-of-mutton sail the gunner was conveyed by his guide from the clubhouse to a blind, which, the direction and force of the wind being considered, was best located for the purpose in view.

In hunting curlew, fowlers often dug a pit at the edge of a sand point in the marsh where the birds were accustomed to feed as the receding tide exposed the mud flats. When the tide was rising, the curlews followed the narrow channels through the island, alighting to rest on the grassy flats along either side. In such places, the hunters, well concealed behind grass blinds, could enjoy flight shooting.

These birds were favorites with many sportsmen because of their size and slow, steady flight. Their large, compact flocks could be seen a mile or more away, as they came in to their feeding or resting places. If the hunter wished to shoot yellow-legs or willets, he would occupy a bush blind close to the edge of a little fresh-water pond, in the mud and shallow water of which the decoys would be placed in such spots as these birds commonly frequented when feeding.

The turnstones gathered on the mud banks bordering the larger bays in company with the smaller sandpipers that preferred the open shores. Because of the small size of these birds and their habit of flying in compact flocks, the gunners were able to bring them down in such numbers, sometimes a dozen or more at a shot, that they provided the material for many a delicious potpie, a welcome relief from the products of the frying pan.

Toward the end of the season, about the middle of May, flocks of robin snipe frequented the exposed sea beaches, and for years they afforded excellent shooting. After a time I became seriously alarmed about the future of these handsome birds, for they began to decrease rapidly in numbers, and late in May, 1904, I made a special trip to Revels Island to obtain pictures of what I feared might be a doomed species.

All day I remained in a blind with my camera before a flock circled over the decoys. The marked difference between hunting with a gun and with a camera was here demonstrated. Had I discharged a gun at this flock, a few birds might have been dropped, and the rest would have hurried on in wild alarm toward their far northern home. As it was, I obtained a fine series of pictures of the entire flock as its members circled back time after time to satisfy their innocent curiosity concerning the strange wooden counterfeits.

During the days I passed in the blinds I was much interested in noting the skill with which some of the local guides imitated the notes of these birds. Often when the birds were passing on their northward flight, or were merely seeking new feeding grounds after having been disturbed by a rising tide, they would pass our decoys, which were strung out near shore, without paying them the least attention.

The guide at my side in the blind would imitate the note peculiar to the species that was passing, and very commonly the flock would respond by swinging in on a graceful curve that would bring them within gunshot. If we did not shoot, they would alight among the decoys, where we could photograph them at our leisure.

The [Revel's Island Club] buildings were surrounded by several acres of tall, thin grass that afforded some grazing for Jerry, the ox, in addition to harboring myriads of mosquitoes that could not be dislodged, even by the heaviest winds off the ocean. If a person wearing black garments passed through this grass in the spring, in a few minutes the black on his back would turn to a uniform brown from the host of mosquitoes alighting on it. Fortunately, in the daytime these insects were not very vicious, and at night well-screened windows prevented them from being annoying.

Ospreys, or fish hawks, have long frequented the large salt marshes along the eastern shore of Virginia, where the meadows are penetrated by small bays and tidal creeks in which there are many fish that attract them. In many parts of the marshes, however, no woody growth is found other than bushes too frail to support the bulky nests, and the ospreys must carry their catches miles away to their young.

Several years after a life-saving station had been established on Parramore Island and a telephone line had been built across the Revels Island marsh, the ospreys began building their nests, precariously balanced on the top crossbars of the telephone poles. These interfered so seriously with the working of the line that all the nests were destroyed. Sometimes the birds built nests on the roofs of cabins in the marshes.

I often neglected to take the picture of bird or animal when occasion offered, believing that this could be done, possibly more conveniently later. Delay, however, is poor policy when dealing with wild things, for they are subject to many more vicissitudes than are tame creatures.

As a striking illustration, I might cite my failure to photograph the largest osprey nest I have ever seen. It was in the top of a tall dead pine on Revels Island, where during many successive seasons I saw the structure grow in bulk by annual additions. The tree was an outstanding one in a grove north of the clubhouse, and so large and elevated was the nest that it constituted a conspicuous landmark for visitors seeking the island.

Year after year I passed this tree always with the thought that some day I would photograph it with the osprey perching on its huge structure or circling over it. Time passed without my doing so, however, until one afternoon in the spring of 1902 I examined the locality to determine the best place in which to conceal the camera in order to obtain the long-desired picture which I planned to take the next morning.

An unusually heavy northeaster occurred that night. The club buildings creaked and rattled under the strain, but, comfortably sheltered, we enjoyed the rush and shrieking of the wind and the booming of the surf along the shore.

The following morning dawned clear and warm, and, shouldering my tripod and camera, I set out to photograph the osprey's home. Reaching the spot, I found the gaunt dead pine prone on the ground and the nest reduced to a great mass of sticks and other material. That the tree had sunk slowly to the earth under the force of the wind was indicated by the three unbroken brown-blotched eggs of the hawk that lay on the ground beside the nest. Among the debris were seven or eight smaller, bluish eggs of grackles, which had been unceremoniously ejected from their big, rent-free apartment house by the catastrophe that had overtaken their landlord.

Millions of shots are fired every season at ducks passing over decoys, or on flights to feeding or resting grounds. Unless a duck is shot through the head or other vital organ, or comes down with a broken wing, it may not be apparent that it has received a wound that will cause death in a few minutes by internal hemorrhage. Every gunner, therefore, should observe closely a departing bird that may have been hit, although it shows no evidence of injury.

Frequently a wounded bird will suddenly drop after it has flown several hundred yards, very commonly when the gunner is reloading his weapon or has his attention otherwise distracted. I recall an instance of retrieving two black ducks that if they had not been watched in their flight of about a mile would not have been found. This occurred during an unusually low tide in Revels Island Bay, when much of the bottom was exposed for a couple of hours.

Knowing that under such conditions black ducks were likely to come in considerable numbers to feed in the few places, I built a small blind at the edge of the marsh in the hope that some would pass within range. After a while a pair of black ducks headed in my direction, but dropped to a pile of seaweed nearly a hundred yards away.

Substituting for the cartridges in my gun others containing No. 3 shot, I stood up in the blind. As I expected, the pair arose almost perpendicularly, quacking loudly. I fired at the upper duck and then took a shot at the other.

I saw the birds leave, apparently unscathed. I could not be sure of this, however, and I watched them fly north toward the end of the bay.

When they were so far away that they looked like two tiny black spots, one of them turned and came back along the opposite shore. Its high and undeviating flight suddenly ended; it stopped abruptly and fell straight down with a splash on the surface of the muddy pool, directly in line with a distant stunted cedar.

By its actions I knew that the duck had died in mid-air before it fell. While pulling up my hip boots to go for it, I happened to notice that the surviving duck was returning along the same course as that followed by the first. Within a hundred yards of its dead mate it, too, collapsed and fell with a splash. A few minutes later I made the trip across the muddy flat and without difficulty found both birds.

Bald eagles are rather common about Revels Island. They seldom harmed the other birds, but one once caused great excitement at the clubhouse. Captain Wickes, then superintendent, was returning to the club through the "swash" channel in a small ducking boat when he saw one of these handsome birds flying overhead within easy gunshot. Thinking it would make a good specimen to mount as a trophy, he fired and dropped it near the boat.

Picking up the apparent lifeless form, Captain Wickes stowed it between his legs and continued rowing toward the clubhouse. Suddenly one of his legs was gripped by the long talons of the bird, which sank into the flesh, causing great pain.

At such close quarters he could neither shoot the bird nor hit it with an oar. He did what seemed to be the best thing—leaped overboard, hoping to drown his assailant and thus cause it to release a grip that would only enlarge his wounds if he tried to pull the bird away while it was alive. As he came to the surface, he found the eagle had let go its hold and was standing erect on the bow seat of the boat.

No wind was blowing at the time, and the boat continued to drift with the tide toward the clubhouse. The captain swam ashore and limped along after the drifting boat for a quarter of a mile, expressing his feelings meanwhile in violent language.

The boat at length touched the bank at a bend, and the ousted skipper was able to get on board. Seizing one of the small oars, he gave the defiant bird a knockout blow, and it sank to the bottom of the boat, apparently with a broken neck.

On reaching his destination, the captain carried his trophy ashore, and threw it on the porch back of the kitchen.

While binding his bleeding wounds, for a small artery had been opened, he heard loud shrieks from the rear of the kitchen. Hastily tying on a temporary bandage, he hurried back to learn the cause of the uproar. A colored maid, with bare feet, while examining the bird, had given it a kick to turn it over for further inspection. Thereupon the apparently lifeless bird had sunk his talons deep into the calf of her leg. She shrieked and jumped about on one foot until she fell down the back steps to the ground. Picking up a piece of stove wood, the captain finished the eagle.

There were days in the spring when the migrating shore birds were not in flight, and then I turned my attention to nesting gulls, skimmers, herons, and oyster-catchers, or to such land birds as the osprey, fish crow, flicker, brown thrasher, tree swallow, grackle, and bluebird. Seldom at this season of the year need the camera be laid aside for want of subjects, and thus the period lost by the devotees of hunting, now that spring shooting is necessarily prohibited throughout the country, can be utilized by the true lover of the out-of-doors.

The next to my last trip to the island was made to photograph the robin snipe and the Hudsonian curlew, for it seemed to me as if they were going the way of the wild pigeon and would soon be exterminated.

My last visit to the island was in May, 1923. The purpose of the trip was to check up on the reported increase of shore birds as a result of their protection under the Migratory Bird Law.

The launch had no sooner put out from the little town of Wachapreague, on the mainland side of Wachapreague Inlet, north of Parramore Island, than Hudsonian curlews began springing up on all sides, and we observed nearly a thousand on the six-mile trip. Yet this bird had nearly become extinct ten years before.

In our several days on the marshes and mud flats we found that the protection given the birds by the Federal law had resulted in an increase in the numbers of most of the shore birds, including the willet, the black-breasted and smaller plovers, the knot or robin-snipe, dowitcher, calico-backs, or turnstones and many varieties of sandpipers. The yellow-legs, however, were scarce, since an open season still permitted shooting of this species.

Subsequently, the Advisory Board, of which I was a member, a committee of game commissioners and sportsmen appointed to offer recommendations for drafting regulations relative to the administration of the Migratory Bird Law, advised that the season be closed on yellow-legs. This suggestion was adopted by the Department of Agriculture in 1927.

From Hunting Wild Life with Camera and Flashlight, 2 vols. (Washington, D.C.: National Geographic Society, 1935), 2:63–96

1907
Hog Island, Virginia

ALEXANDER HUNTER

Islands exude a seductive charm. Discovering a place and a way of living so different from their own, mainland writers often relax their critical faculties. They romanticize the island as a paradise and the islanders as a bit more virtuous than the common run of people. Alexander Hunter, however, refused to be seduced. This sportsman and conservationist cherished no illusions about Hog Island and its inhabitants.

Next to Jamestown, the first settlement made in Virginia, the most interesting spot in that State, to the antiquarian, is Hog Island, on the Atlantic Coast. It was the redoubtable John Smith who first discovered this place. The second day after he landed at Smith's Island and planted the English flag for the first time in the New World, he started out on a voyage along the coast, when a great storm arose, his boat filled and he escaped, as he said, "by ye mercy of God."

He named the island upon which he landed, Shooting Bears Island, as the small species of bruin which to this day abound in the cane-brakes of the Dismal Swamp were numerous on the new-found isle.

It is a great pity that this place did not retain its beautiful Indian name, "Machipongo Island," which, translated, means "fine dust and flies"—literally, fine sand and mosquitoes. These two inflictions plagued the natives, and made the island uninhabitable to the thin-skinned, thinly clad Indians, who only visited it at certain periods of the year to fish and hunt.

The origin of the name "Hog Island," and the person or people who applied the harsh, ugly name to the place, is unknown. The islanders say that in colonial days a vessel was wrecked near the shores, and a large number of hogs swam safely to land, and some matter-of-fact person named the spot Hog Island. There are certain antiquarians of Northampton County, however, who claim that the people of the mainland named the place Hog Island simply and solely because the inhabitants were more like hogs in looks, manners, and way of living than anything else. Certainly there never was, is not, and never will be anything like *entiente cordiale* between the people of the mainland and the islanders.

Hog Island is about four miles long, and varies from one to two miles in width. On the south side runs the Great Machipongo Inlet, whose average depth is forty feet. It is a noble sheet of water. The life-saving station is built on the banks of this inlet, close to where it empties into the ocean. The chart of the Coast and Geodetic Survey shows that the sand shallows for one or two miles, making the place very dangerous to those "who go down to the sea in ships," and mariners give the place a wide berth. The beach is five miles long, with firm sand.

I have made many visits to this island, for the spot always had a peculiar charm; it excites the imagination, stimulates the fancy, and the old colonial ghosts haunt the spot. It is well worth a visit to the tourist.

The early history of the place is in the musty, worn and tattered records of Virginia, in the State Capitol. There is a document bearing date of 1672, which consists of a "letter patent" to Sir Henry Chinchley, of the island known as Machipongo, and his grant of the same to certain colonists, whose names are Henry Patrick, Thomas Hewes, William Mainey, Henry Meadow, William Taylor, John Harbush, Thomas Cooke, Edward Young, George Griffin, John Parson, Richard Bagley, Thomas Shermingham, John Baker, William Bannister, Grace Winter, Abraham Hill, Matt Morgan, John Corry, Richard Hyde, Upham Holt and Ann Emmerson.

These settlers presumably had families, and they resided there no one knows how long. Certainly they must have had a different life and one in marked contrast with the colony at Jamestown, who were many times on the brink of actual starvation; for on the fruitful Machipongo Isle no man need work and no man need starve.

There were no newspapers in those days to chronicle events and to "show the very age and body of the times," nor was there any local historian among the lot; so that their lives and their adventures are not known. They were as isolated from the world as were the mutineers of the merchant ship *Bounty* on Pitcairn Island, and they were lost to the outside world, and in that lone, forgotten spot—

"The world forgetting and by the world forgot."

The colonists disappeared—man, woman, and child. What they suffered, endured, or enjoyed will never be known. But doubtless the tale would bear telling and would make fascinating reading.

There must have been a conflict with the warlike tribes of Accomacs, who would not be likely to submit to having their most fruitful isle seized, like the brightest jewel torn from a crown. The Indians may have closed in upon the island with a great fleet of canoes and massacred and tortured or slain the last one of the settlers; or the mosquitoes may have routed the colony; but if they left the island of their own accord, some of them would undoubtedly have remained in the vicinity. But there is not one of their descendants on the Atlantic Coast to-day. There is not the slightest clew to the fate of these people, and their disappearance is as unfathomable as that of the lost colony of Sir Walter Raleigh, which vanished from Roanoke Island. Certain it is that they left not a token or relic behind; nor is there a grave or mouldering bone to show that the white man lived there long before the Pilgrims built their first village.

The earliest settler of Hog Island who has a real record was a man by the name of Labin Phillips, who settled the place during the Revolutionary War.

Shortly after the surrender of Cornwallis, Labin built the first habitable home on the island, which is still standing and is an object of great interest to the sportsmen and tourists who visit the place.

The dwelling is built of red cedar and is of a quaint, odd style of architecture, such as the early colonists erected, and is worthy of preservation as an object-lesson in proof of the durability of the red cedar, which, after a hundred years, remains firm and sound; whereas, oak, pine, hemlock or black Jack would long since have rotted and fallen to pieces in the damp sea air.

The house would delight an antiquarian. The chimney takes in one entire side of the structure, and is built of clay and wood, corn-cob fashion, and of course liable to catch fire at the smallest provocation. In this house was a barrel of water, and leaning near by was a long sapling with a great bunch of rags tied to one end, looking for all the world like the sweeps that the "chimney devils" of the last century used. Whenever the sticks in the chimney burst into a blaze the rags were plunged into the barrel, the pole was thrust upwards and the incipient flame quenched.

There died on the island a short time ago an aged citizen named Samuel Kelly, aged eighty-two years. Even when a boy he showed a decided bent for making money, and for keeping it also. When he reached manhood he united the characteristics of Daniel Dancer, the miser, and that of the famous Captain Kidd; for he hoarded his money, and then buried it.

"Sam" Kelly became the most unique character on the island. He established a little store, but, paradoxical as it may seem, he could never be found there; no man's foot was allowed to cross the threshold. The owner would call on the natives every morning, get their orders, and deliver the goods in the evening. There never lived a more thorough miser. He visited nobody, never entered a church, never gave a cent to charity, never had a decent coat on his back, and probably never sat down to a well-prepared meal.

As there was no other store on the island, his neighbors knew that he must be making money and hoarding it. Every man, woman, and child was aware that there must be a fortune hid away somewhere in his cabin, for some of his neighbors had caught a passing glimpse through the window of the miser gloating over a great pile of gold coin.

As the years glided by the hoard increased. Never spending a cent, and saving every dollar, it was a matter of much speculation among his neighbors as to how much he was worth.

But the talk was all among themselves; they never breathed a word of old Sam Kelly's hoard to the fishermen and lightermen who stopped at the island. It is marvelous that a decrepit, defenceless miser should live in a dilapidated cabin for years, his gold unsecured by safe, vault, or strong-box, easy for the first strong hand to clutch, and yet there was never a single attempt made to rob him.

Samuel Kelly lived to see nearly all his contemporaries buried, and that "fell sergeant, Death, so strict in the arrest," seemed to have forgotten him, but at last Samuel was summoned to appear before the Bar. On his deathbed his friends and only surviving relative besought him to reveal the secret of his hiding-place; but the ruling passion was strong in death. Shrouds have no pockets, but if the miser could not carry his treasure with him, no one else should have it, and so he died carrying his secret to the grave. The house was searched, and under the counter in his little store were found two boxes, one containing three thousand dollars in gold, the other, two thousand in currency. Then a thorough search was organized and every possible or likely spot was examined, but not another cent was ever discovered. His only relative and heir was his sister, Miss Nancy Kelly, now ninety-four years of age, and who is to-day the richest person on the island.

There are at this writing (1907) forty-two dwellings on the island, and every householder seems to be above want. Each year the island exports 150,000 bushels of oysters, the average price being fifty cents a bushel. The fish and game bring almost as much, so it appears that there is a good deal of money floating around Hog Island.

To a student or a thinker with archaeological proclivities the people of Hog Island present a curious study. Here is a community of forty-two families, averaging six children to each. Most of these households have, father and son, existed on the island for three centuries. Now what kind of people has this intermingling and intermarrying produced? Living in a land where no one need work, and where Nature has given them a fine climate, the ocean and land, and food in plenty, we might expect to find as ideal a community as ever existed in Rasselas's Happy Valley; but such is not the fact. The islanders are below mediocrity. There are some bright examples, but the majority are slothful, and their dispositions mean and malicious. There are no criminals among them, for the reason that they have not the energy or spirit to commit a crime, except in the breaking of the game laws. They fish and hunt, and labor for a few weeks gathering oysters, and this labor gives them enough money to live in ease and comfort. Most of these islanders hibernate like an animal; they eat heavily, and then doze for hours. Some of them recline and repose twenty hours out of the twenty-four.

I had one hunting experience at Hog Island that I will never forget. I turn over the pages of my diary and find it was the 18th of December, 1905. I was staying with the assistant light-house keeper. That morning we went to the blinds about a couple of miles from the island, and some three or four hundred yards from a sand spit that divided the ocean from the inlet.

We soon had the decoys spread, and the sport was good from the start, for the wind was blowing furiously, and the way the black-ducks came darting in from the ocean was good for the sportsman. We were both so busy shooting that we failed to notice that the tide was ebbing fast, and that meant being caught on the flats. When the little boat in the blind began to thump on the bottom we awoke to the fact that we would have to hustle if we were to get back to the island that day.

We jumped out and piled the decoys into the boat with frenzied haste, and then started to pull the boat through the shallow water a couple of hundred yards to where our sailboat was anchored in the channel; we had not gone half the distance when the batteau, heavily weighted by the decoys, stuck in the mud. The water was only a few inches deep, and we pulled and hauled with all our might until every sinew was strained; but all in vain. Now here was a nice state of affairs, a "purty predicament," as the keeper expressed it, in an open boat with the icy wind that came unchecked from Spitzbergen; the thermometer below the freezing point, and our wraps all left in the sailboat!

"Jerusalem! but it is cold," said the keeper, and he humped his spine, thrust his hands in his pockets as far as they would go, sank his neck between his shoulders until only the top of his cap was visible, and lapsed into gloomy silence.

There was nothing to do but sit on the side of the craft, and wait. The mud, black, plastic, and adhesive, was fully two feet deep, and only a web-footed bird could have stood upon it without sinking.

If my companion had been a congenial spirit we could have whiled the hours away, but as the keeper never vouchsafed any answer save a grunt or groan, I might as well have attempted to philander with a "Marble Wenus" as to get up any conversation with him.

"A watched pot never boils," and measuring time—waiting—is worse than the most violent physical toil.

It is in just such situations that the sportsman's old brier-root becomes his best comforter; and, by the way, the art of lighting a pipe in a high wind, when everything is wet except the matches, is only known to old campaigners. How can one light a match when there is nothing dry to scratch it against? It is very simple. Take off your hat, open your knife and place it inside, and rub the match along the sharp edge; so there you are.

It is only in trying situations that the pipe is truly appreciated; like the jewel in the toad's head, it shines brightest in adversity. To those who face hardships tobacco is a boon; it banishes dull care, it soothes the nerves, it brings hope to the wearied heart and rest to the tired brain. The stem of the pipe is sweeter to the taste of the used-up sportsman than the kiss of the rosy-lipped maiden, and the odor of the smoke more fragrant than the odor from a bank covered with flowers. At least it appears that way when one is stuck in a mud bank, with the mercury below freezing, and the wind blowing sixty miles an hour.

We remained in that spot for five hours, and I never felt more overjoyed to reach a well-warmed, well-lighted house, for we were half frozen and wholly starved.

"Quick the measure, dear the treasure,
Sweet is pleasure after pain."

That night the worst hurricane in the memory of man swept over the island. It was a little after two o'clock in the morning when the assistant keeper rushed into my room, clad in oil-skins, with a lantern in his hand, and told me in excited tones that the brant were flocking by the thousand around the light-house, and to dress and go with him to the tower.

I was soon ready, and reaching the four-acre enclosure in which the light-house stood, the full force of the raging wind, filled with sleet and snow, struck us with such force that we staggered like drunken men. Inch by inch we worked and battled our way until we reached the tower. Climbing the spiral steps we reached the keeper's room, just under the revolving light. The place was well-warmed by a red-hot stove, and a table of books and magazines gave the place a cozy, comfortable, homelike look. One of the keepers was keeping watch and ward, his head surrounded by a halo of tobacco smoke. It was a scene of peaceful content; but one step through the door and it was chaos on the rampage—Old Boreas raging and running amuck. To stand, as it were, in mid air, enveloped in a hurricane, was certainly a new sensation. It seemed as though the final moment had come, the "*Dies Ira,*" the convulsive throes of Nature in the wreck of matter, and the crash in the crucible of the world.

The round tower was encircled by a narrow iron balcony just below the lantern. On the south side where we stood clutching the railing, the wind, which struck the tower on the north side, almost with the force of the ocean billows, was fended off. I doubt if any man could have lived for five minutes on the north side of the tower.

The brant, driven by the furious wind, and bewildered, buffeted and frightened by the warring of the elements, were naturally attracted by the flashing lamp high in the air, and they aimed for it from all points of the compass.

It was a sight worth taking a long journey to see. The brant, the shyest, wildest, most timid of water fowl, were within five feet of us, but, evidently blinded by the light, they could see nothing. Some would circle around the tower, others dart by; and wonderful to relate, some would remain stationary in the air, their wings moving so rapidly that they were blurred like a wheel in rapid motion. I thought at the time what a tremendous power must lie in their wings to enable them to nullify the wind that the instrument inside indicated was blowing sixty-five miles an hour.

What a treat to be able to gaze on those wild birds and study them at close range, when they were free and unfettered in their native element two hundred feet above the earth!

The lamp in the tower revolved every forty-five seconds, and for a short time every bird was in the vivid glare, which displayed every graceful curve of neck and head, and the set and balance of the body, and enabled one to look into their brilliant eyes.

The brant is not a glossy, showy bird like the wood-duck or mallard, but in the driving rain and under the powerful rays of the lamp they were exquisitely beautiful; their plumage looked like ebony, and the tints changed to many an iridescent hue. It was enthralling to watch them dart in the midst of the Argand's refulgent gleams, one second vivid and tangible, the next swallowed up in Cimmerian darkness. Every few seconds, above all the rush of the wind, would be heard a loud tinkling sound as a blinded brant, dazed by the rays, would strike the double two-inch plate-glass that surrounded the burner, and fall dead from the impact; sometimes dying on the platform of the tower, but more often falling to the ground.

Sterling, the keeper, picked up twenty-eight that night, and at the base of the tower there were several islanders with their dogs, who secured dozens of the water fowl, the exact number they never divulged.

Some of the islanders asked the keeper on duty to allow them to ascend the tower and shoot the hovering birds. Certainly a man using a small gauge gun could have killed hundreds that night. I told the keeper that if such a murderous act was permitted the Government would dismiss every one of the light-house employees.

After two hours spent in the tower I returned to bed, and in my dreams I could still see the darting, circling brant.

Nature has richly endowed Hog Island. I question whether there is any other one spot on earth where fish, flesh, and fowl are more abundant. In the winter the flats are the haunt of the brant, and the sloughs, of the black-duck; in the spring are the snipe, and in the summer and autumn the bay-birds. The oysters and clams are countless. In the creeks, channels, and inlets are found every variety of fish, especially the delicious sheepshead and hog-fish; and the garden produce is far superior to that of the mainland. The shooting around the island should be very fine; but the State game laws are treated with contempt, and the wild fowl are driven from the vicinity. When President Cleveland was serving his second term he visited Hog Island, and was much impressed with the game outlook, and some of his friends built a large commodious club-house a short distance from the life-saving station, and several sportsmen bought parcels of land and erected handsome shooting-lodges.

Then there was a golden chance for the Hog Islanders to make the place a great tourists', yachting and sportsmen's rendezvous, which would have yielded a handsome return without labor; but these people, actuated by jealousy or malice toward the strangers, instead of preserving the game, deliberately practiced night shooting, which of course drove the wild fowl from their feeding-grounds. It is a well-known fact that no matter how much shooting is done in the daytime, if the birds are undisturbed at night they will cling to their favorite flats during the whole season; on the other hand, if they are hunted in the night they rise high in the air and head for some distant point, often hundreds of miles away. The clubmen left the place in disgust, and the shooting-boxes are now rotting on the ground.

In 1905 I went there in the early part of the season, and there were immense flocks of brant all around the place. Standing on the tower I swept the broadwater with a powerful field-glass, and saw Machipongo Inlet black with wild fowl.

I expected to have fine sport, and was at the life-saving station early the next morning, when Harry Bowen, one of the crew, an exceptionally bright native of the island, was to take me to the blinds.

The captain of the station told me that there would be no sport, that he had heard the reports of the guns all night, and he called up several of the surfmen who had patrolled the beach, and they said that from ten o'clock p.m. until near daybreak some of the islanders were shooting the brant and black-duck.

Harry came to the station from his house about a half mile distant, and gave me the names of three of the islanders who had made a big killing, as he expressed it.

I went to the look-out and used the glass, and could not see a duck in the whole inlet. These islanders knew that the game laws expressly prohibited night-shooting in any form or manner, yet they contemptuously ignored the statutes.

Perhaps a word here about the game laws will not be untimely.

Until 1878 there were no game laws in Virginia, and any one could shoot at will all the week and Sundays too, day or night.

While a member of the Legislature, in 1875, I framed and formed the first game laws for the State, and met with a great deal of opposition, especially from the mountaineers. One member gravely informing me that he would have to oppose me for the reason that the swallows tumbling down the chimney scared his children.

The Virginia sportsmen have succeeded in passing good, honest laws to protect the game, and that King of Sportsmen and Prince of Good Fellows, Polk Miller, has worked for years to not only enact laws to protect the game of Virginia, but to see that the enactments are carried out. It would be a good investment to have a game warden reside at Hog Island during six months of the year.

The game laws should be strictly enforced against night-shooting. All law-abiding citizens of both Virginia and the Carolinas agree to this, and the great majority agree that spring-shooting should be abolished.

Maryland, Virginia and North Carolina all have a navy to protect their fish and oysters, and if the same amount of money was spent in protecting their game there would be an abundance for the next half century.

From *The Huntsman in the South*, vol. 1, *Virginia and North Carolina* (New York and Washington, D.C.: Neale, 1908), pp. 300–314

1913

The Island of Chincoteague

MAUDE RADFORD WARREN

In the years following the coming of the railroad to Chincoteague Bay in 1876 the feverish harvesting of seafood brought prosperity to Chincoteague Island. The good times created change, but Maude Radford Warren (d. 1934) also recognized continuity in the islanders' customs and in their habits of work and thought. Maude Warren was a Canadian essayist, short story writer, and children's

author. She was the first white woman to cross Great Bear Lake in the Northwest Territory, and, as a World War I correspondent, her service under fire earned her the honorary rank of major in the Rainbow Division.

The attitude of most island folk toward their sea is that of the primitive savage toward his god, whom he fears, craves forgetfulness of, and if he loves, loves perforce. Men need the sea, which gives generously, but takes a heavy toll of the bodies of drowned fishers and the hearts of sad wives. When the hours of fishing are over, island people usually turn their backs and pay an unsought homage to the earth in little gardens, sheltered against the angry, scouting winds of the sea.

But if she is a bitter step-dame to most of the land she rules, the sea has taken for a favorite child the Island of Chincoteague. She cherishes the islanders from babyhood to old age, offering them her choicest fruits, asking of them only the lightest labor, tempering the winds, subduing the tidal waves, so that almost nobody is sick or poor, and even the old are not sad. And from babyhood to old age they love her and belittle the earth, so that their gardens are few, and tended, if tended at all, by women and girls, who, more conservative than the men, are carrying out the Old World tradition that the fruits of the earth shall sustain men.

Chincoteague is counted as part of the eastern shore of Virginia, that peninsula which bounds the Chesapeake Bay. The island, which is nine miles long by perhaps a mile and a half wide, is sheltered not only by the long mainland to the west, but to the east by Assoteague, which is called an island, but which is really a slim peninsula running up through Maryland. There is scarcely any place in the country where the traditions are older; but they are not, as in the other parts of Virginia, the traditions of the aristocrats whose ancestors came early to Jamestown and who can show old tombstones, old silver of King Charles's time, and old chairs made in the reign of Queen Anne. Behind the voice and views of the average Southern aristocrats there is always the flavor of another land and other sentiments than our own. But these Chincoteague people have kept the flavor of American pioneer conditions, of a simple living that made its own precedents and accepted its own ideals without consciousness that these might have limitations.

Moreover, in other parts of Virginia, poverty is housemate with gentility. The silver was more plentiful before the war; many of the chairs were sold to buy food. One sees high-bred faces touched with the inalienable shadow of privation and sacrifice, and often with a sorrow that reaches beyond the personal. But in the fortunate island there is nothing of this. Living has come easily always; simplicity, primitiveness have gone hand in hand with standards of plenty. The great national crises, the Revolutionary War and the Civil War, have apparently left no impressions of grief; they have afforded not one tale of death, no fireside tragedy, only some humorous tales and a few flattering pensions. Some gracious chance has lined out for these people a pleasant plane of living marked only faintly with any crossing of evil or pain.

It is supposed that the eastern shore of Virginia began to be settled as early as 1615, for the records show that in 1622 there was a population of seventy-six whites. The planters started at the lower end of the peninsula and extended upward along the watercourses, each finding some wide creek so as to have a landing of his own. Old dim traditions still hold of the visiting that was carried on by boat among families who would travel a whole day to see one another and prolong a call for weeks. But for some decades no one sought Chincoteague. The island has never been a great plantation, nor has it ever sheltered any of the famous families of the South.

Some of the islanders vigorously oppose the tradition that Chincoteague was originally settled by convicts, but the evidence tends in that direction. In the old days a planter was allowed fifty acres of land for each settler he introduced. In 1687 Captain Daniel Jenifer brought over a number of convicts, perhaps seven, perhaps thirty-five, and in return Chincoteague and Assoteague were patented to him. Twice the patent of Chincoteague lapsed, but finally, in 1692, twenty-five hundred acres of the lower half were given to John Robbins and twenty-five hundred of the upper half to William Kendall, and from these two men almost all the people now on the island got their titles. For more than a century only a few people lived on the island whose old names still survive—Jesters and Birches, Thorntons, Bowdens, and Wheeltons. Seventy years ago, the oldest inhabitant says the settlers numbered five hundred. Then, the story goes, an islander was cast away from a fishing-boat on the new Jersey coast, and a few families, lured by his stories of the island paradise, came down to settle. After the Civil War others came, so that the population must have reached a thousand. Since then the islanders have multiplied rapidly. There are now more than three thousand, about a thousand being children of school age.

This is not so surprising as it seems, for the people marry early, the girls sometimes at the age of fourteen, the men at eighteen, and they have large families. One woman is pointed to as the mother of eighteen children; another was a grandmother at thirty. In such a kindly climate it would be strange indeed if life did not flourish. The very hens and turkeys have larger families than can be seen elsewhere. These people are encompassed by the poetry of life—by the three most ancient cries in the world: the cry of the sea-bird, the call of the wind, and the sighing of the sea. Yet they live according to a happy prose kept resolutely in their blood by the strong Anglo-

Saxon strain in them, which has come down as unchanged perhaps as in any community in the world. And allowing for surface changes, they live much as their fathers did.

Surface changes, however, there have been. Fifteen years ago when one went to Chincoteague one crossed from Franklin City in a little steam-yacht. The flat, green marshes gave way to the sea; then Wallop's Island sprang into view, and then out of the mists came shaping the slim foot of Assoteague, and west and north of it the long, blue line that was Chincoteague. The line widened, darkened; the upper side defined itself into the plumes of magnificent pines, the lower side into a long street of houses sitting by the sea. On closer approach these houses showed the color of a city in a child's fairy-tale—buff and pink, blue and dun, white and red and yellow. Here and there in the water tall stakes or slim, waving branches of trees marked the sites of oyster-beds. Clustering close to the many docks were weather-beaten schooners and sail-boats and lighters and row-boats, the whole of a peaceful holiday effect.

Once on the dock, in those old days one was greeted with smiles, if not words, by a number of inhabitants to whom a stranger was so much of an agreeable rarity that he seemed like a household guest. One walked a few steps and looked up and down a slightly irregular street paved with oyster-shells, a street with somehow a shirt-sleeves or Mother-Hubbard-wrapper effect, but very appealing in its homely and comfortable quality. One entered the hotel, which needed painting and sweeping, but one didn't mind. One had to find the proprietor, who was not expecting a traveler. A baby on the stairway smiled and dropped its cracker—and the cracker stayed there five days. One went into the dining-room in which there was but a single long table loaded (although the month had no "r" in it) with all sorts of sea food. Never was a more opulent table; never a more kindly set of people than the few men who sat about it, exchanging personal repartee and eating heartily. Obeying some sort of premonition, one crimped the edges of one's napkin to be sure of getting it again; one didn't for fifteen meals, but one had all the others. One wandered in the streets, and a perfect stranger offered to lend a row-boat, and upon acceptance half a dozen kindly people saw one off with warnings to avoid the oyster-beds. One drifted into a shop where the stock was arranged in hit-or-miss fashion on the shelves, the boxes half open and the contents peeping over the edges. It took the proprietor some time to find what one wanted; he laid the box out on the counter, and there it still lay a month later, the dust leisurely sifting in. There was no mayor and no prison, and, after the first rage, people forgave easily whatever crime was committed. Never surely was there such tolerance.

That was fifteen years ago, and on revisiting one feared at first that the island was changed. One crossed the same water, but now in a gasoline-launch that screamed and pounded out the wonders of advanced civilization. The same green flats were there, the same mist that shaped itself into Chincoteague Island with the gay-colored houses. But over the oyster-beds were reared at intervals square boxes for watchmen who guarded the stock of the sea. Around the docks were no longer the few water craft with weather-beaten holiday faces, but many large, neat schooners, and instead of the row-boats and lighters everywhere were gasoline launches. One walked along the dock and people only looked casually; no longer are tourists rarities. One reached the hotel, and a chambermaid met one and led one up to the register. But she had a long memory, for as she showed one to one's room she said:

"Things hain't like they were when you came before. We have a bath-room now; you can lie right down in the tub and let the water go all over you." She pushed contemptuously aside a lamp that stood on the table and explained. "We have gas, of course; we just keep a lamp in case." At the door she added: "If you want to telephone to any of your friends you can. We could have a telegraft if we wanted, but I reckon the telephone is quicker."

Quicker! Had haste come to Chincoteague!

She lingered in the doorway, hospitably. "Want anything more?"

"I'll ring if I do, thank you."

The pang was unconsciously delivered, but she surely should have been spared it!

"We hain't go no bells yet," she admitted, reluctantly. "You'll have to holler over the banisters." Then she made a struggle for supremacy. "We got two five-cent theaters; be sure you go to-night." Her parting shot was: "We got five ladies' lodges now besides all the men have, and a mayor, and an iron pen to jail 'em."

The dining-room was enlarged and full of small tables, and evidently a clean napkin was intended for each meal. But, at any rate, the gas wouldn't burn, and the bath-room was out of repair, and the people who went to the five-cent theater were the same happy-go-lucky folk of years before. Three-quarters of a mile of Chincoteague has indeed been incorporated into a town for the sake of law and order, and the population within the limits pay fifteen per cent. of taxes and give their affairs into the hands of a council of six, and a mayor, a clerk, and a sergeant.

It is by the largess of the sea that the islanders live. This is not the strenuous toil of fishing so much as the gentler work with oysters and clams. There is a shoal abreast of Chincoteague about seven miles out which drives the fish off shore, so that most of the fishing is done in the deep sea. Nowadays many tourists come down in the autumn for the blue fish and the mackerel, and in winter for cod. In the traps great sturgeons are caught, sometimes weighing as much as two hundred and fifty pounds, and there is abundance of trout and halibut, roach, perch, and flounders. But the real sea harvest is oysters and clams. There are always people to whom the past is the only golden age, and even in Chincoteague there are old men who say that in the days when there were no oyster laws, and no hundred and fifty watchtowers in a long chain from the island to Cape Charles, and when the oysters multiplied the best they could—then there was more than a man could gather, and no neighbors that had to be kept from stealing. Yet most of the inhabitants consider the laws a protection and a benefit.

Clamming and oystering almost seem like door-yard occupations. Each householder living by the shore has riparian rights as far down as the low-tide mark. In his sands the clams are much surer produce than garden stuff, and are raised with almost no personal trouble to himself. Beyond, lie the oyster "meadows" which the government rents to the islander for fifty cents an acre. Oyster-shells (or "rock") are washed clean and "planted," and from the 20th of March to the middle of September the spawn comes to the surface and catches on the rough substance. It is considered better to plant, if possible, in shallow water for the sake of sunlight twice in twenty-four hours. If a thousand bushels of unshucked oysters are planted, in two years they double. The planters have to reckon on some losses. Perhaps the young oysters "sand" or "mud" or refuse to grow. Perhaps the transplanting, done a few months before the oysters are ready to sell, may have unfortunate results. Perhaps the market fails, and the islanders lose fifty thousand dollars in the season—to them a great sum. But on the whole, oysters are a safe investment; a man with an acre would make from three hundred to five hundred dollars a season, besides what he gets from clams and from the once scorned "scallops," which now bring a dollar and a half a gallon.

The time was when almost every householder in Chincoteague had his plot of water, but by degrees the acreage has passed into the hands of just a few people. Perhaps a man would have a year of bad luck and would sell his rights for some ready money, or perhaps he would think that he could make steadier money by working for one of the large planters by the day. There are now about forty planters on the island, a dozen of them large and the rest small. No one is colossally rich; the greatest man commands possibly three hundred thousand dollars; most of the other "rich" men are worth from twenty to forty thousand dollars, which they have made in twenty or twenty-five years. The population is growing, and the acreage of water stands still, but so far the sea promises an abundant living to all her island children.

Those who work for the planters are called "tongers," because they get the oysters out of two or three fathoms of water with tongs. In shallow water they manage it with feet and hands. They are paid on the average twenty-five cents a bushel for the oysters they bring in, and it goes without saying that they appropriate for themselves anything from a peck to a half-bushel. The oysters are divided according to size into three classes: primaries, culls, and cullenteens. Formerly the oysters were "drinked," or put into fresh water to whiten and "plumpen." There seems to be a pure-food law against this now, but some planters maintain that oysters should be "drinked" to purify them, and that without such fresh water they will not live to reach Baltimore and Philadelphia.

Work with the oysters lasts only about seven months a year, but clamming continues all the year round. It is here that the small man can make a comfortable living even if he works only half a week. Perhaps a further reason, besides a natural love of leisure, why the islanders do not like to spend many days in succession at any of this work is that the tide affects their habits. Sometimes they breakfast at four and sometimes at nine; they do not like to rise early. Some of them have a special gift for clamming. They recognize immediately the little key-like holes made by the clams and can quickly dig them out; or, in their own vernacular, such a man is "right quick to sign and wade them out." There are stories of a man who sometimes makes seven dollars a day clamming at one tide. Many a little boy stays out of school to earn fifty cents or a dollar a day, which he is allowed to spend as he pleases. The clammer sells to the island dealer, who pays by the hundred and according to size—the three-hundred size or four-hundred size, reckoned really by the number which fill a sack.

Thus every one in Chincoteague mints the sea into treasure ample for his use. And money comes in other ways. The government furnishes at least fifty thousand dollars a year, for there are four life-saving stations close at hand: on Wallop's Island, on Assoteague, on Pope's Island, and at Green Run, each with a crew of eight men whose families, as a rule, live on Chincoteague. Besides these are the people from the two neighboring light-houses and the light-ship, who spend their money and their holidays on Chincoteague. Then there are thirty or more old Federal soldiers who draw pensions.

For even in the Civil War the islanders showed their characteristic curious mixture of a *lassier-faire* attitude and a tendency to take enough care for the morrow to be sure of a good living. Chincoteague was one of the first places to be visited by the Federal troops, and something like forty men enlisted; but the island luck held, and it seems that they saw no active fighting. Some houses flew the Confederate flag, two or three men joined the Southern forces; a few sympathizers put out the light-house lamp, but it was promptly lighted again by islanders who wanted permits for their oyster-boats to run up to Pennsylvania and New York. The Federal soldiers tore up a few fence stakes belonging to old ladies and demolished the benches of the Methodist Church. A negro company came but even they were not resented deeply. Chincoteague is almost the only part of Virginia where there are no wounds left, physical or mental, to mark the signs of a civil war. Since there is so much comfort, no real poverty, and very little sickness, it is no wonder that Chincoteague has been called the Island Paradise.

A seeker of causes might argue that the comfortable attitude of the natives toward living and work and even crime is due in part to their ancestry and in part to the ease with which any man can get a living. One or two outsiders, emigrants or travelers, imbued with a spirit of gain, deplore the fact that there is no cotton factory or shirt factory on Chincoteague; the reason is that there is no man who will work ten hours in a factory. Even the laborers who are supposed to carry on the work of the two saw-mills take holiday whenever they please. The oysterers and clammers, working two or four days a week, can usually, besides earning their living, save enough to buy a home and to keep it neatly painted, but their ambition rarely extends beyond this. They like to talk in their free hours about smart boats and horse-races, and to tell stories of the tourists, growing numerous now, who come down for deep-sea fishing and to shoot brant or various kinds of duck and shore birds. They are deeply interested in one another's personal affairs, especially love affairs. It is almost impossible for any one on the island to conduct a love affair secretly. Sometimes they so prolong their days of loafing that they can no longer run bills at the shops, and then they have to respect the shopkeeper's scruples and go to work again.

It is said that a few of the younger people are getting ideas of saving. Perhaps this is due to the advance in educational ideas. In the old days there was no public school at all; there was a private school conducted, when a teacher could be found, for four months a year, and there was a literary fund (kindly term) collected for students who could not afford to pay. About half of the older people on Chincoteague cannot read or write. Nowadays, however, there is an excellent central school with four teachers, and in other parts of the island three primary schools. Various shops sell magazines and books, and a boy cries a Philadelphia newspaper in the streets. Yet he generously tells most of the news in it, and in any case it is bought chiefly for the weather predictions.

In certain ways the people of Chincoteague show a moral strictness. They do not believe in cards or dancing. Their six churches, four white and two colored, are well attended. They believe in a personal God who rewards and punishes, and a personal devil who pesters, and they keep Sunday with the sternness of Scotch convenanters. Indeed, church and prayer-meetings are their chief social relaxation; to church they wear their best clothes, and very fine they are, and here, especially in the Baptist Church, they have revivals, when their emotions rise high, and they shout and dance to the glory of the Lord. One of the most poetic memories one could possess would be the vision of a negro revival on Chincoteague at night before the religious feeling ran too high. The meeting is held in a clearing in the great pine woods through which time has gone so grandly. The more earthly light is given by great pitch-pine torches flaring at the four corners of the inclosure. The soft negro voices sing plaintively:

"Leanin', leanin', safe and secure from all alarm;
Leanin', leanin', leanin' on the everlasting Arm."

The tender, soft-throated music, the deep dome of the sky against which are defined the solemn, still trees, the large Southern stars, the subdued sounds of birds and insects, and the flames flickering over the devoted, dull faces—it all forms a harmony gracious to the soul.

When the outside world hears of Chincoteague, it is usually on account of the half-wild horses that roam over the stretches of the island and of Assoteague: strong, shaggy, small creatures, somewhat larger than Shetland ponies, who plunge boldly into the salt water when they want to swim to some little toothsome islet of marsh grass. These animals are supposed to have been cast away on Chincoteague from some wrecked vessel in the eighteenth or perhaps the seventeenth century, and, in the course of time, to have degenerated in size.

They came to a good haven, for there are five different kinds of natural grass to feed them, and for drink little pools of slightly brackish water in the sands. Some of the cleverest ones make little reservoirs for themselves by digging with their hoofs.

They belong to a few of the islanders, who own from one to seventy-five each. Once a year in July the horses are rounded up in Assoteague and in Chincoteague and are driven down into the town, where they are penned, and the colts are branded. Then some of them are sold to men from the mainland who will give as much as a hundred or a hundred and twenty-five dollars for a "stylish" horse. When the horses are fed with oats and their rough coats are properly curried, they present a very attractive appearance. They are very strong and long-lived; one old inhabitant boasts of a mare, most prolific of colts, which lived to be forty years old and worked almost to the end. No wonder they are hardy, fending for themselves, as they do, and having no other shelter than the pine and myrtle trees. It is a pretty sight to see them roaming past the magnolia-trees of the marsh or through the noble pine woods in the interior of the island, while their little fellow-creatures, the mocking-bird, the cardinal grosbeak, the oriole, and the marsh-wren fly past them fearlessly.

Except through the horses, and through the fishing and shooting stories of a few tourists, Chincoteague is unknown, and to the casual spectator its annals seem simple enough. Yet when one talks to the older inhabitants, the past and the present seem to blend together to form an impression of common but significant living. They tell of the time when the girls and women helped the men fish, and when they spun and wove, and perhaps there is lament that to-day the women do not even knit stockings. Then the women wore simple garments of dyed homespun and the men short jackets and trousers, with long-tailed coats for Sunday. One old man mentions a time, ninety years ago, when his father bought five hundred acres of land for five hundred dollars and when many of the neighbors belonged to the Quaker faith, though every one went to the same church on the rare occasions when a preacher could be had from the mainland. Another speaks of the old days before the islanders gave full allegiance to the sea, depending then on the land, raising corn and wheat and rye, apples and pears, which lasted a long time and were larger than one sees nowadays. And such cooking, done in Dutch ovens! Sea food was as now, but one could buy any amount of it for a few cents; salt-rising bread; crackling bread made at hog-killing time; corn-bread hung up all night on a crane; thick Johnny-cake baked on a board; great pot-pies made of goose and chicken cooked together and hanging on the crane; puddings every day; honey that they made vinegar from; and dried beef which they had killed in the autumn. The children hunted for plovers' eggs and marsh-hens' eggs, much better than the gulls' eggs the people eat now.

In those early days they had log houses a story and a half in height, boarded outside, plastered inside, and supported on great cedar blocks. Most of the houses had great hearths which would hold logs as large as a man, and fine brick chimneys; the poorer people, however, had "andiron" chimneys made of lime and laths. In 1840 there were about five hundred people living in twenty-six houses. They did not build more, for in those times the young people would "win away" to Delaware and Pennsylvania.

They tell of the time when there was a forest on the island a mile long and half a mile wide, and the logs were so valuable that the man who bought them to sell again was able to light his pipe with a hundred-dollar bill! There are stories of old George Connor, the hermit of little Piney Island, who had traveled all around the world, but found the pines and the sea better company than people. Their great curiosity was the old Guinea negro, Ocher Binney, said at his death to be a hundred and thirty years old, the tattooed son of an African prince; stolen by Arabs and sold in Virginia, he was freed at last to live with other free people on the fortunate island, for there were no slaves in Chincoteague till just before the war—a fact due perhaps to the Quaker traditions. And yet the old life they talk of, with their quaint phraseology, such as, "It weren't the custom," "Ten head of children," "I was then seven year old, just in my eight"—this old life is only the life of to-day translated, as it were, into slightly older dialect. The past and the present are as unified as the eastern and western waters, rising and falling in deep suspiration on each side of the island.

One old man can send his memory back especially far in the past, and, repeating the stories of his grandfather and great-grandfather, he speaks of the Revolutionary War almost as if it were an event of yesterday. He loves to talk of ancient times, sitting erect in his tall chair against a background of old-fashioned wall-paper with narrow lines of flowers running up and down in widely separated stripes. His white hair is combed straight back and his nose is aquiline. One could almost fancy that the white hair is fastened in a queue behind. It is a Revolutionary face. It would not be hard to believe that he had lived in his great-grandfather's time.

This man's memory is a storehouse of the common, every-day living of the island, and the little tragedies loom especially large to him, though he has no adequate feeling for the wars. He speaks as if he remembers the hurricane of 1822 which made prey of the island, formed a great tidal wave, capsized a house or two, drowned five people, and terrified several into moving to the mainland. He knows every detail, it would seem, of the four murders that have happened in one hundred and twenty years, and even talks about the first one as if he had been an eye-witness. One can see the great New York "bully" (pugilist) in his silver sleeve-links and silver shoe-buckles, who could carry in his arms to the mill a horse-load of corn and who challenged Tunnell, "of powerful manhood," to a fight. He makes one see the bully drinking rum, and the great Tunnell, enraged at last, saying he wanted no liquor, but just the heart's blood of his enemy; the "second," "supple as an eel," who made a ring with his foot and said that any one who crossed it would lose his sight of the sun; then the fight, "right to the tumble," the bully falling at last with the cry that he was not only whipped but killed.

He makes one see the desolate young man who committed the second murder, killing his friend over a girl, and, in spite of acquittal, thereafter finding life on the fortunate island too melancholy. On the last murders, which led to the departure from Chincoteague of the Sanctificationists, he touches briefly, as if he did not like to think of blood being shed in the name of religion.

A simple tale and simple people. They do not see life in a large historical perspective; their sense is not epic; they cannot generalize further than the limits of their commonplace axioms of religion and morality. They have increased their freedom by reducing their wants, and for them life has few complexities. Birth, a little work, marriage, quiet home life, and again a little work, and after many years death; withal a faith in God and in the future He grants them in time and in eternity. Surely it is a sufficient heritage. Surely the sea and their own traditions and ideals have given them a certain wealth of content which is lacking to many more sophisticated communities.

From *Harper's Monthly Magazine* 127 (1913): 775–85

1933
Honeymoon on Cobb Island

OLIN SEWALL PETTINGILL JR.

Over a career spanning six decades and more than one hundred publications, Olin Sewall Pettingill Jr. (1907–) has been a leading figure in twentieth-century ornithology. Author of the classic text A Laboratory and Field Manual of Ornithology *(1939 and sub-*

sequent editions), Pettingill also is an accomplished photographer and filmmaker. From 1960 to 1973 he served as director of the Laboratory of Ornithology at Cornell University.

In 1933 while waiting word of his first formal employment as an ornithologist, the recently married Pettingill undertook a combined honeymoon and scientific expedition to Cobb's Island.

Early on June 21 we were off [from Middleton, Massachusetts] in my roadster, loaded with camera, film, and necessities. Driving all day, we arrived in the evening at Oyster on Cape Charles, Virginia. There we found a friendly fisherman who would take us out to Cobb Island the next afternoon. While we were away, staying on the island, he said I could leave my car beside the driveway that went down to his boat dock where it would be safe.

True to his word, the fisherman at Oyster was waiting for us late the following afternoon. We were soon aboard his fishing smack and headed east across the shallow Broadwater toward Cobb Island, a long, low barrier of dunes on the ocean side of Cape Charles. The one-cylinder motor pounded strenuously, rattling the craft from bow to stern and making conversation virtually impossible. In the distance a thin yellow line appeared on the horizon.

From the fisherman's gestures and bellowed phrases we learned that the line was "Cobb Island . . . eight miles away . . . Coast Guard Station on it . . . couldn't land there without permission . . . would pull in at Captain Cobb's . . . queer old duck . . . owns the island . . . lives alone." Instead of relaxing, I was plagued by the question: Would we be allowed to land, camp, and study birds as we had planned? In the rush of events before starting on our honeymoon, I had neglected to communicate with Captain Cobb. I simply knew that it was an exceedingly attractive spot for coastal birds.

My growing concern was momentarily diverted by eight long-winged birds flying parallel to us to starboard. Striking creatures they were, jet black above and immaculate white below. As they maneuvered liltingly just above the waves, their bodies jerked up and down by strong wing strokes, I could make out their vermilion beaks with the knifelike lower mandibles protruding grotesquely. My first black skimmers! Of all the birds nesting on Cobb Island, they were the ones I wanted most to photograph.

Slowly the island assumed definite character. Near the southern extremity loomed some buildings. Built high on piles so as to escape the tide, they seemed lifted above the island like a mirage. Golden sunlight reflected from their windows. We soon passed the United States Coast Guard Station and approached a frame house flanked by two small bungalows.

It was then that I caught sight of a man standing squarely on both feet, hands on his hips, and motionless. He wore a blue shirt, khaki trousers, and hip boots; his head, though bald, was dignified by a corona of white hair. As our boatman eased his craft toward the landing and killed the motor, I called, "Are you Captain Cobb?" No reply. We jumped out. The man still did not move or speak. Somewhat unnerved by now, I extended my hand, "My name is Pettingill."

"I'm George Cobb, glad to meet you," was the response in a low pleasant voice. We shook hands, and he nodded graciously to Eleanor. Captain Cobb was the warden posted there by the National Association of Audubon Societies.

I was impressed with his massive build and erect, noticeably stiff posture. Although his tanned face had the deep furrows of a man of sixty, his physique possessed the vigor of one many years younger. His expression, not unkindly, remained immobile and serious.

"We'd like to stay a while," I began cautiously, "to camp and study birds."

At this his face brightened, and I sensed a sudden unbending.

"Do as you wish," he said warmly. "Anyone who likes birds is welcome. Lots of people come here to see them."

Much relieved, we unloaded our duffel. The fisherman then poled his craft from the shore. At no time had he exchanged a word or glance with Captain Cobb. Nevertheless, I arranged with the fisherman before he left shore to return and pick us up on July 10.

Still not having taken a step, Captain Cobb said, "You'd better not camp tonight, it's nearly dark."

His words were persuasive, for night was settling down, but the yellow glow in the west still gave some light.

"The upstairs rooms in my house are empty," he continued.

Uneasy lest I hurt his feelings, I tried to explain. "We want to camp—something we've never done together." Had we not wished to appear seasoned to the rigors of the outdoors, I might have told him that my wife had never camped in her life.

"Do as you like," he said. "There's a flat place over there between two dunes where you can pitch your tent. Come with me."

From our campsite on the southern tip of the island we could see the eastern beach rising to the dunes and the marsh stretching westward. Captain Cobb's house was just north of us on piles overlooking the marsh. A wooden ramp extended from his porch to the dunes. The Coast Guard Station was a quarter of a mile away.

In the semidarkness we set up our tent. Meanwhile, Captain Cobb disappeared and returned shortly with a pail and some pieces of iron pipe.

"Drinking water," he said. "My well filled with salt water during the last storm. Caught this from the roof. It's good."

Just as I thanked him, a breeze rushed by, collapsing the tent.

"Try these for staples," Captain Cobb said, handing me the pipes. "Your's never'll hold in the sand." In no time the tent was up for keeps.

"Sorry we can't offer you a chair," I said, "but how about a cigarette?"

"Never smoke or drink," he replied.

After our uneasy silence, he asked, "You want to see birds?"

We learned that we were just in time. The eggs in the skimmer colony on the beach were hatching; there were many nests of gulls and terns in the marsh.

It was dark when Captain Cobb left. The island was soothingly quiet. Above the light rush of surf on the beach, we heard a few skimmers passing close to shore, their calls suggesting the yelps of beagles in pursuit of unseen prey.

Next morning, as we approached the skimmer colony on the beach, the birds sat peacefully on their nests, all facing into the wind like weather vanes. Even when we were within a few yards of them, they failed to move. But suddenly we passed their limit of tolerance, because into the air they went with a rush of wings and discordant cries. The next moment one resentful bird left the throng and flew toward Eleanor. She screamed, folded her hands over her head, and crumpled in the sand.

"They won't hit you," I assured her; "they're bluffing." Just then another skimmer shot toward me at eye level. Not believing my own words, I ducked as the bird veered sharply upward.

Many birds were soon doing the same thing—shooting downward, veering upward, but never striking. Still confident, but not sure they would not strike, I walked boldly into the colony, followed by my reluctant bride, whereupon some of the skimmers dropped to the ground in seemingly helpless prostration. One rested on its belly with wings limply outstretched; another lay on its side with one wing waving; still another flopped along using its wings as paddles. They were injury feigning, I explained, to distract your attention from their nests. Frankly, I was surprised to see it in colony-nesting birds.

Nests—mere cups scratched in the sand—were everywhere, often within two or three feet of one another. Many contained white eggs boldly splotched with black and brown. In a few nests there were chicks, the color of sand, squatting tightly, their eyes closed.

The sun bore down on us; the sand was painful to touch. Realizing that the eggs and chicks could not long endure exposure to such intense heat, we quickly departed, letting the panic-stricken skimmers return to shade their eggs and young from the burning sun.

That evening Captain Cobb invited us to dinner. When we strolled up the ramp to his house, there were lights in the Coast Guard Station. The air was calm, and from the still unexplored marsh came a medley of bird sounds.

Captain Cobb, fork in one hand and pot holder in the other, greeted us at the door and motioned us into a large unfinished room—kitchen, dining room, and living room in one—plainly furnished but tidy. After we assured him that we had come with appetites, he returned to his oil stove, where oysters sizzled in a pan. In the nearby sink, silvery hogfishes and huge blue crabs still awaited his attention. This was to be a very special meal, of the best the local sea could provide—and it was delicious.

After dinner the captain became voluble, revealing his attitudes and philosophies and, withal, an unexpected sense of humor. Time meant nothing to him. His only timepiece lay somewhere in the marsh where he had flung it in disgust three weeks before. The sun was his clock, he said. Companionship meant little either. He was contemptuous of his only neighbors, the crew at the Coast Guard Station, whom he considered lazy and careless. He hated to think of a ship in distress calling on them for help and pointed to a bullet hole in his wall made during their "target practice." He liked most of the people who came to see the birds, though he found the women in "trousers" comical. Of the social life enjoyed by his wife on the mainland, a few days a year was all he could bear. What he wanted, he told us, was to stay on his island every day for the rest of his life.

Cobb Island was his home, settled by his grandfather, Nathan Cobb, when it was longer and wider with rich topsoil and many trees and shrubs. It teemed with birds. The family farm grew cabbages "as big as baskets" and turnips "the size of watermelons." Artesian wells supplied water. A hotel accommodated pothunters and sportsmen.

Toward the end of the last century disaster struck. The pothunters all but exterminated the birds and a great storm, accompanied by high tides, destroyed the buildings, filled the wells, uprooted the trees, and washed away the life-giving soil and a third of the island. The family moved to the mainland.

Captain Cobb, a stubborn man, returned and built the present house. Now he was renovating the two bungalows for people coming to see birds. As for the birds, most of the breeding species had recovered from the pothunters. His present struggle was against the mainlanders who came to steal the beach birds' eggs for food. They hated him, even shot at him, but the National Association of Audubon Societies had appointed him deputy warden with authority to enforce bird protection on his and a neighboring island, and *that* he was determined to do, even if he had to shoot in return.

The next day Eleanor and I explored the marsh. She turned up her nose at the musky odors, became entangled in the waist-high grass, jumped out of the way of scurrying fiddler crabs and into a pool of black, sticky mud which smeared her new slacks and sneakers. Although she expressed doubts that any bird could nest in such a place, she followed me gamely.

Overhead a few laughing gulls circled placidly, and from the grass came the sharp cackles of clapper rails. Moving gingerly lest we step into some unseen hole, we finally reached a place where a gull cried out in alarm. Immediately, dozens of gulls together with several Forster's terns flushed from the vegetation and milled over our heads. Occasionally they dove at us, but their attacks were so half-hearted that we ignored them.

The nests of the gulls and terns were clustered here and there on clumps of debris—dead sedge stalks, seaweeds, and driftwood washed in by excessively high tides. In each nest on top of the debris were eggs, usually three. Several were pipped; there would soon be chicks.

The clapper rails we did not see, as they cleverly managed to keep out of sight in the vegetation surrounding us. The nests, however, we found easily, for the grasses over the nests were pulled together and entwined at their tips in a telltale knot. Some of these nests contained as many as fifteen eggs.

In the ensuing eight days I divided my time between the beach and the marsh, using blinds so that I might observe and photograph the birds without their showing fear. Many of the eggs hatched. The weather was perfect, nearly always sunny with a slight breeze. Nights were balmy, moonlit, and delightful.

Early on the morning of July 3, I awoke with the tent slapping against my face. Struggling through its opening, I discovered a guy rope loose. After tightening it, I looked about. Overhead from the northeast sped low, thick clouds, blotting out the rising sun already dimmed by an upper stratum of haze. Dark chasms furrowed the ocean's gray surface. The marsh bore a weird olive color, the beach an intense yellow. My deeply tanned hands and arms were sickly amber.

As I stood, pajama-clad, in the wind, I called sharply to Eleanor. At that moment, with a fresh burst of wind, another guy rope gave way, and Eleanor's sleepy, bewildered face peered out of the tent.

"Get dressed and get out," I shouted, struggling with the guy rope. Her head snapped back like a turtle's.

No doubt Captain Cobb had been watching since dawn, had seen me emerge, and later had watched Eleanor, fully dressed, assume the role of the detached guy rope while I had my turn inside dressing. We were glad to see him coming down the ramp, his pace slow, reassuring.

"Better take down your tent and move your gear to my porch," he advised. "There'll be a high tide out of this. Have breakfast with me."

Minute by minute the wind increased; each gust seemed stronger than the one before. The tent blew down. There was no argument. With the wind tearing at us, we rolled up the tent and carried our duffel up the narrow ramp to the house. More than once the wind threw us off balance and against the railing which saved us from a tumble into the marsh.

The tide, which, according to Captain Cobb's battered almanac, was due to be high at eleven, reached its normal high soon after we were safely in the house. But what time was that? None of us knew. Our watches had run down, and there was no sun. Captain Cobb guessed eight o'clock. There would be three more hours of rising tide!

As the tide exceeded its normal mark, the ocean seemed to lift up. Great walls of surf rose above the beach, hesitated menacingly, then collapsed in thunderous roars, sending avalanches of water against the protecting dunes. The swelling tide rushed and swirled into the Broadwater. Small ponds appeared in the marsh; the ponds became lakes; the lakes fused into one vast expanse continuous with the Broadwater. Soon the Broadwater crept up to the dunes and under the house. Waves, whipped by the wind, licked at the piles, higher and steadily higher. The ocean sent long tongues of water between the dunes. Our once cozy campsite became a channel. The ramp drifted away. The Coast Guard Station, its piles invisible, seemed afloat. From the boat at the station dock came exhaust fumes indicating that the crew was ready for any emergency.

The plight of the beach-nesting birds was all too apparent. Above the beach a cloud of skimmers hovered momentarily, settled on the island, hovered again, settled again. Each time they rose, we knew that a wave had swept over their nests, destroying both eggs and young. Above the marsh, now totally flooded, families of clapper rails drifted on the water at the mercy of the gale. Weak swimmers, they floundered helplessly. Parent birds attempted to round up scattered broods by cutting wide circles and giving frantic calls that we could hear above the roar of the storm. One by one the chicks, exhausted, heavily soaked, and already submerged to their heads, were swallowed up by the waves and tidal whirls.

The heaps of debris on which laughing gulls nested now floated like small rafts, often with nest intact and still holding eggs or chicks. While adult gulls fluttered anxiously over them, sometimes attempting to alight, the wind forced the rafts steadily southward away from the island and into the open Broadwater. The mounting waves tore them apart, spilling their live cargo into the sea.

We were suddenly distracted from our dismay over the fate of the birds by a muffled crash. A bungalow had dropped on its side. Moments later the waves began slapping under the floor of our house. Captain Cobb still showed neither emotion nor alarm. The collapse of the bungalow, the destruction of the bird colonies, even the floor boards of our house darkened by rising water, evoked no comment from him.

I was, I remember, looking through a window on the oceanside and watching spindrift whipped from the towering waves, when I realized that the surf was breaking over the grass-tufted tops of the highest dunes—our one remaining barrier against the fury of the sea. Suddenly an enormous wave, its force fortunately eased by the dunes, struck the side of the house at floor level, jarring the structure and spraying the windows.

Eleanor gasped. We turned toward Captain Cobb. Instead of the expected evidence of disturbance, I saw one of his rare smiles.

"Tide's turned," he said, pointing to the water flowing eastward out of the Broadwater.

The following morning Cobb Island sparkled under a sunny sky. Gone, however, were the bird colonies. Nature in one great sweep had rubbed out that which she had so generously fostered. The beach where the skimmer colony had been was as smooth and hard as a floor, without sign of eggs or chicks. Beyond the site of the colony several hundred skimmers huddled close together. When we approached, they rose silently in a body and alighted further away. Nowhere in the marsh was there a gull. We heard a few clapper rails and marveled that they had survived.

"Sorry you must go," Captain Cobb said, as we packed that night, confident that the fisherman would realize our plight and come on the morrow. "Come back next year. There'll be more birds than ever."

The fisherman appeared as we had hoped, along with news that did not surprise me: my car had been under water. After landing at Oyster, he helped me find a garage mechanic who drained the oil pan of sea water as well as the old oil. With new oil poured in and my car, inside and out, cleared of tidal debris, I turned the ignition switch. My car started without a cough or whimper.

Later in August we read how another devastating storm had battered the Atlantic coast. Naturally we thought of Captain Cobb and wondered how he had fared. Weeks later in *Bird-Lore,* the journal of the National Association of Audubon Societies, we were shocked to read:

> George W. Cobb, this Association's warden on Cobb's Island, Virginia, lost his life, on August 23, in the severe storm that lashed the middle Atlantic coast. The meager information received may be all that we will ever learn concerning the fate of this Virginian of well-known pioneer stock, who thus ended his lonely vigils on the wind-swept stretch of dune and marsh which was his ancestral home. Search by airplane and boat has failed, as yet, to reveal his body which, no doubt, rests somewhere among the extensive marshes of the Virginian shores. The storm which took Mr. Cobb's life, we are informed, completely demolished the few buildings on the island, leaving nothing but the drill pole of the United States Coast Guard Station.

From *My Way to Ornithology* (Norman and London: Univ. of Oklahoma Press, 1992), pp. 193–203

1940

The Island

VIRGINIA CARDWELL ELDREDGE

Shortly after the turn of the century, a small island, little more than a sandbar, emerged from the sea just across Loon Channel from the United States Life-Saving Service station on the south end of Cobb's Island. In 1905 William D. Cardwell, an attorney and legislator from Hanover County, Virginia, received from the commonwealth a grant of title to the island, charted as Cardwell's Island but more commonly known as Little Cobb's.

Virginia Cardwell Eldredge (1918–), granddaughter of William D. Cardwell, visited the island every August from 1919 to 1940. The following memoir was written for her grandchildren.

My grandfather, William D. Cardwell, became interested in the Eastern Shore of Virginia while serving in the Virginia Legislature, and was Chairman of a Committee to look into the area with respect to the kinds of sources of waterways, marine life, etc., of that section of the State. He invested in oyster beds there, and took his family on vacations to islands in the area—had even taken a cow on a barge so his youngest daughter, Dorothy, as an infant, could have fresh milk! It was from Bone, or Wreck, Island, which was washing away, that he saw "Little" Cobb's Island being formed, from sands being washed across Loon Channel from the large Island known as Cobb's Island. He bought this little Island from the Commonwealth of Virginia for about $16.00—and it grew from its original six acres to over one hundred acres at high tide. He built a house there and, during World War I, it was used as Headquarters for the U.S. Naval Fifth District's Squadron #7, which patrolled those waters for the duration of the War. Names of the Squadron were stencilled on each bedroom door—perfectly legible the last time I was in that house in 1940. Grandfather was the Commanding Officer of this Squadron, and my Father was one of the officers, and Chief Officer on several boats assigned to the Squadron. Grandmother Jane Cardwell was at the Island much of the time during the war, seeing to the housekeeping and cooking for the "boys." One of the items on the front porch of this house was a mine—a large round object, brought there by members of this Squadron. This Island was named on Geodetic charts as "Cardwell's Island"—and some called it "Little Cobb's Island"—but, by and large, we just always called it *the* Island. The two Islands are located about 8 or 9 miles from Oyster, Virginia, on the mainland of the Eastern Shore.

One of the earliest memories of my childhood was being awakened by Mother before dawn in Richmond to get ready to go to the Island, where we spent the month of August, coming back home in time for the opening day of school. My Father and our "handy man," James, had always left the day before we did to go to Hampton, Va., and take his boat—early on it was the "Baltic," but later it was the "Red Wing"—across Chesapeake Bay to the Eastern Shore. Mother, my two sisters—Elizabeth and Dot—and

Grandmother Fox and Rachel, our cook, would drive to Old Point Comfort and take the ferry—the Virginia Lee—to Cape Charles—a trip of two hours or so. We then got in the car again and drove to Oyster, where Daddy would be waiting to take us to the Island on his boat. It was a long day—but worth it! Sometimes Grandfather and Grandmother Cardwell would be with us on the ferry, and we always felt quite important then because he always "engaged" a stateroom for the crossing. I remember once he took us to the bridge of the ferry, where we could watch the Captain steer the big ship. I can only remember one trip when I was allowed to cross the Bay on the Red Wing, and that made me feel very grown-up indeed—proud of the fact that I didn't get the least bit seasick!

By the time we got to Oyster, all of the supplies would have been loaded on the Red Wing, because we were always "running with the tide," and had to leave Oyster before low tide. We would, occasionally, get stuck in the harbor—and then we would line the railing of the boat and rock back and forth while Daddy "worked" the engine to break us loose from the muddy bottom. The Coast Guard probably would not have approved then—and certainly wouldn't approve these days—but one of the things that we children liked best, as we got older, was to ride on the very tip of the bow, with our legs dangling, to catch the water from the bow wave of the Red Wing. We never wore life preservers. The cushions kept in the cockpit of the boat would have acted as life preservers if the need had arisen.

Since the Island was a good distance from the mainland—and the Red Wing only made about ten knots per hour—coming back "ashore" was not done very often. The shopping memorandums were apt to be lengthy, with all of the necessities of life, but the *important* things as well—such as chewing gum and movie magazines for the younger generation! We girls were always glad to go ashore at least several times during the month, mostly for the ride on the Red Wing, but also to get into Herbert West's store in Oyster and the several "variety" stores in Cape Charles, where we would go to meet our houseguests coming in on the ferry.

None of the usual requirements of civilization were on the Island. We had no running water except for a single spigot in the kitchen, which was connected to a rain barrel outside. The rain water was used for washing and cooking, and it was always an anxious time when we didn't have enough rain to give the supply needed. There were two barrels to catch the rain—huge things—on the back porch of the house, made of cedar, I suspect, with metal hoops around them, and they smelled sort of metallic, since the water came off a metal roof. Drinking water was brought from Oyster in five gallon cans, and 100 pound blocks of ice were brought on the deck of the Red Wing. Each room was furnished with a basin and pitcher, and chamber pots or bucket to be used if needed in the nighttime. During the day we used the "out house" located behind the house—and nobody seemed to mind the inconvenience of such outmoded facilities. We had no electricity either, so kerosene was another item brought from Oyster in five gallon cans. The kerosene oil was used in the lamps, with wicks, for light at night. We children always felt quite responsible when we got old enough to clean those glass lamp chimneys!

There was always company on the dock—friends of Mother and Daddy's, and, as the years went by, friends of we three girls, too. Rachel and James must have cooked endlessly in that kitchen, but since we children were always chased out of that room by Rachel, we weren't aware of what went on there, and didn't care anyhow! All we wanted was to have some of the fresh fish caught each day; some of the batter bread; some of Grandmother's clam chowder whenever she was on the dock; and the endless supply of oysters, shucked on the dock where we children hung around to get some as they were being shucked. We were taken on the fishing trips aboard the Red Wing, 'tho we weren't allowed to go on the early morning jaunts the grown-ups took. They would get up before sunrise, depending on the tide. Fishing in those waters in those days was very good indeed—trout, croaker, spot, hog fish, shark and perch in great quantity. In the Spring, the adults would make a trip to the Island to fish for drum—and on one occasion Mother caught a 50 lb. one, which was quite exciting. We often caught two fish at once—and one memorable time was when Grandmother Cardwell pulled in her line to find two large trout *heads*—the rest had been eaten off by sharks! Another source of food were the birds who nested, and lived, in the marsh behind "big" Cobb's Island, and shooting ducks, curlews, and sedgehens was an early morning activity of the men. I remember that Daddy could whistle exactly like a curlew—and that those birds tasted very good indeed. This area, behind the Coast Guard Station on the big Island, was a hunter's paradise in the 1800s, when the Cobb family were well known to sportsmen, and there was a hotel there, and other rooming accommodations, run by the Cobb family.

Our contact with the outside world was one small radio which was on board the Red Wing, which we children were allowed to go aboard and play from time to time. I remember I was listening to that radio when the news came that Will Rogers and Wiley Post had been killed in the crash of Mr. Post's plane, and I rushed to the house to spread the word—since Will Rogers was the most loved person of that time, so this was "earth shaking" news. Our only telephone contact was at the Coast Guard Station, across Loon Channel. If there was a call for Daddy, they would yell across the water through a megaphone, and he would row over there in a scow—or James would go if it was just a written message. The Coast Guard was our life line in many respects. They were always ready to help out with projects and would bring our mail from Oyster. Of course, we girls were always impressed with the young men in their uniforms—and were happy to be asked to ride in the several boats they had there—a Picket boat and a self-bailer, etc.

Entertainment was non-existent, of course, except what we dreamed up for ourselves. Mother was an expert at keeping us busy with card games, etc. on rainy days, and on good days, we were outside on the beach—playing "house" in the dunes; building sand castles; tying strings around the wooden decoys' necks and pulling them along in the water; digging for clams; chasing the fiddler crabs; and, of course, swimming at every opportunity. Of course, as we got older, we spent hours lying on the dock to get that all important tan! We were allowed to get in a scow tied at the dock, and, with fish heads tied on straight lines, we crabbed for bait to catch fish. We never heard of steaming crabs or picking the meat for salad or casserole dishes—using them for bait was too important. The only crabs we ate were the very small ones, and the soft-shelled ones, not good for bait.

We weren't allowed to walk way up the beach unless a grown-up was along, so we were always delighted when Grandmother Cardwell was there. She loved to ride the waves further up the beach, and always took us children along to enjoy it, too. I don't recall Mother and Daddy going swimming up that way but once—and I remember *that* because Daddy swam all the way back to the house, doing the side stroke for what seemed like miles to me! Usually we swam right in front of the house—and I have a scar on my knee from having bumped into part of a wing of a World War I airplane that had gotten itself buried in the sand off of the point of the beach. This happened when I was about five years old so I'm told. We never swam from the beach on "big" Cobb's, 'tho we walked the long board walk from behind the Coast Guard Station to the beach. I guess we did go in the water there at least once, because the story is told that while we were in the water with Mother and Daddy, Rachel yelled for them to get us out of the water at once because she had seen "marmaids" coming into shore for us. Of course, the "marmaids" were really porpoises, and I don't ever remember seeing any of them there, 'tho I know there were some. I wish somebody had made us pay more attention to things of nature—maybe they did and I've forgotten. One of the loveliest sights was when we walked to the other end of the Island, where there was a large colony of gulls, and they would all get up and fly at once when we got near. The nesting areas on the Island were known—and are known now—to the Audubon Society. There were always a bunch of gulls at the end of the dock when James was cleaning fish! The other show put on by nature were the many beautiful sunsets—and I guess the sunrise colors were as lovely, but I don't ever remember seeing one of those!

The only summer we didn't go to the Island was in 1933, when Grandmother Fox was ill, and we children were shipped off to Camp Allegheny—and, of course, that was the summer of the big August hurricane. Grandfather was proud of the fact that *his* house stood firm, while the Coast Guard house suffered much damage, and another Station had to be built just north of the original one. One of the descendants of the original Cobb family—George Cobb—lived in a small house just south of the Station. He would not go ashore with the Coast Guard when the '33 hurricane hit, and he and his house washed out to sea. I have always wished that we had been there to see that storm, but, of course, the Coast Guard would have not let us stay, and neither would our father! Storms at the Island were really something to see, and to *hear,* when the North Easters blew a gale, and masses of seaweed and other debris would drift by our dock—sometimes with sedgehens sitting on the grasses, getting a free ride! And at the end, a gorgeous rainbow. The storms there never scared me at all, and I still like to be near the ocean during a storm.

During World War II, there wasn't enough gasoline to get the Red Wing over to the Island very often, and Daddy and Mother didn't go back there many times after that. Grandfather sold the Island to his daughter Dorothy and her husband, B. W. Davis, who built another house, just north of the original one, in 1946—a modern one, with running water and their own generator for electricity. I was only there once to spend a week-end with them, in 1950, when Capt. George West was always at the Island with the Davises to run the boat and just generally to look after them and the property. By 1965, the Coast Guard had closed the Station on "big" Cobb's, and B. W.'s physical condition was such that it was not possible to keep going there, so the Island was sold. The gentleman who bought it also had to sell it very shortly, and it was advertised in the paper for *$150,000*—this price for the piece of real estate Grandfather had paid $16.00 for! I understand the Island has since been owned by the Chatham Blanket Co.—and is also part of the Virginia Nature Conservancy—one of the so-called "barrier islands."

When Grandfather built the house on the Island, he also built a one room structure, connected to the main house by a boardwalk. It was known as "Liberty Lodge," although I have no idea why it was called that. He hired Capt. Link Winder of Oyster, to stay in that house, to keep an eye on his oyster beds, and to harvest any that grew. These oyster beds never "paid off" for Grandfather, but Capt. Link stayed on the Island most of the time. I remember him shucking oysters and taking Grandmother Cardwell fishing to the "spot hole," within rowing distance of the house. I don't know when that house vanished—probably during the '33 storm.

Several things have happened in the last few years to bring the Island back to *my* life. In 1982, Gren and I were visiting my college room-mate and her husband at their summer cottage on the Eastern Shore of Virginia—and Tillie and Bill took us, in their boat, out to the Island. Tillie had visited me there in the summer of 1938—and here we were again, after so many years. It brought back many memories, of course—and it was a kind of sad return, too. The original house had gone to sea, and the Davis house showed need of attention—and both of the Coast Guard Stations looked mighty empty, and ready to go to sea, too. However, Loon Channel looked the same—and we found many large conch shells, just as we used to in the old days—and as we were eating lunch, anchored in the Channel, I knew what a great adventure we lived through on the Island—and we took it so for granted, that we didn't even know how great it was!

In 1983, I met Warren Cobb—grandson of the George Cobb who had perished in the '33 storm—at the Bourne Gallery in Hyannis, Ma. He was here to have Dick Bourne auction off two of the decoys carved by his great-

great-grandfather Nathan Cobb—carved at Cobb's Island years ago, and worth thousands of dollars today. Warren and his sister still own the tip of the "big" Island below the original Coast Guard Station. He thinks the rest of that Island is now owned by the Nature Conservancy, guardian of the Barrier Islands.

In June, 1982, nephew Tommy Brown took his wife Sally and daughter Preston to the Island, hiring a man to take them out there from Oyster—and in July, 1984, Billy Brown took his bride Nancy out there. Billy and Nancy found that in those two years since Tommy had been there, the Island was covered with water—just the Davis house, on its piling, was still there.

And so, the migrating sands that had built up the Island under Grandfather's watchful eye seventy years ago have migrated again—and "little" Cobb's Island is now just a happy memory for the Cardwell family. When I think now of the many details of organization done by Mother and Daddy for our August stay at the Island, I realize it was a real labor of love—done for themselves, and for all of us fortunate enough to have been a part of that place.

From *The Island: A Remembrance of Summers at Little Cobb's Island off the Eastern Shore of Virginia* (N.p.: Author, 1986)

1969
While the Islands Are Still There
HERMAN "HARDTIMES" HUNT

Herman "Hardtimes" Hunt (1906–1974), an Eastern Shore oysterman, newspaperman, humorist, and philosopher, is best remembered for his lively sketches of the passing scene in the seaside village of Oyster. When developers proposed a high-density resort community on Smith's, Myrtle, and Ship Shoal islands in the late 1960s, Hunt joined other conservationists in opposition to the project.

The chain of barrier islands, lying in staggered arrangement in a row averaging seven to eight miles offshore from the Virginia and Maryland Eastern Shores, is gradually moving in toward the mainland. The ocean chews on the eastward beaches; the westward (inshore) side gradually builds as sand settles in the quiet sheltered coves and mudflats.

Some say that within 100 years Smith Island will have crept across Magothy Bay and will be sitting on old Brighton Dock. Farther up, other forecasters allow a century and a half before Cobb and Wreck Islands march in and straddle Oyster; and up at Willis Wharf they say it'll take 500 years for Hog Island to walk over and squat on the doorsteps.

Some of us are alarmed about this 100-year prediction. In this climate, if we're careful on deck so's not to slip over and drown, everybody just figures to live forever—almost. If the sand-reefs come into our yards the ocean will be there too, knockin' and growlin'. Noisy, worrisome, uncomfortable. The 500-year predicters don't even look worried.

In the old days—back around 1900 and in a few places even as late as 1933, year of the Big August Storm—all the islands were inhabited. Hog Island had a self-contained settlement, complete with schoolhouse and church, of about 300 people. They netted sturgeon in spring, brined the caviar in five-gallon kegs, shipped it to market in the fall. They planted oysters, loaded the 2,000 bushel bugeyes, the buy-boats which tied up at

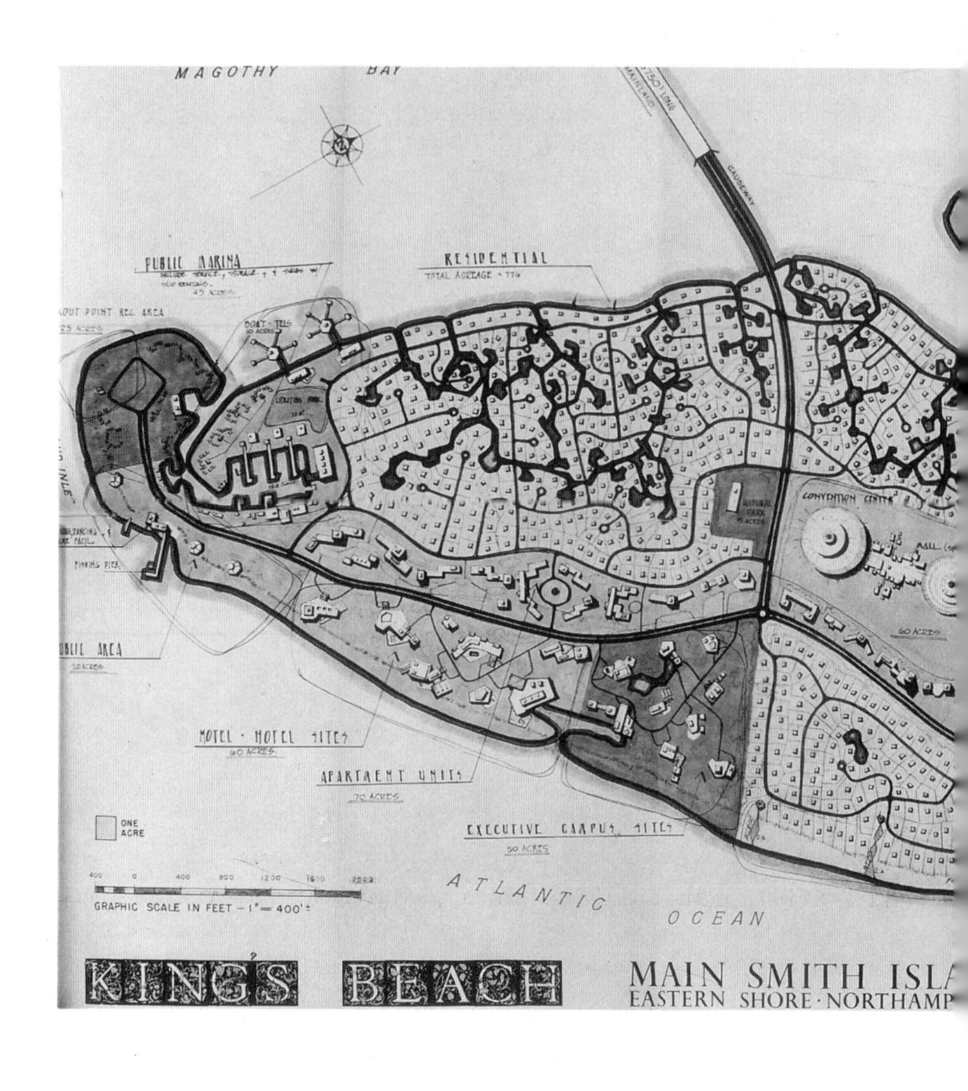
MAGOTHY BAY
CAUSEWAY
PUBLIC MARINA
45 ACRES
BOAT-TELS
RESIDENTIAL
NATURAL PARK
CONVENTION CENTER
60 ACRES
FISHING PIER
20 ACRES
MOTEL · HOTEL SITES
60 ACRES
APARTMENT UNITS
70 ACRES
EXECUTIVE CAMPUS SITES
50 ACRES
ONE ACRE
400 0 400 800 1200 1600 2000
GRAPHIC SCALE IN FEET – 1" = 400'±
ATLANTIC OCEAN
KING'S BEACH
MAIN SMITH ISL
EASTERN SHORE · NORTHAMP

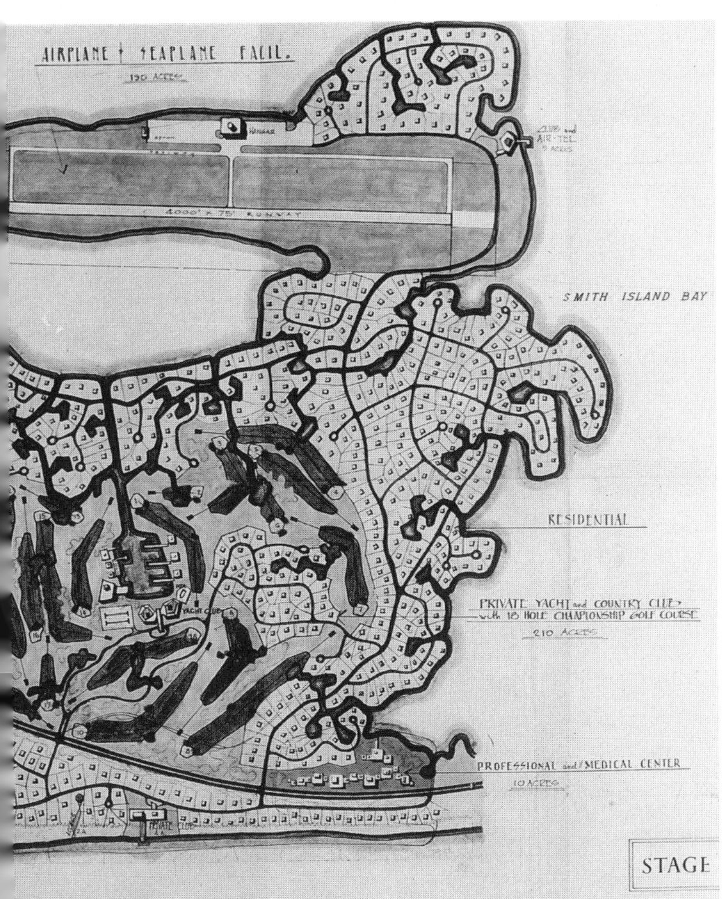
AIRPLANE + SEAPLANE FACIL.
190 ACRES
4000' x 75' RUNWAY
CLUB and AIR-TEL
5 ACRES
SMITH ISLAND BAY
RESIDENTIAL
PRIVATE YACHT and COUNTRY CLUB
with 18 HOLE CHAMPIONSHIP GOLF COURSE
210 ACRES
YACHT CLUB
PROFESSIONAL and MEDICAL CENTER
10 ACRES
PRIVATE CLUB
STAGE
COMPLEX
COUNTY, VIRGINIA
MELVIN M. SPENCE AIA
and ASSOCIATES—ARCHITECTS
4807 COLLEY AVE. NORFOLK, VIRGINIA
EDWARD G. CARSON and ASSOCI
LANDSCAPE ARCHITECTS & PLANN
4505 COLLEY AVE. NORFOLK, VIR

community docks. The storekeeper ran to the mainland once a week for supplies and mail. Mostly the settlement stayed home.

Wes Mitchell said it was a four-mile walk through a big pine forest to go from his father's dock out to Bart Bowen's house, the farthest one out toward the surf. Islanders still speak of the Atlantic Ocean beaches as "The Surf." Wes said when "she began to go" you could lay in bed at night and hear those big tall pine trees popping and exploding as the surf tore them down. They're gone now. Just stumps and roots on the beach.

Grace (Richardson) Tapman, now in her upper 60s, lived on Bone Island when was a small girl. George West Jr., owner of West Oyster Co. in Oyster, lived there during the same time. Grace's father was caretaker for the hunting lodge on the south end of the island and George's father maintained the clubhouse on the north end. Like the others, Bone Island was three or four miles wide with heavy pine forests.

It has since become a sandbar with some marsh hay and "knix" bushes. Some inlets filled and new ones cut themselves in other places so that Bone and Wreck Islands became one. It shows on the chart as Wreck Island.

It's like that with all the islands. They're barren, desolate, wind-eroded and storm-cut now but the "old heads" remember when they were industrious, joyful and sometimes rousing places to live. Each island left a gang of memories within those who lived out there and then moved off when hurricanes began knocking down trees and finally houses.

The Southeast Chapter of Sierra Club, Parkwood Court, Kensington, Md., made a "several months" study of Smith, Myrtle and Ship Shoal Islands, going into the possibility of dense settlement by summer-home owners and concessionaires; explored for availability of adequate water supply, for results from sewage treatment and disposal, for potential damage, silting and redistribution of natural wildlife and seafood habitat—and in a 26-page report expressed total opposition to any development or building on these islands.

The Smith Island Development Corp. is proceeding with surveys and tests to promote the feasibility of selling homesites and commercial resort locations on Smith Island, with anticipated expansion northward to Wreck (formerly Bone, now Ship Shoal Island on the charts) and Myrtle Islands. Their prospectus tells of 5,350 homesites (to be) surveyed on Smith Island, with ocean frontage to sell for $1,000 to $2,000 per front foot. Anticipated total sales from land, before the buyer builds on his lot, is $500 million to $600 million. Profits to the initiators should run $100 million to $300 million; cost of promoting, $15 million. So says the prospectus.

An Army Engineer's report of July 15, 1968, says, in part: "Due to their eroded condition and exposure to full force of Atlantic storms . . . it is not believed that any of the barrier islands should be developed for residential purpose."

In this story, which purposely rambles and dodges all over the years and beaches, so nobody may attribute to it support or dissent for anybody's plans or recommendations, the writer is attempting to link together a series of little experiences typical of the Islands' past, a brief description of their present condition—and the reader's guess about their future is as good as this writer's guess.

On second thought, one brief departure from the no-option method. The Islands are wonderful now, just like they are. You can anchor in an inshore cove and not sleep a wink all night and be glad you stayed awake. The surf booms and bangs over on the other side, gulls fly by and mullet jump and splash. You're out there with peace such as is unknown a few miles to westward in the civilization you just left. Out where there's nobody next door. No neighbor comes cussin' and threatenin' because your kid let the air out of his tires.

On third thought, the Hell with the Impartial Attitude! The Islands can look out for themselves. Nature can maintain its balance. If they're creeping toward the mainland, beaches eroding and inshore side filling, it's a slow creep. They won't be in our laps for many and many a year. It would be to Virginia's everlasting shame and disgrace if trusting people from the cities bought a dream and watched a hurricane knock it down; maybe drown during the watching. A hurricane over the islands is a fearful thing.

Fifty years ago you fought your way across the islands, through the pine forests, with a bush in each hand; slapping your back and fanning furiously at clouds of mosquitos. A mosquito is a frail thing, compared to big trees and houses—but trees and houses went down before the storms and the mosquitos survived.

Back around 1925 Larrimore Cushman, retired owner of Cushman Bakeries in New York, bought Mockhorn Island. This is one of the sheltered ones, lying between Myrtle Island and the mainland—just as Chincoteague lies in the lee of Assateague. Cushman built a splendid dwelling; built big barns, cleared off fields and planted alfalfa hay. Bought a herd of Angus cattle. It was real pretty. Green fields, Western-style barns. A herd of Angus cattle out on the sandbars, standing in water over their backs. Mosquitos. People say that up on Assateague where the "wild" ponies breed, sometimes the ponies run all night to brush off the insects.

Fortunately the state bought Mockhorn Island for a game preserve. Most of Assateague is a federal preserve. That's their best use, for the birds and beasts. A duck can eat a mosquito and a mink can go underground if they attack. Cows and ponies can't do either.

Cobb Island had a life-saving corps, forerunner of the Coast Guard; men who went out in whale boats propelled by oars to rescue survivors from sailing ships that missed the entrance to Chesapeake Bay. Smith Island had another corps. The last vessel to go aground was the *Massassoit,* a five-master running light to Norfolk to load fertilizer. She lay on her side on the outer bar for two years, finally breaking up.

While the *Massassoit* lay on the bar Paul Travis and three associates sailed a four-master right through the bar and out to deep water. This one had come ashore in a heavy blow and washed across the bar into an inshore slough. Paul and associates contracted with the underwriters to return her to deep water. They stayed aboard. Whenever there was an offshore wind they'd put up all sails and let her push into the bar. For inshore winds they'd kedge her, keeping the windlass taut. Surge and surf washed around her, loosening sand at the bow and compacting it in space opened astern. Paul says every now and then you'd feel her "slip an inch ahead."

It took six months to sail-and-kedge 12 feet of draft through six feet of water, and six feet of sandbar. On the day of liberation they split $5,000. Time sold cheap in the old days.

Besides its lifesaving corps, Cobb Island had a settlement north of the station and a resort hotel complex—hotel, barroom, dance hall—and church at a respectable distance on the inshore side. Bill Nottingham, oldest man anywhere around before he passed away ten years ago, remembered that "ol' man Cobb" spent most of his time planting bushes and marsh hay to hold the sand around his property. He recalled that a New

York outfit came down, bought the hotel rights and cleaned up the place. Scraped off every bush and tuft of grass. Left only clean, white sand. That's when she began to go.

Oscar Brady, now 82, lived in the Cobb Island settlement when his father, Frank Brady, was caretaker at the hotel. Oscar says they had a ferris wheel—"prettiest thing you ever saw; painted red, white an' blue"—installed on pilings at the edge of the inlet. The tide turned it; turned one way on flood tide an' the other way on ebb tide. There was a braking arrangement for stopping the wheel so people could get on seats set above the paddle wheel blades. It was free. Part of the hotel's service.

People who came from the barroom could only ride the wheel on flood tide. If they slipped off on ebb tide they'd go out to sea but on flood tide they'd take up on a mudbar somewhere.

"All in one week," says Oscar, "the whole business slid right in the inlet. Sand had blowed away and tide undercut the bank. When you clean up a beach it don't stay there. A few stayed in the barroom until she began to slide but they got out. Stood on the church steps an' cried."

Oscar estimates that no less than 10 people have drowned around Cobb Island during his lifetime. Tide is treacherous, strong undertow around the inlets. Last couple that drowned there was back around 1930 when people still went on picnics, dressing in the abandoned church and in the remaining outbuildings. The girl got in trouble in shallow water. Boy went out to help and undertow—maybe a shark—got him. Girl drowned in three feet of water, just rolling over and over. Boy was never found.

Hog Island had three burying grounds. When the first Old Settlers went over and set up a settlement on the south end the Indians just moved northward and let them have half the island. Cliff Doughty, proprietor of Doughty's Solid-and-Liquid Grocery store in Oyster, says accounts of the settler-and-Indian occupancy came down through his family from the earliest Doughty.

Cliff says the Indians smoked their dead; put them on pole racks and smoked them like a Smithfield ham. After the curing, the earliest known embalming, was completed they'd build a dome of poles and sod over the deceased. Cliff says when he lived there before the 1933 storm some of the old Indian mounds were still up in the brambles and thorn bushes on the north end of Hog Island.

The strangers Burying Ground, for those who washed ashore off ships and wrecks, was in the island's center. Their own cemetery was down toward the south end, well inshore from the beach. In 1955 Cliff and Granville McCready and the writer went over to Hog Island. Cliff showed us where the pine forest had been. Pointed way out there in the surf, saying that some houses had been as much as a mile out there—when it was forest instead of ocean. The graveyard was on the beach, caskets tipped and washed in every direction. Cliff hasn't been back since but he guesses they're all gone now.

On that day we saw some mink on the beach and some muskrat in the inshore coves. Mink would run down the beach and up to the top of a stump. The beach is nothing but stumps, some still in place with roots spreading—held in place by taproots. A wave would come in and if a mink saw some little fish or shrimp get caught in the roots he'd dash down and grab it—returning to top of stump before the next wave.

Looked right pitiful. Just mink, muskrats, white heron standing in the coves. Caskets tipped every which way.

Years ago somebody released some jackrabbits on Cobb Island. These have increased rapidly, despite periodic hunting. Some have crossed channels to the other islands, presumably on debris during storms because nobody has ever seen a jackrabbit swim. Hunters who go after them with dogs say if they run a jack down to water's edge he will turn and fight his way through the dogs before he'll wet a foot.

It is unreliably reported that somebody lost a female beagle hound on one of the lower islands and later crossbreeding produced some jackhounds. Nobody has seen these animals, everybody tells of someone else who has seen one. Through the relay, it's said to be a strange sight to see a black and white spotted jackrabbit wagging his tail, barking on the trail of a deer.

There is also a story about a "great speckled bird," usually seen at night around Myrtle or Wreck Islands. At least a half dozen people have seen this monster but each description varies. Averaged together, this bird stands 6 feet tall on heron legs; has a head like a fishhawk and mottled gray-and-brown feathers somewhat like the big winter gulls. He flies low over the marshes and coves, looking for fish or jackrabbits. When he sees a rabbit in the high marsh he whistles, like a man whistling to his dog.

The whistling stops the jack in his tracks. Bird goes over and plucks rabbit from the grass.

It just goes to show that animals and birds, conventional or outrageous breeds, naturally gravitate to the islands. Some fly there, some swim there and some go by raft. It's a place for wild things. Man hasn't civilized the Islands yet. They're clean—and peaceful.

From the *Washington Post*, 11 December 1969

1987

The Ultimate Edge

TOM HORTON

Tom Horton (1945–), a native of the Eastern Shore of Maryland, has written about the environment for the past two decades for the Baltimore Sun. *His lifelong interest in the Chesapeake Bay region has found expression in* Bay Country *(1987), a series of essays for which Horton won the John Burroughs Medal; in* Turning the Tide *(1990), a report card on the ecological health of the Chesapeake; and in* An Island out of Time *(1996), a memoir of life on Smith Island, Maryland. In 1987 a visit to Parramore Island moved Horton to reflect on change and continuity on the barrier islands.*

Even as we moor on the island's marshy backside, miles from the beach, the Atlantic surf murmurs, a gentle stimulus that urges us forward, beckons on levels remote from our everyday senses. Some birds, more acute receptors of subsonic vibrations than we, are thought to tune in on such surfy mutterings for orientation from hundreds of miles away as they follow age-old migratory flight paths up and down the interior of North America. We feel on no less urgent business this early spring day, eager to be on the edge of things. Edges have always produced phenomena that are among the most interesting in nature—the great migrations of fish and fowl triggered by the intersections of the seasons; the abundance and diversity of wildlife known to any hunter who stalks the junctures of forest and field; and the fantastic habitats of the tide marshes at the merge of land and water. Parramore Island is one of the literal and most unsullied edges of the American landscape, lying five miles off the mainland of Virginia's Eastern Shore and sixty miles south of Salisbury.

At seven thousand longitudinal acres extending about twelve miles between Wachapreague and Quinby inlets, it is the largest and most magnificently forested in a fifty-one-mile chain of coastal barrier islands preserved from development during the 1970s by the Nature Conservancy. In a third of a century the conservancy has purchased many of the most environmentally precious parts of America. Of the approximately one million acres of marsh, mountain, prairie, forest, bog, and barrens thus protected, the Virginia barrier islands are considered by many of its officials to the crowning effort, and Parramore Island the jewel in the crown. The Conservancy calls its acquisition the Virginia Coast Reserve, as if it were some uncommon and treasured old spirits; and indeed this is vintage wild seacoast, an unspoiled ecosystem of beach and dune and salt marsh that can only rarify with age as the trend to make more Ocean Cities, Hilton Heads, and Miami Beaches continues to spread throughout the rest of the barrier islands that stretch from Labrador to Corpus Christi.

In the acquisition of Parramore and its sister islands there seems hope for humanity, a hearteningly ironic recycling of capital. The purchases were enabled by substantial grants from the foundation of Mary Flagler Carey, whose grandfather, Henry Morrison Flagler, made the family fortune by pioneering the development of a set of similar coastal islands farther south at a place called Miami. Parramore easily could have met the same fate. "Were it located 100 miles north it would become one of the most famous resorts in the world; Atlantic City, Cape May, Asbury Park, would all sink into insignificance when compared with this favorable isle," trumpeted a history of the region published in 1903. Since that was written, there have been schemes to log the island, to drill it for oil, and to use it as a military bombing range. The only thing that succeeded was goats. Left there by early settlers, their population had grown by the 1940s to where passing ships often remarked on the white-flecked shores of Parramore. The goats met their Waterloo when the island's private owner imported several dozen crack cowhands and sheepdogs from Texas. The roundup was spectacular enough to draw coverage in the 23 January 1950 issue of *Life.* More than three thousand goats were corralled and sold for meat and for the manufacture of antirabies serum.

Last Memorial Day weekend, when a reported half-million people were packing onto a dozen or so miles of sand just north, in Ocean City, Maryland, conservancy officials flew over the chain of beaches in the Coast Reserve, which are open to day use. They counted ninety people in more than fifty miles, and forty-five of those were in one party. That kind of isolation, now assured in perpetuity by the conservancy, still rankles certain development interests and elected officials on the sleepy, lower part of the Delmarva Peninsula. They had dreamed of bridges, with Disney Worlds and a generally unlimited tax base to follow.

The mood of the local boomers was not helped by what happened to Metomkin Island, whose owners had refused to sell it at any price for inclusion in a reserve that would only "lock it up forever." When a company calling itself Offshore Islands, Inc., finally bought Metomkin, more than a few locals cheered to see the nature lovers get their comeuppance—until they found out that Offshore Islands was a dummy corporation created by the conservancy. The Accomack County commissioners, in retaliation, voted not to recognize the Coast Reserve's designation as an "internationally important biosphere" by the United Nations. The United Nations stated that in years to come the reserve would serve as an example against which we may compare the long stretches of overcrowded, despoiled, and ravaged coastlines of our continent.

So it is that there is no hotelier, no marina, no human occupant to welcome us to Parramore, only a great blue heron who startles up from a tidemarsh gut, rasping with all the indignation of a rightful owner. That the herons are the duly appointed sentinels of every edge where land and water effect a marshy interface, I have never had a doubt. From the smallest headwater bogs of the bay's tributary creeks to the eye-stretching sweeps of Atlantic salt marsh, a heron is present in every season. The heron's family, *Ardeidae,* which includes egrets and bitterns, is old even as their fellow birds go, having emerged during the lower Eocene some sixty million years ago. The race has proven astoundingly adaptable. The fossil and historical record shows that of seventy-seven lines along which the heron's clan evolved throughout all its time on earth, sixty-one still survive, and only one of these is considered endangered today. The great blue heron fits better than any creature I know with our region's thousands of miles of shoreline. He is lord of the edge, and we acknowledge his sovereignty: "Other birds have nicknames, glossies for ibis, seaswallows for terns, etc.," writes Phillip Kopper in his fine book on beaches, *The Wild Edge,* "but some things never get nicknames—Oliver Wendell Holmes, Martin Luther King . . . Great Blue Heron."

We have come from Quinby on the mainland in a sixteen-foot flat-bottomed skiff with a 9.9-horsepower Evinrude, which is laboring to push the four of us with field gear and fifty pounds of lunch (a bushel of oysters). The skiff has many times proven adequate transportation on the bay side of the peninsula, but it seems uncomfortably frail out here, even though the day is calm enough. There simply is more and rawer energy flowing around these sea islands than on the gentler Chesapeake. Tides are several feet greater and currents rip at a fierce pace; and the inlets of the gray-green Atlantic, wracked with shoals and breakers, are never far from sight or mind. We hang the bushel of oysters from an old piling in one fast-running tidal gut. The oysters, tonged that morning near Kent Island from water that was nearly fresh, will have become salty as Chincoteagues from filtering the seawater when we return for them in eight hours. The marshes where we debark on the island are unexpectedly firm footing to one accustomed to sinking thigh-deep into similar-looking terrain on the bay side. Even the bottoms of the tidal guts are swept clean of muck by the amplitude of the tide.

The biotic production here is enormous; the marsh crunches beneath every step of our hip boots. I estimate that in one area covering several acres there is close to a pound of shucked meat from just the mussels and oysters growing on every square foot. Add to that a thick crop of periwinkles and fiddler crabs, the estimated ten tons per acre of organic matter flushed annually into the aquatic food chain, the habitat for nesting black ducks and the nursery provided the young of ninety-six species of fish. Agriculture can yield some pretty impressive production figures too—we raise our chickens to four pounds in eight or nine weeks, in only a square foot or so of space per bird; but those systems take constant inputs of purchased energies like feed, heat, light, medicines, and human labor. The sea island does it all for the price of being let alone; and does it more prettily than any chicken farm I have known.

A second surf, the breeze in the tops of old growth pines that stretch eighty feet or more, rolls far above our heads as we enter the forest of Parramore Island. Spaced well apart, the pines preside over a cinnamon carpet of needles so thick that no seedling, and scarcely even a greenbrier, penetrates their surface for acre after acre. No landscaped and tended English park could be neater, or more ordered, airy, and spacious. Some of the scientists brought here by the conservancy say this is an ecosystem forged by frequent natural fires, which keep all undergrowth from gaining a hold, but cannot damage the mature pines with their inches-thick bark. At least a partial explanation, others say, has to be the foraging on the undergrowth that went on so long by the goats prior to the 1950 roundup. The island's abundant deer herd seems to have taken up the goats' lawn-mower role, as every shoot of greenbrier that has poked through the needles appears to have been browsed. It is an eerily quiet hike for some distance. Footfalls are muffled by the needles, and the cathedral effect of the great forest suppresses conversation; but in the hush, all around us rage the storms of centuries ago, frozen in fantastic, windsculpted forms of dead and dying giant cedars interspersed among the pines. The cedars, traditional early colonizers of sand dunes on barrier islands, far predate the pines, which themselves are more than a century old. When the cedars were young, the ancient dunes on which Parramore's forest grows were hard by the ocean, rooted in barely stabilized agglomerations of sand and beach grass, bearing the full brunt of waves and storms.

Now they are more than a mile back from the modern beach front. One great cedar, still living, is buried in the dune up to its first crotch, where it still measures a full twelve feet around. Its limbs and the grain of its trunk have grown corkscrewed in a clockwise direction. To rest in the silent, storm-sculpted forest, beneath the sixty-foot spread of such a tree is like entering a temple; it invites contemplation. How did you come here, old cedar? How many years have you seen? And what furies shaped you like this?

It makes invigorating walking to cut a sinewy cedar staff that will come about nose-high, and inhaling with every step the incredible aromatic essence, a perfume several centuries in the making. It takes a little while longer in the forest to realize why there is something different about this island than any place we have been before. This is not a walked-in place. Unlike the other islands in the reserve, it is closed to the public entirely because of a private owner's retention of recreational rights from the conservancy for several years. You come upon things here you don't find in other outdoor spots— the delicate plumes of a snowy egret hanging from a pine branch; and the skeleton of a red-tailed hawk, complete down to the talons. The bear, wolf, bobcat, and puma that once prowled these sea islands are said to be extirpated here, but it is easy to imagine different. Animal sign from fox, raccoon, and white-tailed deer is all over, not yet confined by human intrusions to narrow trails through the thickets as in most "natural" places.

It might not seem that most forests or parks, even in eastern America, are all that overrun, or disrupted, but consider just one aspect of our expedition to Parramore. The four of us, almost unthinking, broke off perhaps a half-dozen branches from the island's magnificently gnarled cedars for walking sticks in the space of an hour. Multiply that by, say, fifty visitors a day, a light usage for a twelve-square-mile island, and it adds up to thousands of branches stripped off each year. In a decade or two, the appearance of that forest would be substantially different from the way we found it, although few newcomers would think the island much altered. And egret plumes and hawk skeletons, as well as the delicate sand dollars and lustrous conch shells that now litter the beaches, would be rare finds indeed. After talking this over at lunch, we carefully picked up the peanut shells we tossed away earlier. They would degrade after a while, but one begins to feel more obligation than that after a short time here.

Some day the Nature Conservancy may face a decision on whether to allow public use of Parramore, and to what degree. Their current programs range from the last refuge for a blind salamander in Texas, from which even most researchers are prohibited, to a tract thirty miles from Manhattan that is only closed temporarily whenever foot traffic threatens to wear out the trails. As for Parramore, I, who have already had the pleasure of it so unspoiled, would prefer it remain just that way, with, of course, just one visit permitted me every spring. As for the other ten million or so people within a day's drive of the Coast Reserve, I suspect they would agree—as long as each of them, too, could visit occasionally . . . "Just me, maybe a couple of friends, we'll keep it quiet; too many people, sure, it would spoil the place in a minute . . ."

It seems strange to talk of preserving anything unchanged on a coastal barrier island like Parramore, because constant alteration and everlasting impermanence is the order of the day on these, the most dynamic land forms know to geology. It is most obvious on the ocean side, where Atlantic breakers of palest, icy jade pound a broad, firm-packed beach wide enough to land 747 jets. All this horizontality, stretching uncluttered as far as the eye can see in either direction, is fully as pleasing and renewing to the spirit as any snow-capped mountain wilderness.

The wreck of a nineteenth-century schooner, her bones protruding from the surf, draws our attention. She is built so massively, double-planked with foot thick timber, fastened to 14-by-14 inch ribs with wooden pegs an inch in diameter, surely she must have borne gold or other heavy treasure (an inspection of the records later downgrades that somewhat—her cargo was guano fertilizer). During the decades the wreck has disappeared and reemerged as ocean storms and currents played serve and volley with the island, fattening the beach here, gnawing at it there, breaching the entire island in a single storm, closing the inlet back up in the next one.

The emerging specialty of coastal geology is documenting in places like Parramore how the barrier islands actually depend on storms, and on their own instability, to survive. The periodic overwash of the islands by storm tides carries sand to the islands' backsides, providing the marshes there enough substrate to keep ahead of a sea level that has been rising, trying to submerge them, since the glaciers of the last ice age began to melt. In a time when the seas were lower, and miles more of the continental shelf was high and dry land, the barriers existed, in much the same shape as they do now, miles offshore of their present location. They have survived by literally rolling over themselves, migrating ever landward as the mainland submerges. Ecological banana peels, they have been called. Someday, if sea level continues to rise, the Atlantic rollers may lap at the shores of the Appalachians; and there, a few miles offshore, will likely be a version of Parramore Island and its sisters in the coast reserve. The current island, with its unusually extensive forests, seems more secure than that; but Hog Island just to the south once was similarly forested and seemingly just as secure. Now uninhabited, it held four hundred people as recently as 1933. Since 1871 parts of Hog retreated toward the mainland nearly a half-mile, even as other portions of the island advanced seaward by 3,300 feet. Dunes there that towered an impregnable 80 feet, sheltering a forest behind them, have been reduced to nubs.

Parramore has not exactly stood still either. Although the long-term net movement, driven by rising sea level, has been landward, the islands tend to wander widely in both directions, controlled by shorter shifts in the currents, which bring them the sand that is their lifeblood. In 1852 Parramore was nearly a mile further seaward at its southern tip than it is now; and from 1852 to 1911 it accreted 600 feet in its midsection. In a film shot in geologic time, the barrier islands would flicker back and forth across the screen like Keystone Kops, or a cancan line. What the Nature Conservancy has acquired out here on the continent's wildest edge goes well beyond the usual plants and animals. It is preserving a natural process of land formation so dynamic as to constitute a living system in its own right. The process is correctly known as migration, because for the most part it does not involve an overall loss of sand, only shifts in its shape and location. It is only when people try to anchor their condo-castles on these, earth's most dynamic land forms, that the barrier islands are said to be "unstable," and natural migration becomes an "erosion problem."

The light is beginning to fall in long, oblique slants across the island now. Up and down the beach the rich, late-afternoon rays pick out auburn little foxes detaching themselves from the shadows of the dunes to forage on whatever the sea has tossed up. Walking back, we notice a small pine forest being enveloped by dunes, cresting over it in slow motion as if transmitting the rawer, faster fury of the ocean combers. The trees are dying, bent toward the mainland, bare branches entreating skyward. Nothing that is too well-rooted can last here, I think, and I think about the billions of dollars poured into stabilizing the barrier islands at Miami, Cape Hatteras, along the Jersey coast, and other places in this lovely, shifting chain of sand that runs intermittently from Labrador to Texas.

During the boat ride back to the mainland, a sea fog begins rolling in through Quinby Inlet. No "little cat feet" to this dreadnaught. It has on seven-league boots, moving lots faster than a 9.9-horsepower Evinrude can push a skiff. By the time we dock, you cannot see the mouth of the harbor one hundred feet away. The next day's forecast is high winds and near freezing. You can't count on late March in these regions; but we have plucked enough blossoms from the Virginia sea islands on this voyage to stead us well into warmer weather.

From *Bay Country* (Baltimore: Johns Hopkins Univ. Press, 1987), pp. 127–34

1993

Beachcombing

CURTIS J. BADGER

Curtis J. Badger (1945–), a native Eastern Shoreman whose "seaside" roots extend back several generations, is the former editor of the Eastern Shore News *and of* Wildfowl Art. *His award-winning writing has appeared in several hundred magazine articles and nearly two dozen books. Here, Badger muses on the sensual nature of the wild beaches, the fidelity of the tides, and the limitless possibilities of nature.*

In Tom I see myself, as if I were looking at an old photograph from the family album. I stand next to our black Ford sedan while Jim, my father's English setter, nuzzles my leg. I'm wearing my Sunday suit and smiling at the camera. It must have been Easter.

I see the same smile in Tom, the innocence and trust of a six-year-old. He is experiencing what I experienced, and through him I relive my childhood. I am my father. I am my son.

Out of school, Tom spends the summer with me. In the early mornings I work as he sleeps, then he has a leisurely breakfast, watches TV, rides his bike, plays in the woods behind our house. A stick becomes a sword, a gun. His bike is a motorcycle, a truck. Our yard, so familiar, can be instantly transformed in the mind of a six-year-old to something exotic and adventurous. It is a kind of alchemy. In the half-light of the pine woods, shadows become friend and foe. I know them well.

In the afternoons we run errands—go the post office, buy groceries—and then we'll go out in the boat, perhaps fish for a while, go clamming, or hike the island beaches. Tom enjoys fishing if the fish are plentiful, but he prefers to be on the beach. When he is older, he will learn that part of the pleasure of fishing comes from waiting. But at six, Tom is not a good waiter. His relationship with the islands is sensual, not intellectual or contemplative. He likes the feel of coarse, wet sand on bare feet; the cold of the ocean; the power of the current; the thunderous noise of breaking surf, which is unlike any sound man can make. He likes the cries of the terns and skimmers; the discovery of jingle shells glistening at the water's edge; the delicacy of surf foam; the immensity of the ocean, sky, and beach; the thrill of being part of something wild and undefinable.

Those were my feelings, too, when my father first brought me to the islands. I must have been Tom's age. I remember most of all the power of the ocean, the wonderful thunder of crashing surf, the wildness of it all, as if we were being allowed to witness some private and intimate side of nature . . . as if we were voyeurs.

That first impression left an indelible mark on me, as I hope it will on Tom, something of a birthmark, a birthright. It would not have been the same if we had gone to a seashore resort with thousands of people, restaurants and amusement parks, hotels, boardwalks, lifeguards, and signs warning us away from the carefully built dunes. Perhaps the reason we are unwilling to preserve the last of America's wilderness beach is that we simply don't know better. Most of us are introduced to the beach at an ocean resort or, at best, a state park or national seashore, where the senses are bombarded with screaming children, pungent suntan oil, and hot asphalt. We share the beach elbow to elbow with too many near-naked strangers, each group establishing its own little community marked by a beach blanket and umbrella, intending and desiring no communication with the others. Eye contact is avoided, as if attempting to perpetuate the illusion of being alone.

As wild beaches have disappeared, more Americans have been denied the intimacy with nature—the voyeurism—that imprints upon us at an early age the wildness and power of the ocean, of the planet. At age six, tuned in to the sensual, we see beaches not as extraordinary places but as just another amusement park were we must stand in line to use the toilet.

Tom responds to the ocean by taking off his shoes, jumping out of the boat as soon as it is beached, and racing to the surf. Like a little sandpiper, he runs toward the breakers as they retreat, then races them up the berm of the beach as they come crashing in. In August his legs and back are tanned by the sun, his hair bleached nearly blond. His eyes flash as the cold water laps at his ankles, as a breaker catches him from behind.

Tom doesn't talk about the power of the ocean, the evidence it provides of the immensity and infinity of the universe. He is storing up sensual elements—sights, smells, textures, sounds—and these will over the years blend together, mixing flavors and aromas, until one day he will realize that the sum of the parts is a wonderful whole.

Forty years after I began collecting the sensual elements, I'm still trying to define them, to explain the joy that comes from being there. Perhaps now it goes beyond my sensual inventory, the sounds of the surf, the beauty of the ocean, the wild birds. It is a blend of these, yet more. It is important to be alone, I think, and to have as few reminders as possible of the nearness of civilization—that is, no roads, parking lots, boardwalks, hotels, tourists. Then I can concentrate on the real issues: the ebb and flood, the empty horizon, which requires the power of imagination to see around; the ocean's remarkable physical power, which comes from no discernible source. Some call the experience religious, spiritual. Perhaps it is. Perhaps standing alone at the sea's edge we are close to something we cannot define or comprehend, beginning to get our feet wet.

I enjoy learning more about it. I read the field guides and scientific papers, and I talk to experts. I study coastal dynamics, watch the island birds come and go, examine grains of beach sand with a hand-held microscope bought at the local Radio Shack. These are rewarding little tasks, but they do not satisfy me completely. I store facts as if I were laying in supplies for a hurricane: flashlight, radio, extra batteries, food, water. Yet it gives me a surprisingly incomplete amount of satisfaction that I can identify the birds wading in a salt pond or can explain the workings of marsh grass.

When walking the beach, what I enjoy most is not the process of identification and cataloging but the prospect that I might stumble upon something remarkable, a spear point, perhaps, or the fossilized bone of some extinct creature, some tangible link between our time and another, a totem of sorts. Once I found the fossilized inner ear bone of a whale lying at the base of a dune, washed up by a recent storm. It looked at first like a small, misshapen human skull. Then it looked like a giant tooth. An anthropologist from the Smithsonian Institution visited a few weeks after I found the bone and identified it. He gave me a diagram of the whale skull and highlighted the inner ear bone with a yellow marker.

Twelve thousand years ago forests grew on what now is ocean floor. The barrier beaches and salt marshes were fifty or sixty miles east of here, and prehistoric creatures grazed on ancient grasses where we now fish for tuna. This tickles the imagination, to know that a northeast storm could dislodge some wonderful artifact and send it to shore.

But they are rare. Mostly we find common treasures: jingle shells, limpets, cockles, moon snails, arks, clams, scallops, and tiny snails such as wentletraps and ceriths. Jingle shells are thin, fragile, and nearly transparent. Pick up a few and put them in your pocket, and they jingle like loose change. When wet with seawater, they glitter like shiny coins. Some are white, some orange, some nearly black. They are related to razor clams, the long, thin, bivalves shaped like straight razors. Tom picks them up as we walk the beach. He wants to string them together to make a decoration for the Christmas tree.

The beach, when unpaved and untrammeled by human visitors, is a busy community. In May, terns, skimmers, and plovers nest in the shell litter beyond the berm of the beach. Sea turtles lumber ashore at night and laboriously dig cavities in the sand in which they deposit dozens of leathery eggs. Predators are at work. A fish crow digs up turtle eggs as soon as the exhausted mother disappears at dawn into the breakers. A great black-backed gull steals a tern chick. A fox raids a plover nest.

On a day in late August, Tom and I found a dead herring gull. It was an immature bird, with the smoky gray markings of youth. It had probably hatched earlier in the summer and had somehow met its demise off Metomkin Island. It could have been caught in a fisherman's net and drowned, then washed ashore. There were no visible markings indicating a violent death.

Beneath the gull a ghost crab had dug a den and was going about the process of dismantling the bird, beginning with the most accessible morsels, the eyes and brain. The crab hid in its den as we inspected the bird, no doubt wishing we would leave before another flood tide swept his catch back out to sea. All around the gull were the tracks of the busy ghost crab, and I could imagine him, once his den was built, circling and inspecting his great find, probing it here and there, not actually settling down to feed yet but prancing about in some sort of ghost crab wonder, thanking whatever crab deity he believed in for his great good luck.

On the beach is the beginning of life. The sea turtles that survive detection eventually hatch, and like miniature versions of their mothers plod down the berm of the beach toward the sea. The piping plovers that survive the tides, foxes, fish crows, and ghost crabs become adult birds, and in the fall they fly south. Also on the beach are other signs of success. The black egg casing of a clearnose skate has washed up. The casing has been split open and its occupant has departed, presumably to begin feeding on the small fish and shrimp of the estuary.

We find egg casings of channeled and knobbed whelks; each case, about the size of a quarter, is attached to the next by a stout membrane. Some strings of egg casings may be two feet or more in length, and each translucent compartment holds, or held, dozens of miniature whelks. The casing of the knobbed whelk has a flat edge, while the edge of the channeled whelk casing is sharp. Now and then, if you slice open a casing with a knife, you can find a few tiny whelk shells inside, homes of the few animals that did not make it. But mostly the casings are filled with sand, which they picked up while tumbling around in the surf.

At summer's end our back porch is filled with island treasures. We have dozens of limpets, fascinating little shells in gray or orange that look like miniature volcanoes. We have bits of coral and lacy little stones that actually are colonies of tiny animals called bryozoans, which often build their communities around a pebble or shell. Large clam shells or the shells of sea scallops are put to use in the kitchen as individual serving dishes for deviled crab or clam. I collect a few large ark shells for a friend who carves wooden decoys. Arks have well-defined ribs, which my friend uses to paint the vermiculated feather detail on the sides of duck decoys. He dabs the shell in paint, then presses it onto the wooden carving, transposing a likeness of feathers. There are sand dollars; the purple-specked shells of lady crabs; an unidentified fossilized bone, possibly a shark vertebra; and the jagged tail of a horseshoe crab. It is an eclectic and totally worthless collection, valuable only for the reminders it provides of the beach.

The charm of a wilderness beach lies not in what is there, but in the promise of what it might yield on the next trip or in what might lie around the next set of dunes. The value of an island wilderness is not measured by the known, but by the unknown. The real worth of wilderness is that it keeps alive the six-year-old in us; it demands imagination, curiosity, faith, trust, and a childlike ability to see beyond the horizon.

In an ancient and fossilized oyster shell, much larger than those currently growing in the marsh, we have a link with that world now covered by the sea and separated from us by some twelve thousand years. The oyster grew in the Pleistocene marshes and fed some hunter-gatherer who plucked it from a cluster of shells, chipped its edge with a stone, and sucked out its salty meat and juices. He lived somewhere off the present coast, building fires in an ancient forest long flooded, scavenging the marshes and beaches as I do today, prying clams from the mud for his dinner. I wonder what he thought as he walked along the beach. With his belly full of oyster meat, did he look to the ocean, at the horizon curving away, and wonder?

People who have lived along the coast tend to be religious. Perhaps it has something to do with our nearness to the unknown, the constant reminders of the infinity of the universe, the presence of powers beyond our control. To survive, we must have faith. We must believe that the tides will flood only so far, and then they will ebb. It is high water at noon today, and by six this evening it will be low. Tomorrow, the cycle will advance by about forty minutes. We know the truth of tides, and we live to their rhythms, although we can do nothing to alter the ebb and flood, which is connected to the spin of the earth, the orbit of the moon, barometric pressure, the mysterious push and pull of unseen powers. Yet the process is precise and predictable; those of us who live on the coast stake our lives on it.

Storms often push the tides higher than normal, flooding low areas of the mainland, but such occurrences are business as usual for the estuarine system. A northeaster, for example, blows the water toward the land while the moon's gravity pulls it, building tides higher than normal. Water becomes "stacked up" in the salt marsh creeks because the wind pushes it in during flood tide and hampers its departure as the tide ebbs. But still the tide will turn at approximately the appointed hour, and although it might not recede as much as usual, it will eventually recede.

We trust implicitly in the tidal cycles, planning our fishing and clamming trips to coincide with the period of tide that gives us the best advantage, even choosing our homesites just beyond the reach of the highest tides. We seldom stop to comprehend the efficiency and dependability of the phenomenon. What if one day it were to fail? What if one day the tide neglected to ebb and instead reached the point of high tide and continued to rise, pressing landward for another six hours, and another six after that? If the average tidal change is five feet, then by missing a single ebb cycle, the tide would rise ten feet above mean high water. The result would be catastrophic. In populated areas, businesses, homes, and schools would be flooded, damage would be in the millions, and there would be loss of life. In rural areas, fertile farmland and forests would be poisoned by salt water, waterfront villages inundated, boats torn from their moorings, docks and piers uprooted, and inlets and channels resculpted. A single lapse in the mechanics of tidal change would devastate the landscape, at least temporarily, and it would destroy our faith in the powers of the coastal system. Families would pack their station wagons and head for Nebraska. Great bargains would be found in waterfront property.

So strong is our faith in the immutability of the tides that we gather by the millions just out of harm's way, building our homes, playgrounds, offices, and schools just beyond the longest lick of high water. Building on the ocean beach, however, has more to do with foolishness than faith. While the process of ebb and flood is dependable, its exactness is cushioned by a margin of storms and other atmospheric conditions that blur the precision of the tide tables. While the ebb and flood are dependable, nature sometimes adds surprises.

The surprises, I think, are important. On the beach, we sense a nearness to a force of great power and mystery. It is as if we were testing a sleeping giant, tickling his feet as he slumbers. A northeast storm, or the approach of a hurricane, excites us in a peculiar way, and although we acknowledge the danger, we are somehow drawn to it, as if being allowed to witness one of nature's more intimate moments, a rare opportunity to become voyeurs once again.

While studying the barrier islands and salt marshes provides evidence of things seen, I think it is important also to experience the islands on a different level, and this can be done in a wilderness setting, where the distractions are kept to a minimum. The most important discoveries we make are those not found in field guides and scientific literature. Like belief in the supernatural, the islands force us to use our imagination to see beyond the horizon, to see beyond the barrier of years to a world that once existed here and that someday will return. Like religion, the islands require childlike innocence. The power of the ocean thrills us, frightens us, and feeds and nurtures us.

To find and identify a shell or a bird is satisfying because in a small way it helps us to comprehend this vast interlocking system of ocean, beaches, dunes, marshes, bays, and mainland. Yet the most compelling aspect of the islands lies not in the things we find and identify, but in those not yet found, in that which lies beyond the horizon. The possibilities, when imagined, are without limit. It is not until they are described and identified that the limits are enforced.

I think Tom senses this as he races into the surf, feeling the cold, powerful breakers crash around him and pull at him. He knows he's at the edge of something remarkable, and he doesn't know what it is. That, as I remember, is how I felt when my father first took me to the islands.

From *Salt Tide: Cycles and Currents of Life along the Coast* (Harrisburg, Pa.: Stackpole Books, 1993), pp. 61–72

Notes

Short History of the Barrier Islands

page 6 *currents dramatically reshaped its shoreline* Tom Horton, *Bay Country* (Baltimore: Johns Hopkins Univ. Press, 1987), p. 133.

6 *placid waters of the coastal bays* Herbert Keightley Job, *Wild Wings: Adventures of a Camera-Hunter among the Larger Wild Birds of North America on Sea and Land* (Boston: Houghton Mifflin, 1905), p. 117.

6 *mosquitoes, ticks, chiggers, and horseflies* William W. Warner, "Of Beaches, Bays, and My Boyhood with the Colonel," in *Heart of the Land: Essays on Last Great Places,* ed. Joseph Barbato and Lisa Weinerman (New York: Pantheon, 1994), pp. 68–69; Raymond D. Dueser, William C. Brown, Sue Ann McCuskey, and Gregory S. Hogue, "Vertebrate Zoogeography of the Virginia Coast Reserve," in *The Virginia Coast Reserve Study: Ecosystem Description* (Arlington, Va.: The Nature Conservancy, 1976), p. 455.

7 *almost all of the barrier islands* James R. Perry, *The Formation of a Society on Virginia's Eastern Shore, 1615–1655* (Chapel Hill: Univ. of North Carolina Press, 1990), pp. 34–35; Anne Floyd Upshur and Ralph T. Whitelaw, "Some New Thoughts concerning the Earliest Settlements on the Eastern Shore of Virginia," *Virginia Magazine of History and Biography* 50 (1942): 193–98; Joseph Douglas Deal III, "Race and Class in Colonial Virginia: Indians, Englishmen, and Africans on the Eastern Shore during the Seventeenth Century," Ph.D diss., University of Rochester, 1981, p. 2; Susie M. Ames, *Studies of the Virginia Eastern Shore in the Seventeenth Century* (Richmond: Dietz, 1940), pp. 32–35 (quotes John Custis), 52–53, 58–60, 133–38; Ralph T. Whitelaw, *Virginia's Eastern Shore: A History of Northampton and Accomack Counties,* 2 vols. (Richmond: Virginia Historical Society, 1951), 1:91, 135, 214, 368, 588, 2:780, 880, 1139, 1140, 1242, 1377, 1382, 1383, 1384, 1385.

7 *quantities of food and liquor* Deal, "Race and Class in Colonial Virginia," p. 4; George Washington Parke Custis, *An Address to the People of the United States, on the Importance of Encouraging Agriculture and Domestic Manufactures* (Alexandria, Va., 1808), pp. 16–19; Ames, *Studies of the Virginia Eastern Shore,* pp. 59–60; T. Holmes, "Some Account of the Wild Horses of the Sea Islands of Virginia and Maryland," *Farmers' Register* 3 (November 1835): 417–19.

page 8 *bottles stuffed with red flannel* Kirk Mariner, *Once upon an Island: The History of Chincoteague* (New Church, Va.: Miona Publications, 1996), p. 19; P. Wilson Coldham, ed., "The Wreck of the Schooner *Kitty*," *Virginia Magazine of History and Biography* 82 (1974): 48; George Corbin to Governor, September 4, 1779, in *Calendar of Virginia State Papers and Other Manuscripts Preserved in the Capitol at Richmond*, ed. William P. Palmer (Richmond: Secretary of the Commonwealth, 1875–93), 1:326–27; Whitelaw, *Virginia's Eastern Shore*, 1:368–69; Donald G. Shomette, *Shipwrecks on the Chesapeake: Maritime Disasters on Chesapeake Bay and Its Tributaries, 1608–1978* (Centreville, Md.: Tidewater Publishers, 1982), pp. 77–78; Frances Bibbins Latimer, comp., *1860 Census for Northampton County, Virginia* (Eastville, Va.: Hickory House, 1994), pp. 12, 24–25, 26, 69–70; Charles Lanman, *Haw-Ho-Noo; or Records of a Tourist* (Philadelphia, 1850), pp. 32–33; E. Thomas Crowson and Susan Crowson Hite, *Accomack County, Virginia, 1860 Census* (Bowie, Md.: Heritage Books, 1987), pp. 128–41; Maude Radford Warren, "The Island of Chincoteague," *Harper's Monthly Magazine* 127 (1913): 782; Alexander Hunter, *The Huntsman in the South*, vol. 1, *Virginia and North Carolina* (New York: Neale, 1908), pp. 303–4; Howard Pyle, "Chincoteague: The Island of Ponies," *Scribner's Monthly* 13 (1877): 739.

8 *his interest in material gain* Holmes, "Some Account of the Wild Horses," p. 418; Robert E. Lee to George Washington Parke Custis, May 22, 1832, Robert Edward Lee Papers, Duke University, Durham, N.C.; *Accomac Court House Peninsula Enterprise* (hereafter cited as *PE*), March 27, 1886; Warren, "The Island of Chincoteague," p. 782; Coldham, "The Wreck of the Schooner *Kitty*," p. 54; Pyle, "Chincoteague," p. 738.

8 *to attempt to buy the ship for salvage* Arthur Pierce Middleton, *Tobacco Coast: A Maritime History of Chesapeake Bay in the Colonial Era* (Newport News, Va.: Mariners' Museum, 1953), p. 226; Whitelaw, *Virginia's Eastern Shore*, 1:369; Coldham, "The Wreck of the Schooner *Kitty*," pp. 49, 50, 54; Shomette, *Shipwrecks on the Chesapeake*, pp. 77–78 (quotes *Annapolis Maryland Gazette*, June 7, 1787); *New York Herald*, October 18, 1891.

9 *smashed the machinery in the Smith's Island lighthouse* Middleton, *Tobacco Coast*, p. 206; Donald G. Shomette, *Pirates on the Chesapeake: Being a True History of Pirates, Picaroons, and Raiders on Chesapeake Bay, 1610–1807* (Centreville, Md.: Tidewater Publishers, 1985), pp. 112–13, 194; Dave Horner, *Shipwrecks, Skin Divers, and Sunken Gold* (New York: Dodd, Mead, 1965), pp. 22–23; deposition of James Lemount, August 7, 1687, George Corbin to Governor, September 4, 1779, in *Calendar of Virginia State Papers*, 1:30, 34, 326–27; Peter V. Bergstrom, *Merchants and Markets: Economic Diversification in Colonial Virginia* (New York: Garland, 1985), pp. 79–80; Susie M. Ames, "The Revolutionary Era," in *The Eastern Shore of Maryland and Virginia*, 3 vols., ed. Charles B. Clark (New York: Lewis Historical, 1950), 1:168–69; James Egbert Mears, "The Virginia Eastern Shore in the War of Secession and in the Reconstruction Period" (MS, 1957, Eastern Shore Public Library), p. 226.

page 9 *the efficient satisfaction of that demand* John R. Wennersten, *The Oyster Wars of Chesapeake Bay* (Centreville, Md.: Tidewater Publishers, 1981), pp. 14–16.

9 *"and in the lead in prices"* Lanman, *Haw-Ho-Noo,* p. 30 (quotation); Kirk Mariner, "Ghost Town on the Marsh," *Chesapeake Bay Magazine* 10 (December 1980): 41–42; Ernest Ingersoll, "The Oyster Industry," in *The History and Present Condition of the Fishery Industries,* ed. G. Brown Goode (Washington, D.C., 1881), p. 183; *PE,* June 2, 1888, July 20, 1889, April 5, 19, 1890, October 24, 1891, June 11, July 16, 1892, June 2, 1894, February 27, 1897 (quotation).

10 *and other western markets* Henry V. Poor, *Manual of the Railroads of the United States for 1882* (New York, 1882), p. 512; *PE,* March 15, 1884, November 22, 1890, August 8, 1891, February 13, 1892, November 17, 1894, March 7, 1896; *Richmond Times-Dispatch,* January 1, 1906.

10 *by rail to urban restaurants and fish markets* *PE,* July 27, 1882, May 17, 1883, June 20, July 11, 1885, October 27, 1888, April 18, November 7, 1891, June 29, 1895, October 18, 1902; George Toy to William Mahone, February 21, 1882 (quotation), William Mahone Papers, Duke Univ.

10 *anything from flounder to shark* *PE,* May 22, 1886, May 18, August 10, 1889, May 17, 24, July 26, October 11, 1890, May 30, June 6, 1891, May 21, November 26, December 10, 1892, June 3, July 22, 1893, May 26, 1894, February 29, May 9, 1896; Virginia Lee Hutcheson Davis, *Tidewater Virginia Families: A Social History* (Urbanna, Va.: Author, 1989), p. 191; William J. Mackey Jr., *American Bird Decoys* (New York: Dutton, 1965), p. 152; Amine Kellam, "The Cobb's Island Story," *Virginia Cavalcade* 23 (spring 1974): 23.

11 *had appreciated to an estimated $100,000* *PE,* October 27, 1881, May 4, 1882, July 20, 1889, November 15, 1890, August 6, 1892, June 24, 1893, June 9, September 15, 1894, July 13, 1895, May 20, 1905, December 21, 1907; *Eastville Eastern Shore Herald,* October 21, 1904; Charles A. Sterling, *Hog Island, Virginia* (N.p.: Author, 1903), pp. 37, 39; Kellam, "The Cobb's Island Story," pp. 20, 22–23; Nathaniel H. Bishop, *Voyage of the Paper Canoe: A Geographical Journey of 2500 Miles, from Quebec to the Gulf of Mexico, during the Years 1874–5* (Edinburgh, 1878), p. 144.

11 *"bedraggled, headachy and woe begone"* Whitelaw, *Virginia's Eastern Shore,* 1:370, 588; Thomas G. Reidenbaugh, "Land-Use History of Wallop's Island, Virginia" (MS, 1978, Eastern Shore Public Library), p. 3; *PE,* January 22, March 12, 1887, June 2, 1888, May 18, 1889, March 29, May 24, 1890, May 14, December 10, 1892, April 14 (quotation), 1894, June 6, 1896.

12 *every man, woman, and child on the island* *PE,* February 28, 1885, June 2, 1888; Ingersoll, "The Oyster Industry," pp. 160, 182; Alexander Hunter, "Cobb's Island in Summer," *Forest & Stream* 7 (August 31, 1876); Nora Miller Turman, *The Eastern Shore of Virginia, 1603–1964* (Onancock, Va.: Eastern Shore News, 1964), p. 183; Richard A. Pouliot and Julie J. Pouliot, *Shipwrecks on the Virginia Coast and the Men of the United States Life-Saving Service* (Centreville, Md.: Tidewater Publishers, 1986), pp. 6–8; Record of Appointment of Postmasters, 1832–September 30, 1971, microfilm, National Archives, Washington, D.C.

page 12 *on the Eastern Shore as a whole* *PE,* June 21, October 11, 1883, October 31, 1885, July 21, 1888, May 10, 1890, August 22, October 3, 1896; United States, Department of the Interior, Census Office, *Statistics of the Population of the United States at the Tenth Census (June 1, 1880)* (Washington, D.C., 1883), p. 356; Accomack County 1900 Manuscript Census; Accomack County 1880 Manuscript Census.

12 *watchhouses manned by shotgun-toting guards* *PE,* February 29, April 11, 1896, May 3, 1905; George Shiras, *Hunting Wild Life with Camera and Flashlight: A Record of Sixty-five Years' Visits to the Woods and Waters of North America,* 2 vols. (Washington, D.C.: National Geographic Society, 1935), 2:80; Warren, "The Island of Chincoteague," p. 777.

12 *quit the islands in disgust* Ella B. Huff to editor, October 26, *Loudonville (Ohio) Democrat,* November 4, 1897; Maria Ann Graham, "Land Use History: A Study of Man's Influence on Virginia's Barrier Islands," in *The Virginia Coast Reserve Survey,* pp. 57, 58, 63; *PE,* January 23, 1897; Shiras, *Hunting Wild Life with Camera and Flashlight,* 2:69, 72; Pyle, "Chincoteague," p. 742; Hunter, *The Huntsman in the South,* pp. 312, 313; Frank M. Chapman, *Camps and Cruises of an Ornithologist* (New York: Appleton, 1908), pp. 63–64.

13 *"levelled [Cedar Island] to a mere flat breath of sand"* *PE,* March 24, December 8, 1888, September 28, 1889, November 11, 1893, November 23, 1895, October 17, 1896, February 13, October 30 (quotation), 1897, February 18, 25, March 4, 11, 1899; *Richmond Dispatch,* April 10, 11, 1889; Pouliot and Pouliot, *Shipwrecks on the Virginia Coast,* pp. 111–12, 127; Hunter, *The Huntsman in the South,* p. 309.

13 *history had come to a close* Howard Pyle, "A Peninsular Canaan," *Harper's Magazine* 58 (1879): 811; *PE,* May 23, 1891, August 18, 1894, September 19, 1896, March 20, September 11, 1897; *Baltimore Sun,* October 20, 1896; Ella B. Huff to editor, October 26, *Loudonville (Ohio) Democrat,* November 4, 1897; Hunter, *The Huntsman in the South,* p. 158.

13 *increased numbers of hitherto depleted species* Graham, "Land Use History," p. 58; *PE,* March 14, 1895, November 17, 1906; William Dutcher, "Results of Special Protection to Gulls and Terns Obtained through the Thayer Fund," *Auk* 18 (1901): 77; Olin Sewall Pettingill Jr., "Honeymoon on Cobb Island," in *Discovery: Great Moments in the Lives of Outstanding Naturalists,* ed. John K. Terres (Philadelphia and New York: Lippincott, 1961), p. 297; Shiras, *Hunting Wild Life with Camera and Flashlight,* 2:96.

13 *the efforts of the scientific bureaucracy* *Richmond Times-Dispatch,* August 25, 1907; L. S. Corbin to editor, *PE,* June 29, 1945; Kirk Mariner, *Wachapreague, Virginia: Then and Now* (New Church, Va.: Miona Publications, 1995), p. 27.

14 *traffic in vacation and retirement properties* Robert L. Krieger, *The Chincoteague Toll Road and Bridge Company* (Wallops Island, Va.: Wallops Flight Center, 1980); Nathaniel T. Kenney, "Chincoteague: Waterman's Island Home," *National Geographic* 157 (1980): 822, 823; Turman, *The Eastern Shore of Virginia,* pp. 259–60; *Eastern Shore News,* July 27, 1996.

page 14 *National Aeronautics and Space Administration* "Chincoteague: Strategic Refuge for American Waterfowl," *Virginia Wildlife* 8 (September 1947): 8; *Eastern Shore News,* October 1, 1970; Reidenbaugh, "Land-Use History of Wallop's Island," pp. 6–7; Turman, *The Eastern Shore of Virginia,* p. 248; James E. Mears, "Supplement to the Eastern Shore of Virginia in the 19th and 20th Centuries," in Mears Scrapbook 19 (1966–67), p. 24, Eastern Shore Public Library.

15 *conservation and sustainable development* Donnel Nunes, "How Nature Conservancy Saved the Barrier Islands," *Washington Post,* December 25, 1975, in *Virginia Conservancy News* 7 (March 1976): 5, 6; *Eastern Shore News,* February 19, December 3, 10, 1970.

15 *a subsequent storm of 1936* Claudia Turner Bagwell, *Tidal Surge: The Ash Wednesday Storm, Chincoteague, 1962* (Onancock, Va.: Eastern Shore Printers, 1983), p. 2; United States, Army, Corps of Engineers, *Flood Plain Information, Coastal Flooding: Town of Wachapreague, Virginia* (Norfolk, Va.: Author, 1971), pp. 22, 27–29; Graham, "Land Use History," pp. 58–62, 77–78; Reidenbaugh, "Land-Use History of Wallop's Island," p. 4; Whitelaw, *Virginia's Eastern Shore,* 1:370, 2:780–81.

15 *A cycle had been completed* Northampton County 1920 Manuscript Census, pp. 249–50; *PE,* August 30, 1930; Graham, "Land Use History," pp. 77–81; James Wharton, "Virginia's Drowned Village," *Virginia Cavalcade* 7 (winter 1957): 10.

15 *How many hopes lie buried here* Wharton, "Virginia's Drowned Village," p. 11; A. Parker Barnes, "For the Barriers, an Ancient Conflict Continues," *Norfolk Virginian-Pilot,* January 10, 1971.

Voyage to Virginia

17 *were objects of both hope and fear* Maryland historians place the landfall of the *Virginia Merchant* near the present Delaware-Maryland boundary (Louis Dow Scisco, "Norwood in Worcester County in 1650," *Maryland Historical Magazine* 18 [June 1923]: 130–34; William B. Marye, "The Sea Coast of Maryland," *Maryland Historical Magazine* 40 [June 1945]: 94–118). The small size of the island, the nearby village of the Kickotank tribe of Indians, and the difficulties of seventeenth-century travel indicate that the *Virginia Merchant* made landfall farther south, perhaps on Virginia's Assawoman Island.

18 *Morrison* Francis Moryson (d. 1680 or 1681) survived his island ordeal and before leaving Virginia for England in 1663 served as Speaker of the House of Burgesses (1656) and acting governor (1661–62). He returned briefly to Virginia in 1677 with the royal commission investigating Bacon's Rebellion (Jon Kukla, *Speakers and Clerks of the Virginia House of Burgesses, 1643–1776* [Richmond: Virginia State Library, 1981], pp. 54–57).

20 *Francis Cary* After reaching the safety of the English settlements, Francis Cary (1628?–?) disappeared from the historical record ([Fairfax Harrison], *The*

Virginia Carys: An Essay in Genealogy [New York: De Vinne Press, 1919], pp. 141–42).

page 21 *curlieus* Whimbrel.

21 *Oxeyes* Black-bellied plover.

27 *Kickotank* The Kickotanks, residing on the seaside of the mainland across Kegotank Bay from Assawoman Island, were one of several Eastern Shore tribes known collectively as the Accomacs (Christian F. Feest, "Nanticoke and Neighboring Tribes," in *Handbook of North American Indians,* vol. 15, *Northeast,* ed. Bruce G. Trigger [Washington, D.C.: Smithsonian Institution, 1978], pp. 240–41).

27 *Smith's travels* John Smith, *A Map of Virginia With a Description of the Countrey, the Commodities, People, Government and Religion* (Oxford, 1612).

29 *as plentiful a condition as they could wish* Having enjoyed a few more days of the Indians' hospitality, Henry Norwood and his party safely reached the English settlement at Nandua in what is now lower Accomack County on the Eastern Shore.

Smith's Island

37 *Hitchings* Probably David Hitchens (d. 1881), who later served as keeper of the Smith's Island Life-Saving Service station (1879–81) (George and Suzanne Hurley, *Shipwrecks and Rescues along the Barrier Islands of Delaware, Maryland, and Virginia* [Norfolk, Va.: Donning, 1984], 28). Hamilton, Hamby (perhaps Hanby), and Thomas Roberts remain unidentified.

38 *Dr. Simkins* Dr. Jesse J. Simkins (d. 1866, aged 62).

38 *sedge hen* Clapper rail or marsh hen.

Christian Guardians

50 *the Rev. Thomas Smith* For Smith (1776–1844) and the great Methodist revival of 1800–1814, see Kirk Mariner, *Revival's Children: A Religious History of Virginia's Eastern Shore* (Salisbury, Md.: Peninsula Press, 1979), pp. 34–51.

51 *supplied by the Virginia Conference* Pullen's Chapel Methodist Episcopal Church, South, was established on Hog Island in 1883 by the Rev. Thomas G. Pullen on land donated by Samuel Kelly (b. 1824) and his sister Nancy (b. 1811). For the history of churches on the island, see Mariner, *Revival's Children,* pp. 421, 545–46.

Hog Island

54 *a fine light house* The Hog Island lighthouse was completed in 1854 (Francis Ross Holland Jr., *America's Lighthouses: An Illustrated History* [New York: Dover, 1988], pp. 126–27). For the pro-Union activities of Jean G. Potts and David N.

Boole (d. 1896, aged 71), see James Egbert Mears, "The Virginia Eastern Shore in the War of Secession and in the Reconstruction Period" (manuscript, 1957, Eastern Shore Public Library, Accomac, Va.), pp. 49–52.

page 55 *"Teach's Island"* Edward Teach (d. 1718), better known as Blackbeard. Parramore Island also was known as Teach's Island (Ralph T. Whitelaw, *Virginia's Eastern Shore: A History of Northampton and Accomack Counties,* 2 vols. [Richmond: Virginia Historical Society, 1951], 2:780).

56 *Alexander Selkirk* Selkirk's sojourn (1704–9) on one of the South Pacific islands of Juan Fernández inspired Daniel Defoe's *The Life and Strange and Surprising Adventures of Robinson Crusoe* (1719).

Chincoteague

60 *degenerated into a peculiar breed of ponies* The origin of the Chincoteague ponies is more prosaic. The early settlers of the Eastern Shore mainland put them out to pasture on Chincoteague and other barrier islands. For a commentary on the Chincoteague pony legend, see Phil Holleran, "Chincoteague's Wild Horses," *Virginia Explorer* 12 (summer 1996): 9–12.

62 *Turner's daub of red in his gray sea picture* Joseph Mallard William Turner (1775–1851), English landscape painter.

63 *Kendall Jester* For a biographical sketch of Jester (1815–1898), see Kirk Mariner, *Once upon an Island: The History of Chincoteague* (New Church, Va.: Miona Publications, 1996), p. 167.

65 *Mr. English* Joseph J. English built the Atlantic Hotel in 1876. He fled the island in 1878 after he shot and killed a former guest in a dispute over an unpaid bill. John Caulk (1811–1882) in 1861 became Chincoteague's first collector of customs (Mariner, *Once upon an Island,* pp. 42, 68–69).

68 *snipe* Shorebirds.

69 *sea-mews* Gulls, most likely the ring-billed gull.

70 *by his waistband twenty feet from the ground* For the hurricane and tidal wave of 1821, see Kirk Mariner, "The Great September Gust," *Virginia Cavalcade* 32 (summer 1982): 20–29.

70 *the only loyal portion of the eastern coast of Virginia* Brig. Gen. Henry Hayes Lockwood (1814–1899) led the Union invasion of Virginia's Eastern Shore in November 1861. For John A. M. Whealton (1831?–1912) and the secession crisis and Civil War on Chincoteague, see Mariner, *Once upon an Island,* pp. 46–58, 182–183.

Cobb's Island

74 *Nathan Cobb* Nathan F. Cobb Sr. (1797–1890), a native of Eastham on Cape Cod, came with his family to the Eastern Shore in the early 1830s. Warren D.

Cobb (1833–1903) was the second of Nathan's three surviving sons (Amine Kellam, "The Cobb's Island Story," *Virginia Cavalcade* 23 [spring 1974]: 18–27).

page 76 *Nathan F. Cobb* In 1839 Nathan F. Cobb Sr. purchased Cobb's Island, then known as Great Sand Shoal Island, from William and Elizabeth Fitchett for $150. Salt is not mentioned in the deed (March 11, 1839, Northampton County Deed Book 31, p. 66).

76 *"Col. Sellers"* Col. Beriah Sellers, entrepreneur given to wild schemes in Mark Twain and Charles Dudley Warner's *The Gilded Age* (1873).

77 *showed their lot of birds* Gray-backs are dowitchers; barking gulls are black skimmers; and curlews are whimbrels.

81 *the Lee family of Virginia* Smith's Island came into the hands of the Lees at the death of George Washington Parke Custis in 1857 (Douglas Southall Freeman, *R. E. Lee: A Biography,* 4 vols. [New York and London: Charles Scribner's Sons, 1935], 4:386, 388–390).

82 *"Dry Isaacs"* Probably Adams Island.

83 *John Half* John Haff (d. 1909, aged 60), strongman of the Eastern Shore. "Haff is tall and well-built. He thinks nothing of swimming from Cobb's Island to Norfolk, and has swam from Cobb's Inlet up to Parramores Beach against a strong ebb tide" (*Norfolk Virginian,* July 30, 1889). Once, following the wreck of his sloop in a storm, Haff swam two miles or more while carrying another man on his back (*PE,* November 9, 1882).

Peninsular Canaan

87 *Virginia rail* Clapper rail.

88 *"Gull's Island"* Probably present-day Gull Marsh.

91 *B[rowne]* Orris Applethwaite Browne (1842–1898), Confederate veteran, former inspector in the Virginia oyster police, and agricultural reformer, lived at The Folly on Folly Creek near Accomac Court House. In the mid-1870s Browne obtained Cedar Island by grant from the commonwealth of Virginia (Brooks Miles Barnes, "Orris Applethwaite Browne," in *Dictionary of Virginia Biography,* ed. John Kneebone et al. [Richmond: Library of Virginia, forthcoming]; Ralph T. Whitelaw, *Virginia's Eastern Shore: A History of Northampton and Accomack Counties,* 2 vols. [Richmond: Virginia Historical Society, 1951], 2:880).

Robb's Island Wreck

95 *United States Life-Saving Service* For the Life-Saving Service on the barrier islands, see Richard A. Pouliot and Julie J. Pouliot, *Shipwrecks on the Virginia Coast and the Men of the United States Life-Saving Service* (Centreville, Md.: Tidewater Publishers, 1986).

96 *Robb's Island* In an author's note, Meekins acknowledges that the fictional Robb's Island is modeled on Cobb's Island.

Along Shining Shores

page 110 *jack-curlew* Whimbrel.

111 *calico birds* Ruddy turnstone.

113 *grayback, blackbreast* The grayback is the dowitcher, and the blackbreast is the black-bellied plover.

113 *red-breasted snipe* Red knot.

114 *George Hitchens* George David Hitchens (1850–1936), keeper of the Life-Saving station on Smith's Island (1881–1914) (George and Suzanne Hurley, *Shipwrecks and Rescues along the Barrier Islands of Delaware, Maryland, and Virginia* [Norfolk, Va.: Donning, 1984], pp. 27–28).

Cobb's Island

117 *Cobb* Nathan F. Cobb Sr. (1797–1890), a native of Eastham on Cape Cod, came with his family to the Eastern Shore in the early 1830s (Amine Kellam, "The Cobb's Island Story," *Virginia Cavalcade* 23 [spring 1974]: 18–27). In 1839 Cobb purchased Cobb's Island, then known as Great Sand Shoal Island, from William and Elizabeth Fitchett for $150. Salt is not mentioned in the deed (March 11, 1839, Northampton County Deed Book 31, p. 66).

118 *Cobb's Island a summer resort* The Cobbs had been accommodating sportsmen and tourists for decades before the Life-Saving station opened in 1875 (Kellam, "The Cobb's Island Story," pp. 18–27).

118 *Warren Cobb* Hunter scrambles the birthorder of the Cobb sons. Nathan F. Cobb Jr. (1825–1905) was followed by Warren D. Cobb (1833–1903) and Albert F. Cobb (1836–1890).

119 *Christopher Sly* The drunken tinker in William Shakespeare's *Taming of the Shrew.*

121 *the 21st* Hunter's date is incorrect. The hurricane battered Cobb's Island on October 22, 1878 (*Onancock Eastern Virginian,* October 26, November 2, 9, 1878).

125 *Gull Island* Probably present-day Gull Marsh.

125 *mussels, clams, and the like* Brant fed not on mussels and clams but on the eelgrass that grew in extensive beds on the Eastern Shore seaside. When in the 1930s a fungus destroyed the eelgrass, the flights of Atlantic coast brant were greatly diminished.

128 *A rich syndicate* Hunter is mistaken. In 1890 and 1891 a Lynchburg syndicate purchased for $18,000 the hotel, the Baltimore House, and approximately thirty-one acres of land. The syndicate also agreed to pay $360 per annum for a twenty-five-year lease on the island's fishing, shooting, and bathing rights (October 3, 1890, January 28, 1891, Northampton County Deed Book 45, pp. 35, 38, 203).

128 *October 4, 1896* Hunter again gives an incorrect date. The hurricane struck Cobb's Island on October 11, 1896 (*PE,* October 17, 1896).

Extinction of Cobb's Island

page 133 *a Lynchburg syndicate* Purchased in 1890 and 1891 for $18,000 the hotel, the Baltimore House, and approximately thirty-one acres of land. The syndicate also agreed to pay $360 per annum for a twenty-five-year lease on the island's fishing, shooting, and bathing rights (October 3, 1890, January 28, 1891, Northampton County Deed Book 45, pp. 35, 38, 203). The correspondent refers to Nathan F. Cobb Jr. (1825–1905) and Warren D. Cobb (1833–1903).

Cobb's Island

136 *Mr. Nathan Cobb* Nathan F. Cobb Jr. (1825–1905).

137 *a hotel was built* In 1860 Charles Scautteberry kept a hotel on Prout's Island (Frances Bibbins Latimer, comp., *1860 Census for Northampton County, Virginia* [Eastville, Va.: Hickory House, 1994], p. 26).

137 *purchased the island in 1837* In 1839 Nathan F. Cobb Sr. (1797–1890) purchased Cobb's Island, then known as Great Sand Shoal Island, from William and Elizabeth Fitchett for $150 (March 11, 1839, Northampton County Deed Book 31, p. 66).

Revel's Island

141 *Little Machipongo Inlet* Present-day Quinby Inlet.

141 *comprises several thousand acres* The Nature Conservancy has owned Revel's Island since 1974 (November 4, 1974, Accomack County Deed Book 356, p. 465).

145 *Hudsonian curlews* Whimbrel.

145 *robin-snipe* Red knot.

149 *a catboat* Actually a bateau, a wide, cross-planked, English-rigged, shallow-draft skiff indigenous to the Eastern Shore seaside (Howard I. Chappelle, *American Small Sailing Craft: Their Design, Development, and Construction* [New York: Norton, 1951], pp. 313–15).

151 *a telephone line* In the summer of 1892, the federal government awarded a contract for the placement of poles for the projected telephone line connecting the barrier island Life-Saving stations (*PE*, August 13, 1892).

153 *Captain Wickes* Shiras refers to Capt. S. J. Wickes.

Hog Island

157 *Hog Island and its inhabitants* Nearly half of Alexander Hunter's account of Hog Island, published in 1907, is lifted directly from a pamphlet entitled *Hog Island, Virginia,* privately published in 1903 by Charles A. Sterling, keeper of the Hog Island lighthouse. Considering dates of publication alone, Hunter appears

to have plagiarized Sterling. Other factors, however, should be considered. First, Hunter had been for years a contributor to magazines such as *Forest & Stream* while the Hog Island pamphlet appears to have been Sterling's first and only published work. Might Sterling have borrowed from some lost magazine article by the more experienced Hunter? Or might Hunter, a frequent visitor to Hog Island and an acquaintance of Sterling, have ghostwritten part or all of the Sterling manuscript? Second, the even tone of Hunter's account suggests the work of one writer, and its literary style is consistent with Hunter's other work. Indeed, to extend the argument, Sterling's style is strongly reminiscent of Hunter's. For a commentary on Sterling's and Hunter's accounts of Hog Island, see Curtis Badger, "The Sporting Life at Hog Island," *Wildfowl Art: The Journal of the Ward Foundation* (fall 1986): 8–11, 13. For Sterling, see James Wharton, "Virginia's Drowned Village," *Virginia Cavalcade* 7 (winter 1957): 6–12.

page 158 *John Smith* Capt. John Smith probably never set foot on Hog Island. After landing on Smith's Island in June 1608, Smith and his party proceeded on a voyage of exploration up Chesapeake Bay, not along the Virginia seacoast (John Smith, "Description of Virginia and Proceedings of the Colonie," in *Narratives of Early Virginia,* ed. Lyon Gardiner Tyler [New York: Charles Scribner's Sons, 1907], pp. 141–43). Neither Smith nor anyone else gave Hog Island the name Shooting Bears Island. Colonial land patents of 1681 and 1687 grant to four patentees "Hogg Island alias Shooting Beach" (Ralph T. Whitelaw, *Virginia's Eastern Shore: A History of Northampton and Accomack Counties,* 2 vols. [Richmond: Virginia Historical Society, 1951], 1:368).

158 *"Machipongo Island"* For similar translations, see Jennings Cropper Wise, *Ye Kingdome of Accawmacke, or the Eastern Shore of Virginia in the Seventeenth Century* (Richmond: Bell Book and Stationary Co., 1911), p. 371.

160 *before the Pilgrims built their first village* Hunter's account of the early history of Hog Island is romantic nonsense based on a misreading of the evidence. In the colonial period, the government of Virginia encouraged immigration by granting a headright of fifty acres of land for every person brought into the colony. In 1681 and 1687 (not 1672), the government issued patents for a total of 3,350 acres on Hog Island to Thomas Hunt, John Floyd, Edmund Bibby, and George Clarke. In return for the land, Hunt, Floyd, Bibby, and Clarke presented evidence that they had paid for the passage into Virginia of sixty-seven persons (at 50 acres a person). The names given by Hunter are not island colonists but an incomplete and inaccurate list of headrights claimed by the patentees. Hunter's Hog Island colony is a chimera that could neither be slaughtered by the Eastern Shore's unwarlike Indians nor routed by mosquitoes. Indeed, until the mid-eighteenth century the only people likely living on Hog Island was the family of the overseer who tended the patentees' livestock (Nell Marion Nugent, comp., *Cavaliers and Pioneers: Abstracts of Virginia Land Patents and Grants, vol. 2: 1666–1695* [Richmond: Virginia State Library, 1977], pp. 225, 310; Whitelaw, *Virginia's Eastern Shore,* 1:368).

page 160 *The earliest settler* Thomas Coffin, overseer for the patentees, probably was the first white person to live on Hog Island (Whitelaw, *Virginia's Eastern Shore,* 1:368).

160 *Dancer, the miser, and . . . the famous Captain Kidd* Daniel Dancer (1716–1794) and William Kidd (d. 1701), English pirate.

161 *His only relative and heir* In 1900 Samuel Kelly (b. 1824) was in the general merchandise business and living in the household of his sister Nancy Kelly (b. 1811) (Northampton County 1900 Manuscript Census, enumeration district 63, sheet 18).

162 *a community of forty-two families* Charles A. Sterling counted 113 persons living in forty-two households on Hog Island in 1903 (Sterling, *Hog Island, Virginia,* pp. 14, 35–36).

162 *"recline and repose twenty hours out of twenty-four"* Charles A. Sterling had a much better opinion of Hog Islanders than did Hunter (Badger, "The Sporting Life at Hog Island," pp. 8–11, 13).

164 *That night the worst hurricane in the memory of man* Hunter's date is incorrect. The storm struck Hog Island on December 15–16 (*PE,* December 23, 1905).

166 *President Cleveland* Grover Cleveland (1837–1908) visited Hog Island in 1892 and in 1893 (*PE,* November 26, December 10, 1892, June 3, 1893).

167 *Polk Miller* Miller (1844–1914) was a Richmond pharmaceutical dealer and lecturer.

Chincoteague

170 *Assoteague . . . which is really a slim peninsula* Assateague remained a peninsula until the hurricane of 1933 created an inlet just south of Ocean City, Maryland (William H. Wroten Jr., *Assateague,* 2d ed. [Centreville, Md.: Tidewater Publishers, 1972], p. 3).

171 *In 1687 . . . Jenifer brought over a number of convicts* Daniel Jenifer patented Chincoteague Island in 1671 and Assateague Island in 1687. William Kendall and John Robins repatented Chincoteague in 1691 and in 1692 (Ralph T. Whitelaw, *Virginia's Eastern Shore: A History of Northampton and Accomack Counties,* 2 vols. [Richmond: Virginia Historical Society, 1951], 2:1377–78, 1384). Like Alexander Hunter, Maude Radford Warren confused headrights with actual settlers. Warren compounded the error by assuming that the headrights were also convicts. For the headright system, see above p. 239.

174 *Chincoteague has indeed been incorporated into a town* Chincoteague incorporated in 1908 (Kirk Mariner, *Once upon an Island: The History of Chincoteague* [New Church, Va.: Miona Publications, 1996], p. 96).

176 *the signs of a civil war* For Chincoteague in the Civil War see Mariner, *Once upon an Island,* pp. 46–58.

178 *These animals are supposed to have been cast away* The origin of the ponies was not from a shipwreck. Early settlers on the Eastern Shore mainland put them

out to pasture on Chincoteague and other barrier islands. For a commentary on the Chincoteague pony legend, see Phil Holleran, "Chincoteague's Wild Horses," *Virginia Explorer* 12 (summer 1996): 9–12.

page 179 *Ocher Brinney* For Ocraw Brinney (ca. 1730–ca. 1840), see Mariner, *Once upon an Island*, pp. 158–59).

180 *the hurricane of 1822* Warren's date is incorrect. For the hurricane and tidal wave of 1821, see Kirk Mariner, "The Great September Gust," *Virginia Cavalcade* 32 (summer 1982): 20–29.

180 *Sanctificationists* In 1892 a Methodist splinter group created on Chincoteague Island Christ's Sanctified Holy Church. Certain of the sanctificationists' doctrines, including the repudiation of marriages previously made with the unsanctified, were perceived by many islanders as tending to licentiousness. Antipathy toward the new church hardened, and, following a fatal shooting in 1894, most of the sanctificationists fled the island (Kirk Mariner, *Revival's Children: A Religious History of Virginia's Eastern Shore* [Salisbury, Md.: Peninsula Press, 1979], pp. 188–98, 329–30).

Honeymoon on Cobb Island

191 *The storm which took Mr. Cobb's life* The Coast Guard was forced to abandon Cobb's Island during the hurricane of August 22–23, 1933, but the station, while severely damaged, was not "completely demolished" (Record of the Miscellaneous Events of the Day, Cobb's Island Station, August 23, 24, 1933, Records of the United States Coast Guard, Record Group 26, National Archives, Washington, D.C.). The guardsmen's failure to rescue George W. Cobb (1869–1933) resulted in an investigation of the station's captain for possible negligence (*Onancock Eastern Shore News*, August 25, September 8, 1933). The report of the investigating officer has disappeared.

The Island

194 *He bought this little Island* William D. Cardwell (1868–1954) recalled his acquisition of Little Cobb's Island and his World War I naval service in "Random Collections" (MS, 1952, Eastern Shore Public Library, Accomac, Va.).

197 *"earth shaking" news* Will Rogers (1879–1935), actor and humorist, and Wiley Post (1899–1935), aviator, died in the crash of Post's airplane near Point Barrow, Alaska, on August 15, 1935.

198 *George Cobb* The failure of the Coast Guard to rescue George W. Cobb (1869–1933) resulted in an investigation of the station's captain for possible negligence (*Onancock Eastern Shore News*, August 25, September 8, 1933). The report of the investigating officer has disappeared.

199 *Chatham Blanket Co.* In recent years members of the Chatham family have transferred their interest in Little Cobb's Island to the Nature Conservancy

(July 19, 1989, Northampton County Deed Book 239, pp. 719, 721; December 29, 1989, Northampton County Deed Book 242, p. 230; December 22, 1995, Northampton County Deed Book 278, p. 653).

page 200 *worth thousands of dollars today* In 1993 the firm of Guyette and Schmidt of Farmington, Maine, sold at auction a decoy carved by Nathan F. Cobb Jr. (1825–1905) for $192,500, the highest price ever paid at auction for a Cobb's Island decoy and the third highest paid for any decoy (Gary Guyette to Barry Truitt, August 13, 1996).

While the Islands Are Still There

201 *about 300 people* Hunt overestimates the population of Hog Island. In 1920 the island was home to 162 people (Northampton County 1920 Manuscript Census, pp. 249–50).

204 *"knix" bushes* Marsh elder. Also known to Eastern Shoremen as "high-tide bush."

204 *a 26-page report* Southeast Chapter, Sierra Club, "A Review of the Proposed 'Development' Plan for Smith, Myrtle, and Ship Shoal Islands in Northampton County Virginia" (MS, ca. 1969, Virginia Coast Reserve, Nature Conservancy, Nassawadox, Va.).

204 *and Myrtle Islands* Hunt is somewhat confused. The Smith Island Development Corporation owned Smith's, Myrtle, and Ship Shoal islands. Wreck Island lies to the north of Ship Shoal and encompasses the formerly distinct Bone Island.

206 *the state bought Mockhorn Island* The commonwealth of Virginia acquired Mockhorn in 1959. For the Larimer A. Cushman compound on the island, see Curtis Badger, "Mockhorn Island: A Different Place in Another Time," *Virginia Wildlife* 52 (July 1991): 4–8.

206 *The Massassoit* The vessel ran aground on Smith's Island on November 15, 1914. Photographs indicate clearly that the ship was a four-master.

207 *a New York outfit came down* The Cobb's Island hotel was not acquired by New Yorkers. In 1890 and 1891 a Lynchburg syndicate purchased for $18,000 the hotel, the Baltimore house, and approximately thirty-one acres of land. The syndicate also agreed to pay $360 per annum for a twenty-five-year lease on the island's fishing, shooting, and bathing rights (October 3, 1890, January 28, 1891, Northampton County Deed Book 45, pp. 35, 38, 203).

208 *white heron* Probably the Great Egret.

208 *jackrabbits on Cobb Island* See Roger B. Clapp, John S. Weske, and Tina C. Clapp, "Establishment of the Black-Tailed Jackrabbit on the Virginia Eastern Shore," *Journal of Mammalogy* 57 (1976): 180–81.

209 *They're clean—and peaceful* The Smith Island Development Corporation sold out to the Nature Conservancy in 1970 (December 4, 1970, Northampton County Deed Book 167, p. 403).

Ultimate Edge

page 213 *a history of the region published in 1903* Horton quotes, somewhat loosely, from Charles A. Sterling, *Hog Island, Virginia* (N.p.: Author, 1903), p. 26.

213 *goats* Brought to Parramore not by settlers but by the island's owners around 1940 (Maria Ann Graham, "Land Use History: A Study of Man's Influence on Virginia's Barrier Islands," in *The Virginia Coast Reserve Study: Ecosystem Description* [Arlington, Va.: The Nature Conservancy, 1976], p. 68).

213 *by the United Nations* Horton is mistaken. The Accomack and Northampton boards of supervisors voted not to recognize the United States Department of the Interior's designation of the thirteen barrier islands owned by the Nature Conservancy as a national natural landmark (*Eastern Shore News,* October 11, 25, 1979).

218 *as recently as 1933* Horton overestimates the population of Hog Island. In 1920 the island was home to 162 souls (Northampton County 1920 Manuscript Census, pp. 249–50).

Index

Photo Credits

Curtis J. Badger	221
Eastern Shore of Virginia Historical Society	jacket, iii, xviii, xix, xx, xxvii, 5, 36
Eastern Shore Public Library	xxix, 85, 95, 108, 116, 130
Kirk Mariner	41, 59
The Mariners' Museum	xxiv
National Geographic Society	xxi, xxi, 140
The Nature Conservancy	xvii, xxii, 73, 211
Mr. and Mrs. Thomas J. O'Connor III	xvii, xxvi, xxvii, xxix, 1, 156, 169
Paradigm Design	viii
Peabody Essex Museum	xxv
Claude Rogers	xxiii
Photographic History Collection, National Museum of American History, Smithsonian Institution	xxv, 30, 48, 53
Melvin M. Spence, AIA, & Associates, Architects, and Edward G. Carson & Associates, Landscape Architect and Planners	203
Barry R. Truitt	16, 183, 193
University of Virginia VCR/LTER program	134
Robert E. Wilson	xx, xxviii, xxviii